THE NEW TESTAMENT IN CONTEXT

Sources and Documents

THE NEW TESTAMENT IN CONTEXT
Sources and Documents

HOWARD CLARK KEE

Boston University

Prentice-Hall, Inc., Englewood Cliffs, New Jersey 07632

Library of Congress Cataloging in Publication Data

KEE, HOWARD CLARK.
The New Testament in context.

Bibliography: p. 232
Includes index.
1. Bible. N.T.—History of contemporary events—Sources. 2. Hebrew literature. 3. Apocryphal books. I. Title.
BS2410.K44 1984 225.9'5 83-26894
ISBN 0-13-615774-2

Editorial/production supervision and
interior design: Patricia V. Amoroso
Cover design: Ben Santora
Manufacturing buyer: Harry P. Baisley

This is a revision of a book previously titled
The Origins of Christianity: Sources and Documents

Printed in the United States of America

10 9 8 7 6 5 4 3 2 1

ISBN 0-13-615774-2

PRENTICE-HALL INTERNATIONAL, INC., *London*
PRENTICE-HALL OF AUSTRALIA PTY. LIMITED, *Sydney*
EDITORA PRENTICE-HALL DO BRASIL, LTDA., *Rio de Janeiro*
PRENTICE-HALL CANADA INC., *Toronto*
PRENTICE-HALL OF INDIA PRIVATE LIMITED, *New Delhi*
PRENTICE-HALL OF JAPAN, INC., *Tokyo*
PRENTICE-HALL OF SOUTHEAST ASIA PTE. LTD., *Singapore*
WHITEHALL BOOKS LIMITED, *Wellington, New Zealand*

Contents

Preface

Changing historical perspectives on the setting in which the New Testament was produced, as well as the recent availability of translations of some ancient texts, provide the occasion for a new edition of this book. Some readers thought that the title of the earlier edition, *The Origins of Christianity: Sources and Documents,* promised a comprehensive historical reconstruction, which was not intended. The present title and new arrangement seek to make clear the aim of the work: to furnish translations of texts and documents that present various facets of the diverse world of the New Testament—politically, culturally, religiously, literarily, and philosophically.

Obviously, in a volume of this size only a selection of potentially relevant material can be included. An effort has been made, however, to preserve a balance between such distinctively Jewish materials as apocalypses and scriptural interpretations on the one hand and wider aspects of Greco-Roman culture on the other. I have brought together documents that show that the world in which the New Testament was produced was dynamic and changing, rather than characterized by set patterns of religious aspiration and expression, as some handbooks on the subject often assume or imply.

Colleagues whose comments and suggestions have been especially helpful include Jacob Neusner of Brown University, Patrick Henry of Swarthmore College, and James H. Charlesworth of Duke University. To them, and to all others who have offered constructive criticism, I express my gratitude. The new edition is dedicated to Janet Burrell Kee, whose support and encouragement have helped me to gain perspective on my work, as well as to get it done.

HOWARD CLARK KEE
William Goodwin Aurelio Professor of Biblical Studies
Boston University

Acknowledgments

We gratefully acknowledge permission to quote the following copyrighted material:

pp. 7–15, *I Maccabees,* from the Revised Standard Version of the Bible, copyrighted 1946, 1952 © 1971, 1973.

pp. 17–26, 35–37, 54–56, *Antiquities of the Jews,* reprinted by permission of the publishers and *The Loeb Classical Library* from *Josephus* III, VII, VIII, trans. by H. St. J. Thackeray, Ralph Marcus, and A. Wikgren, Cambridge, Mass.: Harvard University Press, 1934, rpt. 1966.

pp. 26–34, 57–62, *Jewish War,* reprinted by permission of the publishers and *The Loeb Classical Library* from *Josephus, War,* II, trans. by H. St. J. Thackeray, Cambridge, Mass.: Harvard University Press, 1917, rpt. 1967.

pp. 37–43, *Philo Alexandrinus: Legatio ad Gaium,* excerpts from pp. 76–80, 93–97, 115–16, 118–27, 132–34, 143–51, 155–58, trans. by Mary Smallwood, Leiden: E. J. Brill. Reprinted by permission of the publisher.

pp. 44–45, *Correspondence with Trajan,* reprinted by permission of the publishers and *The Loeb Classical Library* from *Pliny,* trans. by W. M. L. Hutchinson, Cambridge, Mass.: Harvard University Press, 1952.

p. 45, *Life of Nero,* reprinted by permission of the publishers and *The Loeb Classical Library* from *Suetonius,* trans. by J. C. Rolfe, Cambridge, Mass.: Harvard University Press, 1914, rpt. 1965.

pp. 49–53, taken from *Josephus, The Jewish War,* edited by Gaayla Cornfeld. Copyright © 1982 by Massada Ltd., Publishers, Givatayim & Gaayla Cornfeld, Tel Aviv. Used by permission of Zondervan Publishing House.

pp. 64–75, from *The Dead Sea Scrolls* by Millar Burrows. Copyright © 1955 by Millar Burrows. Reprinted by permission of Viking Penguin Inc.

pp. 77–87, *Wisdom of Ben Sira* and *Wisdom of Solomon,* from the Revised Standard Version of the Bible, copyrighted 1946, 1952 © 1971, 1973.

pp. 93–95, from G. Vermes, *The Dead Sea Scrolls in English,* Pelican Books, 2nd ed., 1975, pp. 138–40, 211–12, 212–13, 218–20. Copyright © G. Vermes, 1962, 1965, 1968, 1975. Reprinted by permission of Penguin Books Ltd.

pp. 98–104, reprinted from *The Targums and Rabbinic Literature* by J. Bowker by permission of Cambridge University Press. Copyright 1969.

pp. 105–14, *Mekilta de Rabbi Ishmael,* trans. J. Z. Lauterbach, Philadelphia: The Jewish Publication Society of America. This material is copyrighted by and used through the courtesy of The Jewish Publication Society of America.

pp. 114–18, *The Biblical Antiquities of Philo,* New York: KTAV Publishing House. Reprinted by permission of the publisher.

pp. 118–20, *On the Cherubim,* reprinted by permission of the publishers and *The Loeb Classical Library* from *Philo,* trans. by F. H. Colson and G. H. Whitaker, Cambridge, Mass.: Harvard University Press, 1929.

pp. 120–27, from *The Mishnah,* trans. by Herbert Danby, 1933. Reprinted by permission of Oxford University Press.

pp. 127–30, *The Passover Haggadah,* trans. by Z. H. Gutstein, New York: KTAV Publishing House. Reprinted by permission of the publisher.

pp. 142–44, *History of Rome,* reprinted by permission of the publishers and *The Loeb Classical Library* from *Livy,* trans. by Evan T. Sage, Cambridge, Mass.: Harvard University Press, 1936, rpt. 1965.

pp. 144–46, E. J. and L. Edelstein, *Asclepius,* excerpts from "Testimonies," Baltimore: Johns Hopkins University Press.

p. 150, from Yves Grandjean, *Une Nouvelle Aretalogie d'Isis a Maronee,* Leiden: E. J. Brill. Reprinted by permission of the publisher.

pp. 153–54, reprinted by permission of the publishers and *The Loeb Classical Library* from *Cicero,* trans. by William A. Falconer, Cambridge, Mass.: Harvard University Press, 1923, rpt. 1959.

pp. 154–56, *Moralia,* reprinted by permission of the publishers and *The Loeb Classical Library* from *Plutarch,* trans. by F. C. Babbitt, Cambridge, Mass.: Harvard University Press, 1936, rpt. 1962.

pp. 156–58, *Lives of the Caesars,* reprinted by permission of the publishers and *The Loeb Classical Library* from *Suetonius,* trans. by J. C. Rolfe, Cambridge, Mass.: Harvard University Press, 1914, rpt. 1965.

pp. 158–59, *Annals,* reprinted by permission of the publishers and *The Loeb Classical Library* from *Tacitus,* trans. by J. Jackson, Cambridge, Mass.: Harvard University Press, 1937, rpt. 1963.

pp. 162–63, *Fourth Eclogue,* reprinted by permission of the publishers and *The Loeb Classical Library* from *Virgil,* trans. by H. R. Fairclough, Cambridge, Mass.: Harvard University Press, 1916, 1932, rpt. 1967.

pp. 165–173, *On the Origin of the World; The Gospel of Truth; The Gospel of Thomas;* from *The Nag Hammadi Library,* ed. by J. M. Robinson. Reprinted by permission of the copyright owner, E. J. Brill, Leiden, Netherlands.

pp. 174–82, *Ecclesiastical History,* reprinted by permission of the publishers and *The Loeb Classical Library* from *Eusebius,* trans. by Kirsopp Lake, Cambridge, Mass.: Harvard University Press, 1926, rpt. 1965.

pp. 185–89, *Diogenes Laertius,* reprinted by permission of the publishers and *The Loeb Classical Library* from *Lives of Eminent Philosophers,* trans. by R. D. Hicks, Cambridge, Mass.: Harvard University Press, 1925, rpt. 1958.

pp. 189–92, from *The Fathers According to Rabbi Nathan,* trans. by Judah Goldin, pp. 78–82. New Haven: Yale University Press, copyright 1955.

pp. 192–97, reprinted by permission of the publishers and *The Loeb Classical Library* from *Lucian of Samosota,* trans. by A. M. Harmon, Cambridge, Mass.: Harvard University Press, 1911, rpt. 1961.

pp. 195–96, reprinted by permission of the publishers and *The Loeb Classical Library* from *Epictetus,* trans. by W. A. Oldfather, Cambridge, Mass.: Harvard University Press, 1928, rpt. 1966.

pp. 197–202, reprinted by permission of the publishers and *The Loeb Classical Library* from *Apuleius,* trans. by W. Adlington, Cambridge, Mass.: Harvard University Press, 1915, rpt. 1947.

pp. 202–4, from *Light from the Ancient East* by Adolf Deissmann © 1927. Reprinted by permission of Hodder and Stoughton Limited. Rpt. Baker Book House, 1978.

pp. 210–14, from *The Odes of Solomon,* ed. and trans. by J. H. Charlesworth, © Oxford University Press, 1973. Reprinted by permission of Oxford University Press.

pp. 215–19, from *The Acts of Thomas,* trans. by A. J. F. Klijn, Leiden: E. J. Brill. Reprinted by permission of the publisher.

pp. 220–22, reprinted from *Ritual Magic* by E. M. Butler by permission of Cambridge University Press. Copyright 1949, rpt. 1979.

pp. 225–28, *Moral Epistles,* reprinted by permission of the publishers and *The Loeb Classical Library* from *Seneca,* trans. by J. W. Basore, Cambridge, Mass.: Harvard University Press.

pp. 230–31, from *First-Century Cynicism in the Epistles of Heraclitus* Epistle IV, trans. by Harold Attridge. Reprinted by permission of Harvard Theological Review.

THE NEW TESTAMENT IN CONTEXT

Sources and Documents

Introduction

In a dramatic scene depicting the outpouring of the Spirit of God on representatives of all nations gathered in Jerusalem on the day of Pentecost, the author of Acts comments that the multitude was "bewildered, because each one heard [the apostles] speaking in his or her own language" (Acts 2:6). The symbolic meaning of this story is of great importance for anyone studying the New Testament. For the Holy Spirit—or for any merely human agent—to communicate with others, the language used must be comprehensible to the hearer. But what is included in language is far more than merely the words of the message or narrative. In the words of modern linguistics scholars, language is "the vehicle of socialization, of group solidarity, of tension release, of psychotherapy and of love. Language could not exist without culture, or culture without language."[1] Even while shaping its own distinctive language as a medium of expressing and confirming the new life of faith, Christianity had to address potential members of the new community in terms that were meaningful to them in the context of life and thought where they were. To put it bluntly, the "language of the Holy Ghost," as modern devotees of charismatic speech sometimes call it, is presented in Acts as the ability to speak and to be understood by a vast range of persons of diverse linguistic, cultural, and social backgrounds.

To study the New Testament in context therefore requires us to explore the historical setting, the religious aspirations, the social patterns, and the literary styles that were part of the living experience and outlook

[1]Quoted from David G. Hays, "Language and Interpersonal Relationships," in *Language as a Human Problem,* ed. Einar Haugen and Morton Bloomfield (New York: Norton, 1973), p. 206.

on life of the early hearers of the Christian message. This kind of inquiry will show us what assumptions and styles of expression the early Christians shared with their contemporaries, but it will also help us to focus on what was distinctive about this new movement. The New Testament writers, like any others seeking to communicate to a reader or hearer, do not usually define their terms. Some of the most important phrases, such as *kingdom of God* or even *Messiah,* are employed without clarification on the assumption that writer and reader may disagree about the candidates for messiahship, for example, but they agree in general as to what the role involves. Only by investigating the many possible meanings of such terms can the reader of the New Testament have some assurance of grasping the intention of the writers.

The strategy of the New Testament writers is to persuade, rather than merely to inform. Some of the writings may have been intended to convert outsiders, or at least to evoke a positive attitude toward the claims that Christians were making, but most were written to provide instructions or encouragement for those who were already part of the Christian community. An important factor that has often been overlooked in examining the New Testament as a collection is that during the period in which these writings were being produced, there was not a uniform point of view on many of the basic matters of Christian faith and practice. Some segments of the early church were concerned with maintaining continuity with their Jewish heritage. Others had only minimal connections with Judaism, and stressed rather the inclusiveness of the people of the New Covenant. Still others tried to find a mediating position on the question as to what aspects of Jewish practice were binding on Christians. The view of the world—including the understanding of evil, how God was dealing with it, how human moral responsibility was to be understood, what attitude should be taken toward the Roman political power—that the various groups within the church brought with them from their respective backgrounds profoundly affected the ways in which they formulated their standards for Christian faith and action.

The circumstances under which the various New Testament books were written differ widely as well. Some give evidence of having been prepared in order to put in written form what earlier had been transmitted orally. This seems clearest in the case of the gospels, especially Mark. We shall see that the process of oral transmission of tradition was important in both the Jewish and the wider Greco-Roman worlds. Other New Testament writings are far more sophisticated in style, reflecting knowledge of literary forms and intellectual concepts in wide use among hellenistic and Latin writers. The outline of this book, therefore, moves through four different aspects of the context in which the New Testament was produced.

First is the political setting, where attention is given to the political fortunes of the Jewish people in the last two centuries before the birth of Jesus, including their liberation from the hellenistic rulers that dominated Palestine after the death of Alexander the Great, the coming of the Romans and the consequent period of a puppet monarchy under Herod, and finally the unsuccessful nationalistic uprising of the Jews.

The second and largest portion of the book presents the religious context of the New Testament. This begins with a broad range of evidence concerning Judaism in this period, including such religious institutions as the Temple in Jerusalem, the beginnings of the synagogue, the various Jewish sects that arose at this time (especially the Essenes and the Pharisees), the forms of religious writing, and the modes of interpretation that arose as supplements to and keys to the older Jewish scriptures. A major motif in this material is how Jews maintained identity with their past even while adapting to new circumstances in the Roman world.

The materials portraying Greek and Roman religions in this period include evidence of the popularity of the cults that claimed to offer direct relationship with the divine (such as the worship of Asklepios and Isis), the growing pressure of the Roman empire to exploit the idea of the divinity of the emperor as an instrument of solidarity among its diverse subjects, and the widespread belief in portents and oracles as evidence of the guiding hand of the gods in the movement of human history. Documentation is also included for that movement in the second and subsequent centuries called *Gnosticism.* It claimed to disclose true knowledge (in Greek, *gnosis*) of both the spiritual realm in which the ultimate God dwells and the material world in which human beings are caught, but from which gnosis can effect their deliverance.

The third section begins with excerpts from Jewish and Greco-Roman sources in which anecdotes are offered depicting the lives of famous persons in history. Then there are excerpts of both historical and novelistic styles of writing from this period, including popular rhetoric in the form of speeches and statements made in public defense. The last groups of literary forms offered are hymnic or liturgical patterns. Moving out of the strictly literary forms, we have some examples of personal letters from this epoch, and finally public inscriptions and magical formulas. Of the latter, collections dating from later times but including material from before the turn of our era have been preserved. And finally, in this section there are excerpts (preserved in Eusebius's *Ecclesiastical History*) of tradition about the fate of the apostles and the developments of the church into the second century.

In the fourth section, the philosophical context of the origins of Christianity is sketched in relation to the three systems of Greek philosophy that most directly influenced the New Testament writers and other early Christian thinkers, beginning with Paul. These are Platonism, Stoicism, and Cynicism. In addition to the more specifically philosophical interest, the excerpts provide evidence of the widespread popular concern for raising the level of public and private morality.

The aim of this collection of material is to provide detailed information to the reader interested in knowing more about the setting in which the Christian movement arose and took shape, ranging from the second century B.C. to the end of the second century A.D. The reader may thereby achieve fuller understanding of the forces—political, social, cultural, intellectual, literary, and religious—that shaped the environment in which the early Christians lived. In light of these insights one can gain a heightened awareness of the language and conceptual systems through which the New Testament writers sought to express their convictions to their contemporaries.

NOTE: Throughout this book, references to biblical passages are occasionally printed in the margins. These refer not to direct quotations, but to texts that are relevant—either by way of similarity or contrast—to the documents that are being quoted in the book.

1

The Political Context

The political events that most directly affected the rise of Christianity were the struggles of the Jews, from the second century B.C. to the second century A.D., to establish an autonomous Jewish state, and the Roman efforts to suppress them. Fortunately we have abundant sources, both Jewish and Roman in origin and in outlook, for discovering what went on in the political arena to foster and to frustrate these Jewish political hopes.

THE JEWISH STATE IN THE GRECO-ROMAN PERIOD

I Maccabees

Following the death of Alexander the Great (in 323 B.C.), the struggle for power among his generals left Palestine a buffer zone between the dynasty of the Ptolemies in Egypt and that of the Seleucids, based at Antioch in Syria. By the early second century B.C., the Seleucids were in control of the Jewish territory. Antiochus IV Epiphanes was determined to force the Jews to acknowledge him as a divine ruler, and sent troops in to enforce his decree. The resistance to Antiochus, led by a priest, Mattathias, and his sons, is known by historians as the Maccabean revolt, taking its name from the nickname of one of the sons, Judah (or Judas). From these courageous nationalists arose the royal line that continued down to the coming of the Romans under Pompey in 63 B.C. The best source for our knowledge of this successful revolt and its consequences is known as *I Maccabees.*

Alexander the Great. This son of Philip of Macedon, inspired by a mixture of hunger for power and a philosophical vision of the unity of humanity, brought under military control the whole of the Middle East. His early death in 323 B.C. led to a power struggle among his generals, which resulted in the rise to power of the Seleucids in Syria and the Ptolemies in Egypt. The Jews lived in a buffer zone between these rival centers of cultural and political force. *(Courtesy of the Alexandria Museum)*

The work was probably begun during the reign of Simon the Maccabee (142–135 B.C.), but was completed after his death in approximately 125 B.C. Allegedly composed in Hebrew, it has survived and has been known since ancient times solely in Greek. Based largely on eyewitness accounts and on the author's own detailed knowledge of the land and the events, it is a remarkably accurate and precise documentary account, although the author's knowledge of Roman institutions is understandably but regrettably faulty. Some of the letters purporting to have been written by or to foreign rulers, such as the letters exchanged with the Spartans, are almost certainly later interpolations, made in the interests of attaching international importance to the events of Jewish history. What basis this correspondence has in fact is almost impossible to determine, but even taking into consideration the unqualified admiration the writer has for the Maccabees, he has produced a first-rate historical narrative of the period.

MT. The significance of I Maccabees for the study of the origins of
2:2 Christianity is twofold. It enables the reader to understand why the Ro-
MK. mans were in Palestine at the time of Jesus, and why the charge that Jesus
15:12, aspired to be king of the Jews could not be dismissed as mere fantasy.
26 But it also points up the unresolved conflict among Jews as to whether

their destiny as the people of God required that they form an independent political state, or whether "Israel" was to be a holy people of God in the midst of an alien world. Related to these issues was the further question of whether Jews should seize the initiative in settling the issue of their own destiny, or whether the outcome should be left entirely in the hands of God, who would intervene on behalf of his people. I Maccabees represents one set of answers to these questions. We shall see that the Pharisees and the Essenes came to have very different solutions for the future of the Israelites as the convenant people.

I MACCABEES 1:20–2:28

(1:20) And after Antiochus had attacked Egypt, he returned in the hundred and forty-third year,[1] and went up against Israel and Jerusalem with a great army. (21) He entered arrogantly into the sanctuary and took away the golden altar and the lampstand and all its accessories (22) and the table of the Bread of the Presence and the pouring vessels, and the bowls, and the golden censers, and the veil, and the crowns, and all the golden ornaments that were on the facade of the temple he pulled off. (23) He also took the silver and the gold, and the precious vessels, as well as the hidden treasures, which he found. (24) And when he had carried off the whole of this, he returned to his own land, having caused a great massacre and spoken with great arrogance.

(25) As a consequence, there was great mourning in Israel, in every place where they were.[2] (26) The princes and the elders mourned, the virgins and the young men became weak, and the beauty of women was changed. (27) Every bridegroom took up lamentation, and even the bride sitting in the marriage chamber was in mourning. (28) The land was moved by the fate of its inhabitants, and all the house of Jacob was covered with humiliation.

(29) After two years the king sent his chief collector of tribute to the cities of Judah. He came to Jerusalem with a great host (30) and spoke peaceful words to the people, but the whole thing was deceitful, for when the people took him at his word, he fell suddenly on the city, struck it a severe blow, and destroyed many of the people of Israel. (31) And when he had taken spoils from the city, he set it on fire, and razed its houses and walls on every side. (32) The women and children were taken captive and the cattle were seized. (33) Then the enemy built the Citadel of David with a great and strong wall, and with mighty towers, and made it a stronghold for themselves. (34) In it they placed a sinful people, wicked men, who fortified themselves within it. (35) They stored it also with arms and provisions. When they had gathered together the spoils of Jerusalem, they stored them there as well. In this way they became a severe menace, (36) for it provided them a place to lie in wait opposite the sanctuary, an evil adversary for Is-

[1]The Seleucid era began on October 1, 312 B.C., when Seleucus I, one of the generals of Alexander the Great and heir to Syria in terms of Alexander's will, ascended to the throne. Antiochus's attack on Palestine took place, therefore, in 169 B.C.

[2]That is, the Jews. Many of the cities of Palestine had few or no Jewish inhabitants. This was true of both coastal and inland cities that were dominated by hellenistic culture and considered by pious Jews to be unfit places to live. The old Philistine cities—Ashdod, Ashkelon, Gaza, Ekron, and Gath—were not conquered by the invading Hebrews, and were dominated by hellenistic culture, as the recent excavations at Ashdod have clearly shown.

rael in every way. (37) By this means they shed innocent blood on every side of the sanctuary and defiled it. (38) Because of them, the inhabitants of Jerusalem fled, with the result that the city became a dwelling place for foreigners, and was instead strange to those who were born within her, since her own offspring had left her. (39) Her sanctuary became barren like a desert. Her feasts were turned into mourning, her sabbaths into dishonor, her honor into contempt. (40) As once she had been glorious, so now she filled with dishonor; she who formerly had been exalted was now turned to lamentation.

(41) Furthermore, King Antiochus wrote to all his kingdom that all people should be one,[3] (42) and that every one should abandon his own laws. All the heathen agreed to the king's commandment, (43) and even many of the Israelites were pleased to accept his religion, sacrificing to idols and profaning the sabbath. (44) For the king had sent letters by messengers to Jerusalem and the cities of Judah requiring them to practice regulations that were alien to their land: (45) the messengers were under instruction that they should prohibit burnt offerings and sacrifices and drink offerings in the temple; that they should profane the sabbaths and the feast days. (46) Further, they were to pollute the sanctuary and the holy people, (47) to set up altars and groves and shrines of idols, to sacrifice the flesh of swine and unclean animals. (48) The people of Judah were ordered to leave their sons uncircumcized and to make themselves ceremonially polluted with all manner of uncleanness and profanation (49) with the aim in view that they might forget their Law and change all its ordinances. (50) If anyone would not conform to the king's decree, he was to die.

(51) In the same manner he wrote to his whole kingdom, and appointed overseers over all the people who commanded the cities of Judah to offer sacrifice, city by city. (52) Then many of the people went along with this; in so doing they forsook the Law and committed evils in the land. (53) As a result, the Israelites were driven into hiding places wherever they could flee for refuge. (54) Now on the fifteenth day of the month Kislev, in the one

Antiochus IV, ruler in Syria during the early second century B.C. (175–164). Antiochus insisted that he be called *Epiphanes* (manifestation of the divine), and that all subjects, including the Jews, acknowledge him as such in their sanctuaries. His attempt to enforce this decree triggered the Jewish Revolt, under the Maccabees. *(Courtesy of the American Numismatic Society)*

[3]The unity of all mankind was a major dogma and ideal of the hellenistic rulers from Alexander on. Jews could not accept this view and still continue to regard themselves as the elect covenant community; to accept such a distinction-free view of humanity would have forced them to abandon the laws of separateness that were essential elements in the Mosaic Law.

hundred forty-fifth year,[4] they set up the desolating sacrilege on the altar and built idol altars throughout the whole of the cities of Judah. (55) They burned incense at the doors of their houses and in the streets, (56) and when they had torn in pieces the books of the Law which they found, they burned them with fire. (57) And wherever anyone was found with the book of the covenant or if anyone conformed to the Law, the king's decree was that they should put him to death. (58) Thus they kept performing acts of violence against Israel month by month, against whomever they found in the cities.

(59) On the twenty-fifth day of the month they offered sacrifices on the idol altar, which was placed upon the altar of God. (60) In keeping with the decree, they put to death the women who had caused their children to be circumcized; (61) they hanged their infants about their necks, and slaughtered households and those that had circumcized their children. (62) Many in Israel, however, were resolute and were determined in themselves not to eat any unclean thing. (63) They chose rather to die in order that they might not be defiled by unclean food or that they might not profane the holy covenant; and they did indeed die. (64) And there was very great wrath against Israel.

(2:1) In those days Mattathias, the son of John, the son of Simeon, a priest of the sons of Joarib, moved from Jerusalem and lived in Modin.[5] (2) And he had five sons: John, called Caddi; (3) Simon, called Thassi; (4) Judah, who was called Maccabeus; (5) Eleazar, called Avaran; and Jonathan, whose surname was Apphus.

(6) When he saw the blasphemies that were being committed in Judah and Jerusalem, (7) he said, "Woe is me! Why was I born to see this misery of my people, and of the holy city, and to dwell there when it was delivered into the hand of the enemy, and the sanctuary was given over to strangers? (8) Her temple is become like a man without glory. (9) Her vessels are carried away into captivity, her infants are slain in the streets, and her young men are killed by the sword of the enemy. (10) What nation has not had a part in her kingdom and obtained some of her spoils? (11) All her adornments are taken away; instead of a free woman she has become a bondslave. (12) And behold, our sanctuary, which is our beauty and our glory, has been made desolate, and the Gentiles have profaned it. (13) Why then shall we live any longer?"

(14) Then Mattathias and his sons tore their clothes and put on sackcloth and mourned bitterly.

(15) At that time the king's officers, who were assigned to compel the people to commit apostasy, came into the city of Modin in order that they might coerce its inhabitants to offer sacrifice. (16) Many of Israel came to the officers, as did Mattathias and his sons as well. (17) Then the king's officers said to Mattathias: "You are a leader, an honorable and great man in this city, supported by your sons and brothers; now become the first to fulfill the king's commandment, just as all the other nations have done, as well as men of Judah and those who have stayed in Jerusalem. (18) In this way you

[4]The year corresponds to 167 B.C., and the month, Kislev, is roughly the equivalent of our December.

[5]Modin is a small town located on what was in antiquity the main route leading down through the hills of Judea from Jerusalem on the crest of the ridge to Lydda and Jaffa on the seacoast.

and your sons will be included among the king's friends, and you and your sons will be honored with silver and gold and many rewards."

(19) Then Mattathias replied, speaking in a loud voice: "Though all the nations that are under the king's dominion obey him, and though every one of them departs from the religion of his fathers and gives in to the king's commands, (20) yet will I and my sons and my brothers walk in the covenant of our fathers. (21) God forbid that we should forsake the Law and the ordinances. (22) We will not obey the king's word, to depart from our religion either to the right or the left."

(23) Now when he had finished speaking these words, according to the king's commandment, there came one of the Jews in the sight of all to sacrifice on the altar which was in Modin. (24) When Mattathias saw this, he was inflamed with zeal and his heart quivered. Driven by righteous indignation, he ran and killed the man as he was sacrificing at the altar. (25) And at the same time he also killed the officer sent by the king to enforce his commandment by compelling the people to sacrifice, and he knocked down the altar. (26) Thus he acted zealously for the law of God, as Phineas[6] had done to Zambri, the son of Salom. (27) And Mattathias went throughout the city calling out with a loud voice, "Whoever is zealous for the Law and maintains the covenant, let him follow me." (28) So he and his sons fled into the mountains and left all that they had in the city.

3:1–9

(3:1) Then[7] his son Judas, called Maccabeus, assumed command in his stead, (2) and all his brothers helped him, and so did all those who had sided with his father, and they fought with joy the battle of Israel. (3) So he increased the great glory of his people and put on a breastplate as a giant, and girded his armor of war about him, and fought battles, protecting his troops with the sword. (4) In his deeds he was like a lion, and like a lion's whelp roaring for his prey. (5) For he pursued the wicked and sought them out and consumed with fire those that harassed his people. (6) The lawless drew back for fear of him, and all the doers of evil were put to confusion because salvation prospered in his hand. (7) He brought grief to many kings, but through his deeds he made Jacob glad, and his memory is blessed forever. (8) Moreover he went through the cities of Judah, destroying the irreligious persons in them and thus turning away wrath from Israel. (9) Accordingly, he was renowned to the ends of the earth, and he gathered to himself such men as were prepared to fight to the death.

4:6–61

(4:6) But as soon as it was day, Judas appeared in the plain[8] with three thousand men, who had neither the arms nor the swords that they might

[6]Phineas, according to Numbers 25, on finding an Israelite having intercourse with a Midianite woman, ran them both through with a spear.

[7]That is, after the death of Mattathias in 166 B.C. His dying admonitions to his sons are recorded in I Macc. 2:49–68, and the date of his death as well as his place of burial—at Modin—are given in 2:69–70.

[8]After the Maccabean forces had bested the Syrians in a series of guerilla engagements and battles, Antiochus sent a huge army to crush the revolt (3:10–4:5). The troops of Antiochus were encamped near Emmaus, at a point where the Jerusalem-Jaffa road descends from the hills to the coastal plain.

have wished. (7) They saw the camp of the Gentiles, which was strong and well-fortified, surrounded with cavalry, and with soldiers expert in war. (8) Then Judas said to the men who were with him, "Do not fear their numbers nor be afraid of their attack. (9) Remember how our fathers were delivered at the Red Sea, when Pharaoh pursued them with an army. (10) So now let us call out to heaven, if perhaps the Lord will have mercy on us, and remember the covenant of our fathers, and destroy this army before us this day. (11) Thus all the Gentiles may know that there is one who delivers and saves Israel."

(12) When the foreigners looked up and saw them coming against them, (13) they went out from the camp to battle. Those that were with Judas sounded the trumpets. (14) So the battle was joined, and the Gentiles were overwhelmed and fled into the plain. (15) Those in the rear ranks, however, were slain with the sword. They pursued them as far as Gezer[9] and to the plains of Idumea,[10] and Ashdod,[11] and Jamnia,[12] so that three thousand of the enemy were slain on a single day. (16) With this accomplished, Judas and his army returned from pursuing them.

(17) Then Judas said to the people, "Do not be greedy for loot, since there is a battle before us. (18) Gorgias and his army are near us in the mountains, but stand up now against our enemies and defeat them; after that you may take the plunder."

(19) Just as Judas was finishing his address, a contingent of the enemy appeared coming down out of the mountains. (20) When they perceived that the Jews had put their forces to flight and were burning their encampment—for the smoke that was visible disclosed what had occurred—(21) they were terrified. And when they saw the troops of Judas in the plain ready for battle, (22) they all of them fled into the land of the foreigners.[13]

(23) Then Judas returned to plunder the enemy camp, where they obtained much gold, silver, and blue silk, and sea purple,[14] and other great riches. When they returned home, they sang songs of thanksgiving and praised the Lord of heaven, because he is good, because his mercy endures forever. (25) Thus Israel had a great deliverance that day.

(26) Now all the foreigners that had escaped came and told Lysias what had happened. (27) When he heard this, he was puzzled and disheartened,

[9]Gezer was a stronghold guarding the coastal plain from Bronze Age to hellenistic times.

[10]Idumea was the southern part of the Judean hills (around Hebron) where the Edomites (Idumeans) were forced to migrate by the Nabatean Arabs, who occupied the area southeast of the Dead Sea in the sixth century B.C.

[11]Azotus (or more accurately, Ashdod), a leading city and a major port, is mentioned in the Bible and in ancient literature as a leading city of the Philistines from Iron Age times (ca. 1000 B.C.) on. It provided an important cultural link between the Palestinian coast and the Greek world.

[12]Jamnia (Jabneh) is a small city about midway between Ashdod and Jaffa. Later it became a center of rabbinic learning, after the Jews were driven out of Jerusalem as a result of the revolts that ended in A.D. 70. Jamnia was located in what was traditionally Philistine territory.

[13]That is, of the Philistines. The cluster of cities along the southern Palestinian coast had never been under Israelite control, nor were they later for any extended period of time under Jewish control.

[14]A costly dye made from murex shells. An installation for producing this dye, together with thousands of the shells, has recently been excavated at the site of one of the ports of ancient Ashdod, now known by archaeologists as Tell Mor.

because neither had the things occurred that he had intended for Israel nor did such things as the king had commanded take place. (28) So the next year Lysias gathered together sixty thousand choice infantrymen and five thousand horsemen, in order to subdue them. (29) They came into Idumea and pitched their tents at Beth-Zur,[15] and Judas met them with ten thousand men. (30) When he saw that mighty encampment, he prayed and said: "Blessed art Thou, O savior of Israel, who didst thwart the attack of that mighty man[16] by the hand of thy servant David, and didst give the army of foreigners into the hand of Jonathan the son of Saul and his armor-bearer: (31) Surround this army by the hand of thy people Israel, and let their troops and horsemen be a humiliation to them. (32) Make them be cowardly, and cause the boldness of their strength to dwindle. May they tremble at their own destruction. (33) Hurl them down by the sword of those that love thee, and let all those that know thy name praise thee with songs."

(34) So they joined in battle, and about five thousand men of the army of Lysias were killed; directly in front of the eyes of the rest of the enemy force were they slain.[17] (35) When Lysias saw his army put to flight and observed the courage of Judas' soldiers—how they were ready to live or die valiantly—he withdrew to Antioch. There he gathered together an even larger army of mercenaries with the aim of marching once again into Judea.

(36) Then Judas and his brothers said, "Behold our enemies are overwhelmed; let us go up to purify and rededicate the sanctuary." (37) At this proposal all the troops assembled themselves together and went up to Mount Zion. (38) And when they saw the sanctuary desolate and the altar profaned and the gates burned up and brush growing in the courts as in a forest or on one of the mountains, and the priest's chambers in ruins, (39) they tore their clothes, made great lamentations and threw ashes on themselves. (40) They fell down with their faces to the ground and blew a signal with the trumpets and cried to heaven.

(41) Then Judas appointed certain men to fight against the garrison that was still in the stronghold[18] until he could cleanse the sanctuary. (42) So he chose priests whose manner of life was blameless, who delighted in the Law. (43) These cleansed the sanctuary and carried out to an unclean place the defiled stones. (44) After they had discussed what to do with the altar of burnt offerings that had been profaned, (45) they thought best to pull it down, so that it would not be a reproach against them because the heathen had defiled it. So they pulled it down (46) and stored the stones in the temple mountain in a convenient place, until there should come a prophet to show what should be done with them. (47) Then they took rough-hewn stones according to the Law and built a new altar resembling the former one. (48) They reconstructed the sanctuary and the interior parts of the temple and consecrated its courts. (49) They also made new sacred vessels, and brought into the temple the lampstand, the altars of burnt offerings

[15]Beth-Zur, an important hellenistic stronghold guarding one of the main access routes to the southern Judean hills.

[16]Goliath, the Philistine giant killed by David while he was still a shepherd boy (I Samuel 17:1–58).

[17]The Greek text is elliptical here, but it seems to say that the main body of the Syrian troops was in a position to see 5000 of their comrades fall but not able to come to their aid.

[18]Apparently the reference is to a massive tower that overlooked the temple area and that continued to be occupied by Syrian soldiers even after the rest of the city had been taken over by the Maccabean forces.

and of incense and the table. (50) They burned incense on the altar and they lit the lamps that were on the lampstand to give light in the temple. (51) Then they set the loaves on the table, hung up the curtains and finished all the work they had set out to do.

(52) Now on the twenty-fifth day of the ninth month, which is called the month Kislev, in the one hundred forty-eighth year,[19] they rose up early in the morning (53) and offered sacrifice according to the Law on the new altar of burnt offerings that they had made. (54) At the very time and on precisely the day that the heathen had profaned it, it was dedicated with songs and harps and lutes and cymbals. (55) Then all the people fell on their faces, worshipping and praising the God of heaven, who had given them good success. (56) So they performed the dedication of the altar for eight days offering burnt offerings with gladness and sacrificing the sacrifices of deliverance and praise. (57) They also decorated the facade of the temple with crowns of gold and with shields; they restored the gates and chambers, supplying them with doors. (58) Thus there was very great gladness among the people in that the reproach by the Gentiles had been taken away.

(59) Then Judas and his brothers, with the whole congregation of Israel, established that the days of the dedication of the altar should be kept at the appropriate season from year to year for a period of eight days, beginning with the twenty-fifth day of the month Kislev, with joy and gladness. (60) Also at that time they built up Mount Zion, surrounding it with high walls and strong towers, so that the Gentiles should not come and defile it as they had done before. (61) And they placed there a garrison to guard it. And further, they fortified Beth-Zur, to maintain it as a defense for the people against Idumea.

8:1–32

(8:1) Now Judas had heard of the fame of the Romans, that they were strong and powerful men who regard with great favor all who would make a treaty of friendship with them and who gave assurances of amity to all that came to them. (2) Further, he heard that the Romans were men of great valor, and he was told of the wars and noble deeds they had accomplished among the Galatians, how they had conquered them and brought them under tribute; (3) and what they had done in the region of Spain, for gaining control of the silver and gold mines that are there, (4) and that by their strategy and persistence they had conquered the whole territory even though it was very far from them; and that they had vanquished also the kings that came against them from the ends of the earth, to such an extent that they had overwhelmed them and given them a disastrous defeat with the result that the rest of the kings paid tribute to them year by year.

(5) Besides this he heard how the Romans had defeated Philip[20] in battle and Perseus,[21] king of the Macedonians, and had overcome others who lifted themselves up against them. (6) They heard also how Antiochus,[22] the

[19]This would be 164 B.C.

[20]Philip V of Macedon, who ruled from 220–179 B.C., but who was defeated by the Romans in Thessaly in 197 B.C.

[21]Perseus, an illegitimate son of Philip V, succeeded him as king, but was defeated by the Romans in 168 B.C.

[22]Antiochus III, king of Syria from 223–187 B.C.

great king of Asia, who came against the Romans in battle accompanied by a hundred and twenty elephants, with cavalry, chariots and a very great army, was overwhelmed by them; (7) and how they took him alive and decreed that he and those who reigned after him should pay a heavy tribute, that they should give hostages, and that they should turn over to the Romans such choice lands as were agreed upon. (8) The regions of India,[23] Media,[24] and Lydia,[25] they took from him and gave to King Eumenes.[26] (9) The Greeks had planned to come and destroy them, (10) but since the Romans had advance knowledge of it, they sent against them a certain general who fought with them and killed many of them and carried away as captives their wives and children, and took plunder from them and took over their lands and pulled down their fortifications and made slaves of them down to this day. (11) It was told him further how they destroyed and brought under dominion all other kingdoms and islands that ever offered resistance to them, but with their friends and allies they maintained amity; (12) that they conquered kingdoms near and far, with the result that all who heard of their name was afraid of them; (13) and also they establish as kings those whom they want to help gain the rule, but those whom they do not want to rule they displace.

Finally, he was told that they were a people of supreme power; (14) yet for all this none of them wore a crown or was clothed in the purple of royalty, lest anyone become inflated with pride thereby; (15) and how they made for themselves a senate house in which three hundred and twenty men sat daily, always deliberating in behalf of the people the better to insure public order; (16) and that they committed their government to one man every year,[27] who ruled over all their land, and that all were obedient to him, and that there was neither envy nor jealousy among them.

(17) In consideration of these things, Judas chose Eupolemus, the son of John, the son of Accos, and Jason, the son of Eleazar, and sent them to Rome to make an alliance of friendship and mutual assistance with them, (18) and to urge the Romans to take the yoke from them; for they saw that the kingdom of the Greeks was oppressing Israel with slavery. (19) So they went to Rome, which was a very great journey, and came into the senate house, where they spoke as follows:

(20) "Judas, who is also known as Maccabeus, with his brothers and the people of the Jews, have sent us to you to make an alliance and a treaty of peace with you, so that we might be registered as your allies and friends."

(21) This report pleased the Romans well. (22) And this is the copy of

[23]This is historically impossible, since the Seleucids never controlled India and were therefore in no position to turn it over to the Romans.

[24]The Seleucids were forced by the Romans to turn over to them territory northwest of the Taurus Range.

[25]A rich territory in SW Asia Minor that became a client state subject to Rome.

[26]Eumenes II, king of the rich city-state Pergamos from 197–158 B.C.; his assistance to the Romans against the Seleucids was rewarded by the grant of these rich territories.

[27]Several of the details of the information given here about Rome are inaccurate: the senate sat at stated times, but not daily; there were two consuls, not one; there was considerable rivalry for leadership. But there is no reason to doubt the intention of the writer to give an accurate account or to question the general historicity of this picture of the dealings between the Maccabees and the Romans.

the epistle that the senate wrote back again on tablets of brass and sent to Jerusalem, in order for the Jews to have there a memorial of peace and mutual assistance:

(23) "May things go well for the Romans and for the nation of the Jews, at sea and on land for ever and ever; and may both sword and enemy be far from them. (24) If there should come first any war against Rome or any of her allies throughout all their dominion, (25) the people of the Jews shall help them with all their heart, as the time shall be appointed; (26) neither shall the Jews provide anything for those who make war on the Romans, or aid them with food, weapons, money, or ships, as it has seemed good to the Romans; but they shall keep their agreements without taking anything in exchange. (27) In the same way, if war should come first upon the nation of the Jews, the Romans will help them with all their heart, according as occasion may dictate to them. (28) Neither shall food be given to those who side against the Jews, nor weapons, nor money, as it has seemed good to the Romans, but they shall keep their obligations and do so without deceit. (29) According to these articles the Romans make a covenant with the nation of the Jews, (30) but if hereafter the one party or the other shall think it fitting to add or delete anything, they may do it at their pleasures, and whatever they shall add or take away shall be ratified. (31) And on the matter of the evils that Demetrius[28] is perpetrating against the Jews, we have written him saying, 'Why have you made heavy the yoke upon our friends and allies the Jews? If they have further complaints against you, we will meet our just obligations to them, and fight against you by sea and land.' "

ROMAN POLICY IN THE EASTERN PROVINCES

Josephus, Antiquities of the Jews

Born in the year Gaius Caligula became emperor (A.D. 37), Joseph(us) ben Matthias was descended from priests on his father's side and from the royal Hasmonean (Maccabean) family on his mother's. He was given every advantage as a child, including a thorough education in scriptural learning. In addition to his exposure to the teachings of the Pharisees and the Sadducees, he spent three years in the ascetic community of the Essenes in the Jordan Valley. His own religious position was Pharisaic, which enabled him to combine devotion to the Law of Moses with an attitude of passive accommodation toward Rome.

A visit to Rome in the year 64 impressed on him the wisdom of adopting an attitude of acceptance toward Rome, which had unbeatable power, so when he returned to his native Palestine and found the Jewish nationalists fomenting revolt, he devoted all his energies and powers of

[28]Demetrius I, who reigned from 162–150 B.C. as Seleucid King of Syria.

persuasion to deterring the insurrectionists. His efforts were unavailing, however. When the fighting started, he was given some kind of special assignment in Galilee, which seems to have included achieving a peaceful settlement between the nationalists and the Romans. He was apparently regarded by the insurrectionists as a traitor and by the Romans as a spy. Whatever his connections and motives, he was captured by Vespasian, whose rise to imperial power he had earlier and accurately predicted; attached as a kind of prisoner-advisor to the Roman forces, he accompanied Vespasian to Alexandria and then returned for the siege of Jerusalem, where he functioned as mediator and interpreter between the Romans and his fellow Jews.

After the fall of Jerusalem (A.D. 70), Vespasian having been proclaimed emperor by the army in 69, Josephus was assured of a place in imperial favor, and even of living accommodations in the imperial household. It was in Rome that most of his writing was done, although he seems to have written a first edition of his *Jewish War* in Aramaic, his native tongue, and addressed it to Jews living in the eastern parts of Syria and Mesopotamia, where large numbers of his coreligionists remained from the time of Babylonian exile (sixth century B.C.). The second edition was composed before A.D. 79 with the help of Greek-speaking literary aides, as he acknowledges in the introduction to the Greek version, which alone has survived. His *Antiquities of the Jews* appeared late in the reign of Domitian (probably between 93 and 94 A.D.). In it Josephus shows dependence on other historical sources, such as I Maccabees and records kept in the court of Herod the Great. It was impossible, of course, for him to have been a first-hand observer of so long a span of history.

From the second century on, Christians were disappointed that Josephus paid so little attention to Christianity, mentioning it only twice and then only in passing (*Antiquities* XVIII:63; XX:200). In order to remedy what they regarded as an oversight, some of his Christian readers expanded the references, thereby transforming Josephus into a witness in behalf of Jesus as Messiah. (See discussion of this in H. C. Kee, *Jesus in History,* New York: Harcourt Brace Jovanovich, 1977, pp. 42–45.)

In spite of the absence from his account of information we might wish he had included, and in spite of his pro-Roman prejudices and his attempts at self-vindication, he remains one of our most important ancient sources, not only for the history of Judaism in the first centuries before and after the birth of Jesus, but for detailed knowledge of palace politics both in Jerusalem and in Rome, as well as for information in depth about imperial policy in dealing with an eastern province.

In Book XIII of his *Antiquities,* Josephus describes the reign of one of the most notorious of the descendants of the Maccabees—the family was known as the Hasmoneans—in the person of Alexander Jannaeus.

His reputation rested on the cruelty with which he treated his fellow Jews.

ANTIQUITIES OF THE JEWS XIII:379–383

(379) Alexander[29] thereupon fled to the mountains, where out of pity for him at this reverse[30] six thousand Jews gathered to his side. And at this Demetrius withdrew in alarm. But later on the Jews fought (380) against Alexander and were defeated, many of them dying in battle. The most powerful of them, however, he brought back to Jerusalem; and there he did a thing that was as cruel as could be: while he feasted with his concubines in a conspicuous place, he ordered some eight hundred of the Jews to be crucified, and slaughtered their children and wives before the eyes of the still living wretches. This was the revenge he (381) took for the injuries he had suffered; but the penalty he exacted was inhuman for all that, even though he had, as was natural, gone through very great hardships in the wars he had fought against them, and had finally found himself in danger of losing both his life and his throne, for they were not satisfied to carry on the struggle by themselves but (382) brought foreigners as well, and at last reduced him to the necessity of surrendering to the king of the Arabs[31] the territory which he had conquered in Moab and Galaaditis and the strongholds therein, in order that he might not aid the Jews in the war against him; and they (383) committed countless other insulting and abusive acts against him. But still he seems to have done this thing unnecessarily, and as a result of his excessive cruelty he was nicknamed Thrakidas (the "Cossack") by the Jews. Then his opponents, numbering in all about eight thousand, fled by night and remained in exile so long as Alexander lived. And he, being rid of the trouble they had caused him, reigned thereafter in complete tranquility.

In Book XIV of the *Antiquities,* Josephus describes one of the dark moments in Jewish history: the seizure of Jerusalem and its temple by the Romans under Pompey. Except for brief periods of revolt (A.D. 66–70 and 132–135), the Jews were not again in control of Jerusalem until modern times.

[29]The reign of Alexander Jannaeus as king of the Jews lasted from 103–76 B.C. His cruel and ruthless tyranny, his excesses in suppressing dissent, both from within his own family and from his subjects, included crucifying his political foes and earned him a place as a model of inhumanity. The internal strife within the Jewish state was aggravated by his harsh methods and the way was thus prepared for intervention by the Romans.

[30]The defeat mentioned was the outcome of a battle in which the Seleucid king, Demetrius III, was joined by Jewish troops fighting against their own despotic ruler, Alexander. But the setback for Alexander was only temporary, and he retaliated ruthlessly against the Jews who continued to oppose his rule.

[31]From the sixth century B.C. down into Roman times, the Nabatean Arabs controlled the area bordering the Arabian Desert from Damascus south to the Gulf of Aqaba. Their capital was the spectacular rock-hewn city, Petra. Moab is the mountainous area to the east of the Dead Sea; Galaaditis is geologically similar territory north of Moab and east of the Jordan Valley.

XIV:57–67; 69–73

(57) And Pompey,[32] being seized with anger at this,[33] placed Aristobulus[34] under arrest, and himself went to the city,[35] which was strongly fortified on all sides except on the north, where it was weak. For it is surrounded by a broad and deep ravine which takes in the temple, and this is very strongly protected by an encircling wall of stone.

(58) But among the men within the city there was dissension, for they were not of one mind concerning their situation; to some it seemed best to deliver the city to Pompey, while those who sympathized with Aristobulus urged that they shut Pompey out and make war on him because he held Aristobulus prisoner. It was this party that made the first move and occupied the temple, and cutting the bridge[36] that stretches (59) from it to the city, prepared themselves for a siege. But those of the other faction admitted Pompey's army and handed over to him the city and the palace. Pompey thereupon sent his legate Piso with an army to guard the city and the palace, and fortified the houses adjoining the (60) temple and the places round the temple outside. His first step was to offer conciliatory terms to those within, but as they would not listen to his proposals, he fortified the surrounding places with walls, with Hyrcanus willingly assisting him in all ways. And at dawn Pompey pitched his camp on the north side of the temple, where it was open to (61) attack. But even here stood great towers, and a trench had been dug, and the temple was surrounded by a deep ravine; for there was a steep slope on the side toward the city after the bridge was destroyed, and at this spot Pompey by great labour day by day had caused earthworks to be raised, for which the Romans cut down the timber round about. (62) And when these were high enough, though the trench was filled up with difficulty because of its immense depth, he moved up and set in place the siege engines and instruments of war that had been brought from Tyre, and began to batter the temple with his catapults. But if it (63) were not our national custom to rest on the Sabbath day, the earthworks would not have been finished, because the Jews would have prevented this; for the Law permits us to defend ourselves against those who begin a battle and strike us, but it does not allow us to fight against an enemy that does anything else.

(64) Of this fact the Romans were well aware, and on those days which

[32]Member of the famous Roman triumvirate, along with Julius Caesar and Crassus, Pompey invaded Syria and then Palestine on the pretext of pacifying the local warring populace, but the result was to establish Roman hegemony in the area for the next seven centuries.

[33]The immediate occasion for Pompey's wrath was Aristobulus's refusal to follow through on his earlier promise of three hundred talents to be given to Pompey. When Gabinius, Pompey's general, arrived at Jerusalem to pick up the bribe, Aristobulus refused to admit him to the city.

[34]Aristobulus, son of Alexander Jannaeus and Alexandra, succeeded his mother as king at her death in 69 B.C. by persuading his brother, Hyrcanus, to abdicate in his favor.

[35]That is, Jerusalem.

[36]The temple hill was separated from the wealthy suburbs on the western hill of Jerusalem by a valley that was much deeper then than it is now. A viaduct made it possible to cross to the temple without descending into the valley. The recently discovered piers of what is probably a similar viaduct crossing this valley are associated with Herod's vastly enlarged version of the temple complex, work on which did not begin until a half century after Pompey's invasion.

we call the Sabbath, they did not shoot at the Jews or meet them in hand to hand combat, but instead they raised earthworks and towers, and brought up their siege-engines in order that these might be put (65) to work the following day. And one may get an idea of the extreme piety which we show toward God and of our strict observance of the laws from the fact that during the siege the priests were not hindered from performing any of the sacred ceremonies through fear, but twice a day, in the morning and at the ninth hour, they performed the sacred ceremonies at the altar, and did not omit any of the sacrifices even when some (66) difficulty arose because of the attacks. And indeed when the city was taken, in the third month, on the Fast Day, in the hundred and seventy-ninth Olympiad,[37] in the consulship of Gaius Antonius and Marcus Tullius Cicero, and the enemy rushed in and were slaughtering the (67) Jews in the temple, those who were busied with the sacrifices none the less continued to perform the sacred ceremonies; nor were they compelled, either by fear for their lives or by the great number of those already slain, to run away, but thought it better to endure whatever they might have to suffer there beside the altars than to neglect any of the ordinances.

(69) Now when the siege-engine was brought up, the largest of the towers was shaken and fell, making a breach through which the enemy poured in; first among them was Cornelius Faustus, the son of Sulla, who with his soldiers mounted the wall, and after him the centurion Furius, with those who followed him, on the other side, and between them Fabius, another centurion, with a strong and compact body of men. And there was slaughter everywhere. For some of the Jews were slain (70) by the Romans, and others by their fellows; and there were some who hurled themselves down the precipices, and setting fire to their houses, burned themselves within them, for they could not bear to accept their fate. And so of the Jews there fell some twelve thousand, but of the (71) Romans only a very few. One of those taken captive was Absalom, the uncle and at the same time father-in-law of Aristobulus. And not light was the sin committed against the sanctuary, which before that time had never been entered or seen. For Pompey and not a few of his men went (72) into it and saw what it was unlawful for any but the high priests to see. But though the golden table was there and the sacred lampstand and the libation vessels and a great quantity of spices, and beside these, in the treasury, the sacred moneys amounting to two thousand talents, he touched none of these because of piety, and in this respect also he acted in a manner worthy of his virtuous character. And on (73) the morrow he instructed the temple servants to cleanse the temple and to offer the customary sacrifice to God, and he restored the high priesthood to Hyrcanus[38] because in various ways he had been useful to him and particularly because he had prevented the Jews throughout the country from fighting on Aristobulus's side; and those responsible for the war he executed by beheading.

Antipater, an Idumean adventurer and father of Herod the Great, had served variously as an intermediary between Jewish leaders and the

[37]That is, 63 B.C.

[38]Hyrcanus, son of Alexandra, had been dethroned in the dynastic struggle for control of the high priesthood sketched in Note 33.

Nabatean Arabs of East Jordan, and between the Jews and the Roman invaders. His knack of shifting to the winning side was evident when he abandoned Pompey and helped Julius Caesar gain control of Egypt. Brave and politically adroit, Antipater's son Herod inherited these characteristics, with the result that he was appointed by the Romans as governor of Samaria and northern Palestine. Then in 40 B.C. the Roman senate confirmed him as king of the Jews, with Caesar and Mark Antony jointly sponsoring him. In this capacity he ruled over all of Palestine, as well as over territories to the north and east of the Jordan Valley. He sought to lend legitimacy to his kingship by taking as his wife Mariamne, a woman of the Hasmonean royal line. His love for her was turned to distrust, fed by the rumors perpetrated by those who sought to destroy her, until finally Herod had her put to death. His subsequent remorse and grief brought on what we would call a depression and fostered a neurotic suspicion of everyone, from which he never recovered. His efficiency as an administrator and ruler remained, but his insensitive, even ruthless, attitude toward his subjects engendered their hatred of him. The final paragraph of the section of Josephus's *Antiquities* here ex-

Caesar Augustus, the winner in the contest for power that led to and continued after the assassination of Julius Caesar. While preserving the forms of the Roman Republic, Octavian (on whom was bestowed the title Augustus) became in fact the monarch of the Roman state. His skills, militarily and diplomatically, enabled him to bring peace and relative unity to the entire Mediterranean region under his control. *(Courtesy of the Fototeca di Architettura e Topographia dell'Italia Antica)*

cerpted reports Herod's will, in which he distributed his realm among his surviving sons and daughter.

Not only do Herod and his sons figure directly in the New Testament as the rulers who dominated the land from Jesus's birth until his crucifixion, but the fact that they ruled through collaboration with the Romans was a major factor in the political tensions of the period, and made Jesus's ideas about "the Kingdom of God" take on revolutionary overtones. On the other hand, reconstruction of the Jerusalem temple, begun under Herod the Great and completed much later, was a chief source of Jewish pride, the major factor in the economy of Jerusalem, and the House of God.

xv:267–276

For this reason[39] Herod went still farther (267) in departing from the native customs, and through foreign practices he gradually corrupted the ancient way of life, which had hitherto been inviolable. As a result of this we suffered considerable harm at a later time as well, because those things were neglected which had formerly induced piety in the masses. For in the first place he established athletic (268) contests every fifth year in honour of Caesar, and he built a theatre in Jerusalem, and after that a very large amphitheatre in the plain, both being spectacularly lavish but foreign to Jewish custom, for the use of such buildings and the exhibition of such spectacles have not been traditional [with the Jews]. Herod, however, celebrated the (269) quinquennial festival in the most splendid way sending notices of it to the neighbouring peoples and inviting participants from the whole nation. Athletes and other classes of contestants were invited from every land, being attracted by the hope of winning the prizes offered and by the glory of victory. And the leading men in various fields were assembled, for Herod offered (270) very great prizes not only to the winners in gymnastic games but also to those who engaged in music and those who are called thymelikoi.[40] And an effort was made to have all the most famous persons come to the contest. He also offered considerable gifts to drivers of four-horse and two-horse chariots and to (271) those mounted on race-horses. And whatever costly or magnificent efforts had been made by others, all these did Herod imitate in his ambition to see his spectacle become famous. (272) All round the theatre were inscriptions concerning Caesar and trophies of the nations which he had won in war, all of them made for Herod of pure gold and silver. As for serviceable objects, there was no valuable garment or vessel of precious stones which was not also on (273) exhibition along with the contests. There was also a supply of wild beasts, a great many lions and other animals having been brought together for him, such as were of extraordinary strength or of very rare kinds. When the practice began of involving them in combat with one another or setting condemned men to fight against them, foreigners were astonished (274) at the expense and at the same time entertained by the dangerous spectacle, but to the natives it meant an open break with the customs held in honour by them. For it

[39]The reason was that no members of the Hasmonean line survived to challenge Herod's power or to remind him of his obligation to Jewish traditions.

[40]Probably refers to performers, such as actors or musicians.

seemed glaring impiety to throw men to wild beasts for the pleasure of other men as spectators, and it seemed a further impiety to change (275) their established ways for foreign practices. But more than all else it was the trophies that irked them, for in the belief that these were images surrounded by weapons, (276) which it was against their national custom to worship, they were exceedingly angry.

XV:380–402

It was at this time, in the eighteenth year of his reign,[41] (380) after the events mentioned above, that Herod undertook an extraordinary work, (namely) the reconstructing of the temple of God at his own expense, enlarging its precincts and raising it to a more imposing height. For he believed that the accomplishment of this task would be the most notable of all the things achieved by him, as indeed it was, and would be great enough to assure his eternal remembrance. (381) But since he knew that the populace was not prepared for or easy to enlist in so great an undertaking, he thought it best to predispose them to set to work on the whole project (382) by making a speech to them first, and so he called them together and spoke as follows: "So far as the other things achieved during my reign are concerned, my countrymen, I consider it unnecessary to speak of them, although they were of such a kind that the prestige which comes from them to me is (383) less than the security which they have brought to you. For in the most difficult situations I have not been unmindful of the things that might benefit you in your need, nor have I in my building been more intent upon my own invulnerability than upon that of all of you, and I think I have, by the will of God, brought the Jewish nation to such a state of prosperity as it has never known before. (384) Now as for the various buildings which we have erected in our country and in the cities of our land and in those of acquired territories, with which, as the most beautiful adornment, we have embellished our nation, it seems to me quite needless to speak of them to you, knowing them as you do. But that enterprise which I now propose to undertake is the most pious and beautiful one of our time as I will now make clear. (385) For this was the temple which our fathers built to the Most Great God after their return from Babylon, but it lacks sixty cubits[42] in height, the amount by which the first temple, built by Solomon, exceeded it. And yet no one should condemn our fathers for neglecting their pious duty, for it was not their fault that this temple is smaller. (386) Rather it was Cyrus and Darius, the son of Hystaspes, who prescribed these dimensions for building, and since our fathers were subject to them and their descendants and after them to the Macedonians,[43] they had no opportunity to restore this first archetype of piety to its former size. But since, by the will of God, I am now ruler and there continues to be a long period of peace and an abundance (387) of wealth and great revenues, and—what is of most importance—the Romans, who are, so to speak, the masters of the world, are (my) loyal friends, I will try to remedy the oversight caused by the necessity and subjection of that earlier time, and by this act of piety make full return to God for the gift of this kingdom."

[41]In the year 20–19 B.C.

[42]Sixty cubits equals approximately 90 feet.

[43]That is, the Seleucids who dominated Palestine from their capital at Antioch in Syria.

Model of the Temple in Jerusalem. This large-scale reconstruction of the Temple as it existed in the first century of our era shows how it was positioned on the eastern hill of Jerusalem. On the western hill were the homes of the wealthier citizens, who were able to cross the intervening valley on the viaducts visible in this picture. The older part of the city lies off to the right, below the temple area. The higher part of the complex is the main sanctuary, and the colonnaded portion is the so-called Porch (or Stoa) of Solomon, although it was actually built by Herod the Great just before the turn of the eras. *(Photograph by Howard C. Kee)*

These were Herod's words, and most of the people were (388) astonished by his speech, for it fell upon their ears as something quite unexpected. And while the unlikelihood of his realizing his hope did not disturb them, they were dismayed by the thought that he might tear down the whole edifice and not have sufficient means to bring his project [of rebuilding it] to completion. And this danger appeared to them to be very great, (389) and the vast size of the undertaking seemed to make it difficult to carry out. Since they felt this way, the king spoke encouragingly to them, saying that he would not pull down the temple before having ready all the materials needed for its completion. (390) And these assurances he did not belie. For he prepared a thousand wagons to carry the stones, selected ten thousand of the most skilled workmen, purchased priestly robes for a thousand priests and trained some as masons, others as carpenters, and began the construction only after all these preparations had diligently been made by him.

After removing the old foundations, he laid down others (391) and upon these he erected the temple, which was a hundred cubits in length . . . and twenty more in height, but in the course of time this dropped as the foundations subsided. And this part we decided to raise again in the time of Nero. (392) The temple was built of hard, white stones, each of which was about twenty-five cubits in length, eight in height and twelve in width. And in the whole of it, as also in the royal portico, either side was the lowest, while the middle portion was the (393) highest, so that this was visible at a distance of many stades[44] to those who inhabited the country, especially those who lived opposite or happened to approach it. The entrance-doors, which with their lintels were equal [in height] to the temple itself, he adorned with multi-coloured hangings, with purple colours and with inwoven designs of (394) pillars. Above these, under the cornice, spread a golden vine with grape-clusters hanging from it, a marvel of size and artistry to all (395) who saw with what costliness of material it had been constructed. And he surrounded the temple with very large porticoes, all of which he made in proportion [to the temple], and he surpassed his predecessors in spending money, so that it was thought that no one else had adorned the temple so spendidly. Both [porticoes] were [supported] by (396) a great wall, and the wall itself was the greatest ever heard of by man. The hill was a rocky ascent that sloped gently up toward the eastern (397) part of the city to the topmost peak. This hill our first king, (398) Solomon, with God-given wisdom surrounded with great works above at the top. And below, beginning at the foot, where a deep ravine runs round it, he surrounded it with enormous stones bound together with lead. He cut off more and more of the area within as [the wall] became greater in depth, so that the size and height of the structure, which was square, were immense, and the great size of the stones was seen along (399) the front surface, while iron clamps on the inside assured that the joints would remain permanently united. When this work reached the top of the hill, he levelled off the summit, and filled in the hollow spaces near the walls, and made the upper surface smooth and even (400) throughout. Such was the whole enclosure, having a circumference of four stades, each side taking up the length of a stade. Within this (401) wall and on the very summit there ran another wall of stone, which had on the eastern ridge a double portico of the same length as the wall, and it faced the doors of the temple, for this lay within it. This portico many of the earlier kings adorned. Round about the entire (402) temple were fixed the spoils taken from the barbarians, and all these King Herod dedicated, adding those which he took from the Arabs.

XV:410–423

In the western part of the court [of the temple] there were (410) four gates. The first led to the palace by a passage over the intervening ravine, two others led to the suburb, and the last led to the other part of the city, from which it was separated by many steps going down to the ravine and from here up again to the hill. For the City lay opposite the temple, being in the form of a theatre and being bordered by a deep ravine along its whole southern side. The fourth front (411) of this [court], facing south, also had gates in the middle, and had over it the Royal Portico, which had three aisles, extending in length from the eastern to the western ravine. It was not possible for it to extend farther. And it was a structure more noteworthy than any under the sun. For while the depth of the ravine was great, and no (412) one who bent over to look into it from above could bear to look down to the bottom, the height of the portico standing over it was so very great that if anyone looked down from its rooftop, combining the two

[44]A *stade* is approximately 600 feet, or 180 meters.

elevations, he would become dizzy and his vision would be unable to reach the end of so measureless a depth. Now the columns [of the portico] (413) stood in four rows, one opposite the other all along—the fourth row was attached to a wall built of stone—and the thickness of each column was such that it would take three men with outstretched arms touching one another to envelop it; its height was twenty-seven feet, and there was a double moulding running round its base. The number of all the columns was a hundred and sixty-two, and their capitals were (414) ornamented in the Corinthian style of carving, which caused amazement by the magnificence of its whole effect. Since there were four rows, (415) they made three aisles among them, under the porticoes. Of these the two side ones corresponded and were made in the same way, each being thirty feet in width, a stade in length, and over fifty feet in height. But the middle aisle was one and a half times as wide and twice as high, and thus it greatly towered over those on either side. The ceilings [of the porticoes] were ornamented with deeply cut wood-carvings (416) representing all sorts of different figures. The ceiling of the middle aisle was raised to a greater height, and the front wall was cut at either end into architraves with columns built into it, and all of it was polished, so that these structures seemed incredible to those who had not seen them, and were beheld with amazement by those who set (417) eyes on them. Such, then, was the first court. Within it and not far distant was a second one, accessible by a few steps and surrounded by a stone balustrade with an inscription prohibiting the entrance of a foreigner under threat of the penalty of death.[45] On its southern and (418) northern sides the inner court had three-chambered gateways, equally distant from one another, and on the side where the sun rises it had one great gateway, through which those of us who were ritually clean (419) used to pass with our wives. Within this court was the sacred (court) which women were forbidden to enter, and still farther within was a third court into which only priests were permitted to go. In this [priests' court] was the temple, and before it was an altar, on which we used to sacrifice whole burnt-offerings to God. Into none of these (420) courts did King Herod enter since he was not a priest and was therefore prevented from so doing. But with the construction of the porticoes and the outer courts he did busy himself, and these he finished building in eight years.

The temple itself was built by the priests in a year and six (421) months, and all the people were filled with joy and offered thanks to God, first of all for the speed [of the work] and next for the king's zeal, and as they celebrated they acclaimed the restoration. Then the king sacrificed three hundred oxen to God, and others did similarly, (422) each according to his means. The number of these [sacrifices] it would be impossible to give, for it would exceed our power to give a true estimate. And it so happened that the day on which the work of (423) the temple was completed coincided with that of the king's accession, which they were accustomed to celebrate, and because of the double occasion the festival was a very glorious one indeed.

XVII:188–192

Then because of the change of mind he had undergone, he (188) once more altered his will and designated Antipas, to whom he had left his

[45]The translation of this inscription is given on p. 203.

throne, to be tetrarch of Galilee and Peraea, while he bestowed the kingdom on Archelaus. Gaulonitis, Trachonitis, Batanaea[46] and (189) Paneas[47] were to be given as a tetrarchy to his son Philip, who was a full brother of Archelaus, while Jamneia, Azotus and Phasaelis were given over to his sister Salome along with five hundred thousand pieces of coined silver. He also provided for all his other relatives and left them wealthy through gifts of money and the assignment of revenues. (190) To Caesar he left ten million pieces of coined silver besides vessels of gold and of silver and some very valuable garments, while to Caesar's wife Julia and some others he left five million pieces (of silver). Having done this he died, on the fifth day after having his son Antipater killed. He had reigned for thirty-four years from the time when he had put Antigonus to death, and for thirty-seven years from the time when (191) he had been appointed king by the Romans.[48] He was a man who was cruel to all alike and one who easily gave in to anger and was contemptuous of justice. And yet he was as greatly favoured by fortune as any man has ever been in that from being a commoner he was made king, and (192) though encompassed by innumerable perils, he managed to escape them all and lived on to a very old age. As for the affairs of his household and his relation to his sons, he had, in his own opinion at least, enjoyed very good fortune since he had not failed to get the better of those whom he considered his enemies, but in my opinion he was very unfortunate indeed.

Josephus, Jewish War

Our final excerpts from Josephus are all drawn from his *Jewish War;* they describe the insurrectionist movement and its suppression by the Romans in 66–73 A.D. Josephus was an eyewitness of much that he reports, and although he was ambivalent about the revolt—he fought at first with his fellow Jews and then joined the Romans in defeating them—he was by no means a nonpartisan.

JEWISH WAR IV:147–161

(147) In the end,[49] to such abject prostration and terror were the people reduced and to such heights of madness rose these brigands, that they actually took upon themselves the election to the high priesthood. (148) Abrogating the claims of those families from which in turn the high priests had always been drawn, they appointed to that office ignoble (149) and low born individuals, in order to gain accomplices in their impious crimes; for persons who had undeservedly attained to the highest (150) dignity were

[46]Territories north and east of the Sea of Galilee.

[47]A city located near the main sources of the Jordan. A shrine there to the pagan god, Pan, gave the name to the place, Panias (or in Latin form, *Paneus*).

[48]Equivalent to 4 B.C.

[49]The events here depicted occurred as the Roman invasion of Palestine approached its climax: the attack on Jerusalem. The city was swollen with refugees, who further taxed its already limited supplies of food and water. Torn by warring factions and terrorized by brigands, there was little order to the life of the city and no proper preparations were made for its defense.

bound to obey those who had conferred it. Moreover, by various devices and libelous statements, they brought the official authorities into collision with each other, finding their own opportunity in the bickerings of those who should have kept them in check; until, glutted with the wrongs which they had done to men, they transferred their insolence to the Deity and with polluted feet invaded the sanctuary.

(151) An insurrection of the populace was at length pending, instigated by Ananus, the senior of the chief priests, a man of profound sanity, who might possibly have saved the city, had he escaped the conspirators' hands. At this threat these wretches converted the temple of God into their fortress and refuge from any outbreak of (152) popular violence, and made the Holy Place the headquarters of their (153) tyranny. To these horrors was added a spice of mockery more galling than their actions. For, to test the abject submission of the populace and make trial of their own strength, they essayed to appoint the high (154) priests by lot, although, as we have stated, the succession was hereditary. As pretext for this scheme they adduced ancient custom, asserting that in old days the high priesthood had been determined by lot; but in reality their action was the abrogation of established practice and a trick to make themselves supreme by getting these appointments into their own hands.

(155) They accordingly summoned one of the highpriestly clans, called Eniachin, and cast lots for a high priest. By chance the lot fell to one who proved a signal illustration of their depravity; he was an individual named Phanni, son of Samuel, of the village of Aphthia, a man who not only was not descended from high priests, but was such a clown that he scarcely knew what the high priesthood meant. (156) At any rate they dragged their reluctant victim out of the country and, dressing him up for his assumed part, as on the stage, put the sacred vestments upon him and instructed him how to act in keeping with (157) the occasion. To them this monstrous impiety was a subject for jesting and sport, but the other priests, beholding from a

Coin of the Jewish Revolt. During the brief space of three years when the Jews gained partial control of their land and their capital city from the Romans, they issued their own coinage. On one side it reads "Jerusalem the Holy," and the other side gives the year of the revolt. This would have been after A.D. 66. *(Photograph by James T. Stewart)*

distance their mockery of their law, could not restrain their tears and bemoaned the degradation of the sacred honours.

(158) This latest outrage was more than the people could stand, and as if for the overthrow of a despotism one and all were now roused. (159) For their leaders of outstanding reputation, such as Gorion, son of Joseph, and Symeon, son of Gamaliel, by public addresses to the whole assembly and by private visits to individuals, urged them to delay no longer to punish these wreckers of liberty and purge the sanctuary of its bloodstained polluters. Their efforts were supported by the most (160) emininent of the high priests, Jesus,[50] son of Gamalas, and Ananus, son of Ananus, who at their meetings vehemently upbraided the people for (161) their apathy and incited them against the Zealots; for so these miscreants called themselves, as though they were zealous in the cause of virtue and not for vice in its basest and most extravagant form.

VI:193–219

(193) Meanwhile,[51] the victims perishing of famine throughout the city were dropping in countless numbers and enduring suffering (194) indescribable. In every house, the appearance anywhere of but a shadow of food was a signal for war, and the dearest of relatives fell to blows, snatching from each other the pitiful supports of life. The (195) very dying were not credited as in want; nay, even those expiring were searched by the brigands, lest any should be concealing food beneath a fold of his garment and feigning death. Gaping with hunger, (196) like mad dogs, these ruffians went staggering and reeling along, battering upon the doors in the manner of drunken men, and in their perplexity bursting into the same house twice or thrice within a single (197) hour. Necessity drove the victims to gnaw anything, and objects which even the filthiest of brute beasts would reject they condescended to collect and eat: thus in the end they abstained not from belts and shoes and stripped off and chewed the very leather of their bucklers. (198) Others devoured tufts of withered grass: indeed some collectors of stalks sold a trifling quantity for four Attic drachmas. But why tell (199) of the shameless resort to inanimate articles of food induced by the famine, seeing that I am here about to describe an act unparalleled in the history whether of Greeks or barbarians, and as horrible to relate (200) as it is incredible to hear? For my part, for fear that posterity might suspect me of monstrous fabrication, I would gladly have omitted this tragedy, had I not innumerable witnesses among my contemporaries. Moreover, it would be a poor compliment that I should pay my country in suppressing the narrative of the woes which she actually endured.

(201) Among the residents of the region beyond Jordan was a woman named Mary, daughter of Eleazar, of the village of Bethezuba (the name

[50]*Jesus* is a rough transliteration of the Greek *Iēsous,* which is in turn a transliteration of the Hebrew *Yeshua,* or *Yehoshua,* which means "Yahweh will save." The name was very common among Jews, although it is best known today obviously because of Jesus of Nazareth.

[51]By A.D. 70 the Romans under Titus had surrounded Jerusalem with armies and were in the process of constructing a circumvallation or encompassing wall to prevent the besieged Jews in the city from escaping. In spite of great acts of bravery on the part of the besieged, who sapped the Roman earthworks and attacked the Roman camps during the night, their plight was hopeless, as Josephus told them in lengthy harangues shouted up to the Jews gathered at the top of the city's fortified walls.

means "House of Hyssop"[52]), eminent by reason of her family and fortune, who had fled with the rest of the people to Jerusalem and there became involved in the seige. (202) The bulk of her property, which she had packed up and brought with her from Peraea[53] to the city, had been plundered by the tyrants; while the relics of her treasures, with whatever food she had contrived to procure, were being carried off by their satellites in their daily raids. (203) With deep indignation in her heart, the poor woman constantly abused and cursed these extortioners and so incensed them against her. (204) But when no one either out of exasperation or pity put her to death, weary of finding for others food, which indeed it was now impossible from any quarter to procure, while famine coursed through her intestines and marrow and the fire of rage was more consuming even than the famine, impelled by the promptings alike of fury and necessity, she proceeded to an act of outrage upon nature. (205) Seizing her child, an infant at the breast, "Poor babe," she cried, "amidst war, famine, and sedition, to what end should I preserve thee? (206) With the Romans slavery awaits us, should we live till they come; but famine is forestalling slavery, and more cruel than both are the rebels. (207) Come, be thou food for me, to the rebels an avenging fury, and to the world a tale such as alone is wanting to the calamities of the Jews." (208) With these words she slew her son, and then, having roasted the body and devoured half of it, she covered up and stored the remainder. (209) At once the rebels were upon her and, scenting the unholy odour, threatened her with instant death unless she produced what she had prepared. (210) Replying that she had reserved a goodly portion for them also, she disclosed the remnants of her child. Seized with instant horror and stupefaction, they stood paralysed by the sight. She, however, said, "This is my own child, and this my handiwork. Eat, for I too have eaten. (211) Show not yourselves weaker than a woman, or more compassionate than a mother. But if you have pious scruples and shrink from my sacrifice, then let what I have eaten be your portion and the remainder also be left for me." (212) At that they departed trembling, in this one instance cowards, though scarcely yielding even this food to the mother. The whole city instantly rang with the abomination, and each, picturing the horror of it, shuddered as though it had been perpetrated by himself. (213) The starving folk longed for death, and felicitated those who had gone to their rest ere they had heard or beheld such evils.

(214) The horrible news soon spread to the Romans. Of them some were incredulous, others were moved to pity, but the effect on the majority was to intensify their hatred of the nation. (215) Caesar declared himself innocent in this matter also in the sight of God, protesting that *he* had offered the Jews peace, independence, and an amnesty for all past offences, while *they*, preferring sedition to concord, peace to war, famine to plenty and prosperity, (216) and having been the first to set fire with their own hands to that temple which he and his army were preserving for them, were indeed deserving even of such food as this. (217) He, however, would bury this abomination of infant-cannibalism beneath the ruins of their country, and would not leave upon the face of the earth, for the sun to behold, a city in which mothers were thus fed. (218) Yet, he added, such food was less meet for mothers than for fathers, who even after such horrors still re-

[52]An obscure village; in Hebrew, Beth-ezov.

[53]Peraea, a name that derives from the Greek word *Peran,* which means "beyond"—that is, beyond the Jordan River, on the east bank.

mained in arms. (219) While expressing these sentiments, he had, moreover, in mind the desperation of these men, being convinced that they were past being brought to reason who had already endured all the miseries, to be spared the experience of which they might have been expected to relent.

VI:271–280

(271) While the temple blazed,[54] the victors plundered everything that fell in their way and slaughtered wholesale all who were caught. No pity was shown for age, no reverence for rank; children and greybeards, laity and priests alike were massacred; every class was pursued and encompassed in the grasp of war, whether suppliants for mercy or offering (272) resistance. The roar of the flames streaming far and wide mingled with the groans of the falling victims; and, owing to the height of the hill and the mass of the burning pile, one would have thought that the whole city was ablaze. And then the din—nothing more deafening or appalling could be conceived than that. There were the war-cries of (273) the Roman legions sweeping onward in mass, the howls of the rebels encircled by fire and sword, the rush of the people who, cut off above, fled panic-stricken only to fall into the arms of the foe, and their shrieks as they met their fate. With the cries on the hill were blended (274) those of the multitude in the city below; and now many who were emaciated and tongue-tied from starvation, when they beheld the sanctuary on fire, gathered strength once more for lamentations and wailing. Peraea and the surrounding mountains contributed their echoes, deepening (275) the din. But yet more awful than the uproar were the sufferings. You would indeed have thought that the temple-hill was boiling over from its base, being everywhere one mass of flame, but yet the stream of blood was more copious than the flames and the slain more numerous than (276) the slayers. For the ground was nowhere visible through the corpses; but the soldiers had to clamber over heaps of bodies in pursuit of the (277) fugitives. The brigand crowd succeeded in pushing through the Romans and with difficulty forcing their way into the outer court of the temple, and thence to the city; while what was left of the populace took refuge on the outer portico. Of the priests some, at the first, tore up the (278) spikes from the sanctuary, with their leaden sockets, and hurled them at the Romans, but afterwards, finding their efforts unavailing (279) and the flames breaking out against them, they retired to the wall, which was eight cubits broad, and there remained. Two persons of (280) distinction, however, having the choice of saving their lives by going over to the Romans or of holding out and sharing the fortune of the rest, plunged into the fire and were consumed with the temple, namely Meirus, son of Belgas, and Josephus, son of Dalaeus.

VI:288–300

(288) (3) Thus it was that the wretched people were deluded at that time by charlatans and pretended messengers of the deity; while they neither heeded nor believed in the manifest portents that foretold the coming desolation, but, as if thunderstruck and bereft of eyes and mind, disregarded

[54]Finally in late August of A.D. 70 the walls were breached and the temple complex itself set afire. Josephus claims that this was done by the Jewish defenders, but his view likely reflects his pro-Roman apologetic sentiment rather than the facts.

the plain warnings of God. So it was when a star, (289) resembling a sword, stood over the city, and a comet which continued for a year. So again when, before the revolt and the commotion that (290) led to war, at the time when the people were assembling for the feast of unleavened bread, on the eighth of the month Xanthicus,[55] at the ninth hour of the night, so brilliant a light shone round the altar and the sanctuary that it seemed to be broad daylight; and this continued for (291) half an hour. By the inexperienced this was regarded as a good omen, (292) but by the sacred scribes it was at once interpreted in accordance with after-events. At that same feast a cow that had been brought by (293) someone for sacrifice gave birth to a lamb in the midst of the court of the temple; moreover, the eastern gate of the inner court—it was of brass and very massive, and, when closed towards evening, could scarcely be moved by twenty men; fastened with iron-bound bars, it had bolts which (294) were sunk to a great depth into a threshold consisting of a solid block of stone—this gate was observed at the sixth hour of the night to have opened of its own accord. The watchmen of the temple ran and (295) reported the matter to the captain, and he came up and with difficulty succeeded in shutting it. This again to the uninitiated seemed the best of omens, as they supposed that God had opened to them the gate of blessings; but the learned understood that the security of the temple (296) was dissolving of its own accord and that the opening of the gate meant a present to the enemy, interpreting the portent in their own minds as indicative of coming desolation. Again, not many days after (297) the festival, on the twenty-first of the month Artemisium, there appeared a miraculous phenomenon, passing belief. Indeed, what I am (298) about to relate would, I imagine, have been deemed a fable, were it not for the narratives of eyewitnesses and for the subsequent calamities (299) which deserved to be so signalized. For before sunset throughout all parts of the country chariots were seen in the air and armed battalions hurtling through the clouds and encompassing the cities. Moreover, at the feast which is called Pentecost, the priests on entering the inner (300) court of the temple by night, as their custom was in the discharge of their ministrations, reported that they were conscious, first of a commotion and a din, and after that of a voice as of a host, "We are departing hence."

But a further portent was even more alarming. Four years before the war, when the city was enjoying profound peace and prosperity, there came to the feast at which it is the custom of all Jews to erect tabernacles to God, one Jesus, son of Ananias, a rude peasant, who, standing in the temple, suddenly began to cry out, "A voice from the east, a voice from the west, a voice from the four winds; a voice against Jerusalem and the sanctuary, a voice against the bridegroom and the bride, a voice against all the people."

VI:403–419

(403) The Romans, now[56] masters of the walls, planted their standards on the towers, and with clapping of hands and jubilation raised a paean in honour of their victory. They had found the end of the war a much lighter

[55]Probably April.

[56]By late September the upper part of the city was in Roman hands and Jerusalem was entirely subdued. The remaining rebels fled, and with their leaders took refuge in the Herodian fortresses of Machaerus east of the Dead Sea and at Masada near the southwestern shore. Josephus gives details of the fall of these last strongholds of the insurrectionists in Book VII of the *Jewish War*.

task than the beginning; indeed, they could hardly believe that they had surmounted the last wall without bloodshed, and, seeing none to oppose them, were truly perplexed. Pouring into the alleys, swords (404) in hand, they massacred indiscriminately all whom they met, and burnt the houses with all who had taken refuge within. Often in the course (405) of their raids, on entering the houses they would find whole families dead and the rooms filled with the victims of the famine, and then shuddering at the sight, retire empty-handed. Yet, while they (406) pitied those who had thus perished, they had no similar feelings for the living, but, running everyone through who fell in their way, they choked the alleys with corpses and deluged the whole city with blood, insomuch that many of the fires were extinguished by the gory stream. (407) Towards evening they ceased slaughtering, but when night fell the fire gained the mastery, and the dawn of the eighth day of the month Gorpiaeus[57] broke upon Jerusalem in flames—a city which had suffered such calamities (408) during the siege, that, had she from her foundation enjoyed an equal share of blessings, she would have been thought unquestionably enviable; a city undeserving, moreover, of these great misfortunes on any other ground, save that she produced a generation such as that which caused her overthrow.

(409) (ix.1) Titus, on entering the town, was amazed at its strength, but chiefly at the towers, which the tyrants, in their infatuation, had (410) abandoned. Indeed, when he beheld their solid lofty mass, the magnitude of each block and the accuracy of the joinings, and marked how great was (411) their breadth, how vast their height, "God indeed," he exclaimed, "has been with us in the war. God it was who brought down the Jews (412) from these strongholds; for what power have human hands or engines against these towers?" He made many similar observations to his friends at that time, when he also liberated all prisoners of the tyrants who were found in the forts. And when, at a later period, he demolished (413) the rest of the city and razed the walls he left these towers as a memorial of his attendant fortune, to whose co-operation he owed his conquest of defences which defied assault.

(414) Since the soldiers were now growing weary of slaughter, though numerous survivors still came to light, Caesar issued orders to kill only those who were found in arms and offered resistance, and to (415) make prisoners of the rest. The troops, in addition to those specified in their instructions, slew the old and feeble; while those in the prime of life and serviceable they drove together into the temple and shut them up in the court of the women. Caesar appointed one of his freedmen (416) as their guard, and his friend Fronto to adjudicate upon the lot (417) appropriate to each. Fronto put to death all the seditious and brigands, information being given by them against each other; he selected (418) the tallest and most handsome of the youth and reserved them for the triumph; of the rest, those over seventeen years of age he sent in chains to the works in Egypt, while multitudes were presented by Titus to the various provinces, to be destroyed in the theatres by the sword (419) or by wild beasts; those under seventeen were sold. During the days spent by Fronto over this scrutiny, eleven thousand of the prisoners perished from starvation, partly owing to their jailers' hatred, who denied them food, partly their own refusal of it when offered; moreover, for so vast a multitude even corn failed.

[57]September 26, A.D. 70.

Josephus took up residence in Rome as an army pensioner, as we learn from his autobiography. It is likely that he was a witness of the triumph accorded Titus on his return from the suppression of the Jewish revolt. Titus, who had remained in Palestine to complete the subjugation of the rebellious Jews when his father had returned to Rome to be acclaimed as emperor, had now gone back for the triumphal procession offered him by the grateful Senate and Roman people, as was the custom for receiving victors returning from major conflicts. The sacred objects from the temple that were carried in the triumph are depicted on the reliefs still preserved (though mutilated) on the inner faces of Titus's triumphal arch in the Roman forum.

As may be inferred from the gospels, especially Mark 13 and parallels in Matthew 24–25 and Luke 21, the early Christians regarded the destruction of Jerusalem as a sign of God's judgment on the Jews for the rejection of Jesus. It is likely that some Christians thought that the fall of the city was the final sign that the New Age was about to arrive.

VII:132–152

(132) It is impossible adequately to describe the multitude of those spectacles and their magnificence under every conceivable aspect, whether in works of art or diversity of riches or natural rarities; for (133) almost all the objects which men who have ever been blessed by fortune have acquired one by one—the wonderful and precious productions of various nations—by their collective exhibition on that day displayed (134) the majesty of the Roman empire. Silver and gold and ivory in masses, wrought into all manner of forms, might be seen, not as if carried in procession, but flowing, so to speak, like a river; here were tapestries borne along, some of the rarest purple, others embroidered by Babylonian art with perfect portraiture; transparent gems, some set in golden (135) crowns, some in other fashions, swept by in such profusion as to correct our erroneous supposition that any of them was rare. Then, too, there were carried images of their gods, of marvellous size and no mean (136) craftsmanship, and of these not one but was of some rich material. Beasts of many species were led along all caparisoned with appropriate trappings. The numerous attendants conducting each group of animals (137) were decked in garments of true purple dye, interwoven with gold; while those selected to take part in the pageant itself had about them choice ornaments of amazing richness. Moreover, even among the mob of (138) captives, none was to be seen unadorned, the variety and beauty of their dresses concealing from view any unsightliness arising from bodily disfigurement.

(139) But nothing in the procession excited so much astonishment as the structure of the moving stages; indeed, their massiveness afforded (140) ground for alarm and misgiving as to their stability, many of them being three or four stories high, while the magnificence of the fabric was a source at once of delight and amazement. For many were (141) enveloped in tapestries interwoven with gold, and all had a framework of gold and wrought ivory. The war was shown by numerous (142) representations, in separate sections, affording a very vivid picture (143) of its episodes. Here was to be seen a prosperous country devastated, there whole battalions of

Arch of Titus. With the choice of Vespasian as emperor, Titus took command of the troops battling for control of Jerusalem. His success was marked by his capture of the temple hill, and was publicly displayed in Rome by his bringing back there in triumphal procession the trophies from the temple, including the seven-branched lampstand and sacred trumpets, which are still visible in the relief on the side of this triumphal arch in the Roman Forum. *(Courtesy of the Fototeca di Architettura e Topographia dell'Italia Antica)*

the enemy slaughtered; here a party in flight, there others led into captivity; walls of surpassing compass demolished by engines, strong fortresses overpowered, cities with well-manned (144) defences completely mastered and an army pouring within the ramparts, an area all deluged with blood, the hands of those incapable of resistance raised in supplication, temples set on fire, houses pulled down over (145) their owners' heads, and, after general desolation and woe, rivers flowing, not over a cultivated land, nor supplying drink to man and beast, but across a country still on every side in flames. For to such sufferings were the Jews destined when they plunged into the war; and (146) the art and magnificent workmanship of these structures now portrayed the incidents to those who had not witnessed them, as though they were (147) happening before their eyes. On each of the stages was stationed the general of one of the captured cities in the attitude in which he was taken. A number of ships also followed.

(148) The spoils in general were borne in promiscuous heaps; but conspicuous above all stood out those captured in the temple at Jerusalem. These consisted of a golden table, many talents in weight, and a lampstand, likewise made of gold, but constructed on a different pattern from (149) those which we use in ordinary life. Affixed to a pedestal was a central shaft, from which there extended slender branches, arranged trident-fashion, a wrought lamp being attached to the extremity of each branch; of these there were seven, indicating the honour paid to that (150) number among the Jews. After these, and last of all the spoils, (151) was carried a copy of the Jewish Law. Then followed a large party carrying images of victory, all made of ivory and gold. Behind them (152) drove Vespasian, followed by Titus; while Domitian rode beside them, in magnificent apparel and mounted on a steed that was itself a sight.

MOUNTING RESISTANCE TO ROMAN POLICY

The sources brought together here are of four different types and from four different times, but they have in common the exercise of Roman power in the eastern empire. The first consists of excerpts from Josephus's *Antiquities of the Jews,* in which we learn how Antipater, the Idumean, secured his place as king over the Jews, even though he was not a Jew, and how Caligula decreed special tax regulations for the Jews in order to enable them to meet their obligations to Rome while at the same time to obey their own laws and to maintain their cultic system.

The second group of excerpts is from Philo of Alexandria, from a treatise describing his experiences as head of a delegation that visited Rome to plead with the emperor Gaius Caligula (ruled A.D. 37–41) not to pursue policies that were in direct conflict with the laws and sensibilities of his Jewish subjects in Alexandria and Palestine. Caligula then ordered that his own statue be erected in the Jerusalem temple, to the horror of Jews throughout the Roman world. This plan, which was forestalled by Gaius's death, had an enduring impact on both Jews and Christians, however. It recalled the action of Antiochus Epiphanes, referred to indirectly in Daniel 11:31 and 12:11 as "the abomination that makes desolate." And it appears in Mark 13:14 as "the desolating sacrilege"—the final event before the expected destruction of the temple in Jerusalem, according to the prediction attributed to Jesus.

The excerpts in the third section, also from Philo's treatise, deal with a decree according to which a provincial legislative body in Asia Minor passed a decree honoring the emperor Augustus (ruled 30 B.C.–14 A.D.) as a divine savior. When Caligula claimed later that he was a god, the growing incompatibility of both the Jewish and Christian religions with this idea eventually led to hostility between the young Christian church and the empire, as is reflected in the fourth section of excerpts, the letter of Pliny the Younger, Roman governor in the Black Sea provinces of Bithynia and Pontus, to his emperor Trajan (ruled A.D. 98–117) and Trajan's reply.

Josephus, Antiquities of the Jews

XIV:156–162

(156) Now when Caesar[58] had settled the affairs of Syria, he sailed away. And Antipater,[59] after escorting Caesar out of Syria, returned to Judea and

[58]This was Julius Caesar, who was then (47 B.C.) in the process of conquering the eastern Mediterranean and arranging for his clients to control the territories his troops had conquered.

[59]Antipater was an Idumean opportunist whose skills in diplomacy, political dealings, warfare, and administration were superb. All these capacities were inherited in a heightened degree by his more famous son, Herod.

at once raised again the wall which had been demolished by Pompey, and going about the country suppressed disorders therein by both (157) threatening and advising the people to remain quiet. For, he said, those who were on the side of Hyrcanus[60] would be left in peace and could live undisturbed in the enjoyment of their own possessions, but if they clung to the hope of achieving something by revolution and were counting on any gains therefrom, they would have in him a master in place of a king, and in the Romans and Caesar bitter enemies in place of rulers. For they would not allow any man to be removed from office whom they themselves had placed therein. Through such words he restored order throughout the country by his own efforts.

(158) But as he saw that Hyrcanus was dull and sluggish, he appointed his eldest son Phasael governor of Jerusalem and the surrounding region, and entrusted Galilee to his second son Herod, who was still quite young; (159) he was, in fact, only fifteen years old. But his youth in no way hindered him, and being a young man of high spirit, he quickly found an opportunity for showing his prowess. For on learning that Ezekias, a bandit leader, was overrunning the borders of Syria with a large troop, he caught and killed him and many of the bandits with him. This (160) achievement of his was greatly admired by the Syrians, for he had cleared their country of a gang of bandits of whom they longed to be rid. And so they sang his praises for this deed throughout their villages and cities, saying that he had given them peace and the secure enjoyment of their possessions. And through this action he became known to Sextus Caesar, a kinsman of the great Caesar and governor of (161) Syria. Thereupon the desire to emulate Herod's achievements seized his brother Phasael, and being moved by the thought of the reputation Herod had won, he was ambitious not to be behind him in achieving like fame; and so he made the inhabitants of Jerusalem feel very friendly toward him, and though he kept the city under his own rule, he did not show any lack of discretion in governing it or abuse his authority. (162) This situation made it possible for Antipater to receive from the nation the respect shown a king for such honour as might be enjoyed by one who is an absolute master. With all this glory, however, he did not, as so often seems to happen, in any way alter his friendship and loyalty to Hyrcanus.

XIV:202–204

(202) Gaius Caesar,[61] Imperator for the second time, has ruled that they shall pay a tax for the city of Jerusalem, Joppa excluded, every year except in the seventh year, which they call the sabbatical year, because in this time they neither take fruit from the trees nor do they (203) sow. And that in the second year they shall pay the tribute at Sidon, consisting of one-fourth of the produce sown, and in addition, they shall also pay tithes to Hyrcanus and his sons, just as they paid to their forefathers. And that no one, whether

[60]Hyrcanus, last of the priests of the Hasmonean family. Through cooperation and marriage with the descendants of the Hasmoneans, Antipas and Herod, who were Idumeans (Semitic but not Jewish) sought to give legitimacy to their own non-Jewish family claims to royal leadership in Palestine.

[61]Gaius Caesar, better known by his nickname, Caligula (Little Boot), was emperor briefly from 37–41 A.D. Spoiled as a child by the army, his rule was arbitrary and ended in his madness. This decree in behalf of the Jews, however, was eminently sane, and shows how eager Rome was to make special concessions to the Jews.

magistrate or pro-magistrate, praetor or legate, shall raise auxiliary troops in the (204) territories of the Jews, nor shall soldiers be allowed to exact money from them, whether for winter quarters or on any other pretext, but they shall be free from all molestation. And whatever they may hereafter acquire or buy or possess or have assigned to them, all these they shall keep.

XIV:265–267

(265) Now there are many other such decrees, passed by the Senate and the Imperators of the Romans, relating to Hyrcanus and our nation, as well as resolutions of cities and rescripts of provincial governors in reply to letters on the subject of our rights, all of which those who will read our work without malice will find it possible to take on faith from the documents we have cited. For since we have furnished (266) clear and visible proofs of our friendship with the Romans, indicating those decrees engraved on bronze pillars and tablets which remain to this day and will continue to remain in the Capitol, I have refrained from citing them all as being both superfluous and disagreeable; for I cannot suppose that anyone is so stupid that he will actually refuse (267) to believe the statements about the friendliness of the Romans towards us, when they have demonstrated this in a good many decrees relating to us, or will not admit that we are making truthful statements on the basis of the examples we have given. And herein we have set forth our friendship and alliance with the Romans in those times.

Philo of Alexandria, Embassy to Gaius

Pleas to Caligula

PP. 76–80

People say that at the beginning of the mental derangement [Gaius] used the following argument: "The keepers of the animals, oxherds, goatherds, and shepherds, are not themselves oxen or goats or sheep, but human beings, who have been given a higher destiny and condition; in the same way one must suppose that I, who am the herdsman of the noblest herd, the human race, am a superior being, above the human plane and endowed with a higher and more divine destiny." Having impressed this idea on his mind, the fool began to carry a fantasy about with him, believing it to be an absolute truth. Then, when once his courage had risen and he had risked introduction of this blasphemous deification of himself to the masses, he tried to act in an appropriate and consistent way and advanced little by little to the top as if up a ladder. He began to equate himself with the first so-called demi-gods, Dionysus, Heracles, and the Dioscuri, making a mockery of Trophonius, Amphiareus, Amphilochus, and the rest, oracles, rites, and all, when he compared their powers with his own. Then, as in a theatre, he put on first one costume and then another, sometimes a lion-skin and club, both gilded, when he was arrayed as Heracles, and sometimes a cap on his head, when he dressed up as the Dioscuri; at other times he dressed up as Dionysus with ivy, thyrsus, and fawn-skins. He resolved to differ from the demi-gods in that, whereas each of them had his own honors and did not lay claim to those which the others shared, his jealous greed appropriated the honors of all of them alike, or rather, appropriated the demi-gods themselves.

PP. 93–97

Gaius's madness, his wild and frenzied insanity, reached such a pitch that he went beyond the demi-gods and began to climb higher and to go in for the worship paid to the greater gods,[62] Hermes, Apollo, and Ares, who are supposed to be of divine parentage on both sides. It was the worship due to Hermes first. He dressed up with herald's staff, sandals, and cloak, displaying order amid disorder, consistency amid confusion, and reason amid mental derangement. Then, when he saw fit, he discarded these attributes and changed his appearance and dress to those of Apollo. He wore a radiate crown, grasped a bow and arrows in his left hand, and held out the Graces in his right hand, as if it were correct to have good things ready at hand to proffer and to let them hold the superior position, on the right, while subordinating punishments and assigning the inferior position, on the left, to them. Well-trained choirs at once took up their positions, singing paeans to him—choirs which had shortly before been calling him Bacchus, Evaeus, and Lyaeus, and chanting hymns in his honor, when he assumed the costume of Dionysus. Often he would put on a breastplate and march forth sword in hand with helmet and shield, and be hailed as Ares.[63] On either side of him marched the attendants of this new Ares, a rabble of murderers and executioners, who would undertake despicable services for him when he was in a murderous frame of mind and thirsted for human blood.

PP. 115–116

It was only of the Jews that Gaius was suspicious, on the grounds that they were the only people who deliberately opposed him and had been taught from their very cradles, as it were, by their parents, tutors, and teachers and—more than that—by their holy Laws and even by their unwritten customs, to believe that the Father and Creator of the universe is one God. All other men, women, cities, nations, countries, and regions of the world—I can say almost the whole inhabited earth—although they deplored what was happening, flattered Gaius none the less, glorifying him more than was reasonable, and increasing his vanity. Some people even introduced into Italy the barbaric custom of *proskunesis* [that is, prostrating oneself before a ruler], and thus debased the nobility of Roman freedom.

PP. 118–127

. . . The change being effected was not a small one but an absolutely fundamental one, namely, the apparent transformation of the created, destructible nature of man into the uncreated, indestructible nature of God, which the Jewish nation judged to be the most horrible of blasphemies; for God would change into man sooner than man into God. This was quite apart from the acceptance of the other evils of unbelief in, and ingratitude towards, the Benefactor of the whole world, Who by His own might gives good things in lavish abundance to all parts of his universe.

Accordingly, total and truceless war was waged against the Jewish nation.

[62]The Romans, like the Greeks, distinguished between deified men—usually actual heroes, but including also legendary figures—and the great gods. The former were venerated, but worship was offered to the latter. Gaius was at first content to have himself venerated as one of the deified heroes, but later aspired to be included among the Olympian deities.

[63]Ares, or Mars, the god of war.

What heavier burden could a slave have than a hostile owner? Subjects are the slaves of an emperor, and even if this was not the case with Gaius's predecessors, because they ruled reasonably and legally, yet it was the case under Gaius, who had cut all humanity out of his heart and made a cult of illegality; for he regarded himself as the law, and broke the laws of the lawgivers of every country, as if they were empty words. So we were enrolled not simply as slaves but as the lowest of slaves, when the Emperor turned into a tyrant.

When the promiscuous and unruly Alexandrian mob discovered this, it supposed that a most opportune moment had come its way and attacked us. It unmasked the hatred which had long been smoldering and threw everything into chaos and confusion. As if we had been surrendered by the Emperor to sufferings admitted to be of the severest kind or had been defeated in war, they attacked us with insane and bestial fury. They invaded our homes and drove out the householders, wives and children and all, so as to leave the houses unoccupied. They no longer waited for the darkness of night in fear of arrest, like burglars, to steal our furniture and treasures, but they carried them off openly in broad daylight, and displayed them to those they met, as people who have inherited things or bought them from their owners. If several people agreed to join forces in plunder, they divided out their loot in the middle of the marketplace, often before the eyes of its real owners, jeering and laughing as they did so. This was terrible in itself, of course. Wealthy men became paupers and well-to-do people penniless, suddenly deprived of hearth and home although they were innocent of any crime, and driven out of their houses as exiles, to live in the open air day and night and die either of sunstroke or of exposure by night. Yet this is easier reading than what follows. For the Greeks joined in driving many thousands of men, women, and children out of the whole city into a very small part of it, like sheep or cattle into a pen. They supposed that within a few days they would find piles of bodies of Jews, who had died either of starvation through lack of the necessities of life, since they had no forewarning of this sudden calamity to enable them to make suitable provision against it, or of overcrowding or suffocation. Their quarters were extremely cramped, and moreover the surrounding air became foul and surrendered its life-giving qualities to the respirations, or rather, the gasps of the dying. So, no longer able to stand the lack of space, the Jews overflowed on to the desert, the shores, the cemeteries, longing to breathe pure, healthy air. Any who had already been caught in other parts of the city, or who visited it from the country in ignorance of the calamities which had descended upon us, experienced sufferings of every kind. They were stoned, or wounded with tiles, or battered to death with branches of ilex or oak on the most vulnerable parts of their bodies, especially their heads.

PP. 132–134

The prefect of the country, who could have put an end to this mob-rule single-handed in an hour had he chosen to, pretended not to see and hear what he did see and hear, but allowed the Greeks to make war without restraint and so shattered the peace of the city. They consequently became still more excited and rushed headlong into outrageous plots of even greater audacity. Assembling enormous hordes together, they attacked the synagogues, of which there are many in each section of the city. Some they smashed, some they rased to the ground, and others they set on fire and burned, giving no thought even to the adjacent houses in their madness and frenzied insanity. For nothing is swifter than fire when it gets plenty of fuel. I say nothing about the simultaneous destruction and burning of the objects set up in honor of the emperor—gilded shields and crowns, monuments, and inscriptions—which should have made the Greeks keep their hands off everything else also. But they derived confidence from the fact that they had no punishment to fear from Gaius, who, as they well knew, felt an indescribable hatred for the Jews. . . .

Philo of Alexandria, Ad Gaium

Augustus as Divine Savior

PP. 143–151

What about the nature of the Emperor whose every virtue outshone human nature, who through the greatness of his imperial rule and of his valor alike became the first to bear the title "Augustus," who did not receive the title by inheritance from his family as a part of a legacy, but was himself the source of the reverence paid to his successors also? What about the man who pitted himself against the general confusion and chaos as soon as he took charge of public affairs? For islands were struggling for supremacy against continents and continents against islands, with the Romans of the greatest distinction in public life as their generals and leaders. Again, large parts of the world were battling for mastery of the empire, Asia against Europe and Europe against Asia; European nations and Asian nations from the ends of the earth had risen up and were engaged in grim warfare, fighting with armies and fleets on every land and sea, so that almost the whole human race would have been destroyed in internecine conflict and disappeared completely, had it not been for one man, one *princeps,* Augustus, who deserves the title of "Averter of Evil." This is the Caesar who lulled the storms which were crashing everywhere, who healed the sicknesses common to Greeks and barbarians alike, which descended from the South and East and swept across to the West and North, sowing misery in the lands and seas in between. This is he who not merely loosened but broke the fetters which had confined and oppressed the world. This is he who both ended the wars which were before everyone's eyes and those which were going on out of sight as a result of the attacks of pirates. This is he who cleared the sea of pirate-ships and filled it with merchant-ships. This is he who set every city again at liberty, who reduced disorder to order, who civilized all the unfriendly, savage tribes and brought them into harmony with each other, who enlarged Greece with many other Greek lands, and who hellenized the most important parts of the barbarian world. This is he who safeguarded peace, gave each man his due, distributed his favors widely without stint, and never in his whole life kept any blessing or advantage back.

During the forty years of this wonderful benefactor's rule over Egypt, the Alexandrians neglected him and did not make a single dedication on his behalf in the synagogues—neither a statue nor a wooden image nor a painting. Yet if new and exceptional honors had been voted to anyone, it should have been appropriate in his case. This was not merely because he founded and originated the Augustan dynasty, nor because he was the first and greatest universal benefactor, who ended the rule of many by handing the ship of state over to a single helmsman, namely himself with his remarkable grasp of the science of government, to steer. . . . It was because the whole world voted him honors equal to those of the Olympians. Temples, gateways, vestibules, and colonnades bear witness to this, so that the imposing buildings erected in any city, new or old, are surpassed by the beauty and size of the temples of Caesar, especially in our own Alexandria. There is no other precinct like our so-called "Augusteum," the temple of Caesar, the protector of sailors. . . . The extensive precinct is furnished with colonnades, libraries, banqueting-halls, groves, gateways, open spaces, unroofed enclosures, and everything that makes for lavish decoration. It gives hope of safety to sailors when they set out to sea and when they return.

PP. 155–158

(Augustus) knew that the large district of Rome beyond the Tiber was owned and inhabited by Jews. The majority of them were Roman freedmen. They had been brought to Italy as prisoners of war and manumitted by their owners, and had not been able to alter any of their national customs. Augustus therefore knew that they had synagogues and met in them, especially on the Sabbath, when they received public instruction in their national philosophy. He also knew that they collected sacred money from their "first-fruits" and sent it up to Jerusalem by the hand of envoys who would offer the sacrifices. But despite this he did not expel them from Rome or deprive them of their Roman citizenship because they remembered their Jewish nationality also. He introduced no changes into their synagogues, he did not prevent them from meeting for the exposition of the Law, and he raised no objections to their offering of the "first-fruits." On the contrary, he showed such reverence for our traditions that he and almost all his family enriched our Temple with expensive dedications. He gave orders for regular sacrifices of holocausts to be made daily in perpetuity at his own expense, as an offering to the Most High God. These sacrifices continue to this day, and will continue always as a proof of his truly imperial character. Moreover, at the monthly distributions in Rome, when all the people in turn received money or food, he never deprived the Jews of this bounty, but if the distributions happened to be made on a Sabbath, when it is forbidden to receive or give anything or to do any of the ordinary things of life in general, especially commercial life, he instructed the distributors to reserve the Jews' share of the universal largesse until the next day.

PP. 186–189

While we were considering our case, expecting at any moment to be summoned into (Gaius's) presence, a man came up to us completely out of breath, his eyes bloodshot and troubled. He drew us aside a little from the others—there were a few people standing near—and said, "Have you heard the news?" Then before he could tell us he broke off in floods of tears. He began again, but broke off a second and a third time. When we saw this, we were alarmed and begged him to tell us the business on which he said he
DAN. had come. "For," we said, "you surely have not come just to let us witness
11:31 your weeping. If your news is worthy of tears, do not indulge in grief on
your own. We are used to disasters by this time." With difficulty and still
MK. sobbing he managed to say in a choked voice, "Our Temple is gone! Gaius
13:14 has given orders for a colossal statue to be set up right inside the shrine,
named after Zeus himself." We were amazed at what he said and stood

MT. rooted to the ground in horror, unable to move. We stood dumb and help-
24:15 less on the point of collapse, our whole bodies unnerved.

PP. 263–268

... When Gaius noticed that (Agrippa[64]) was worried and perplexed—he was clever at divining a man's hidden wishes and feelings from his visible expression—he said, "Are you perplexed, Agrippa? I will put an end to your perplexity. . . . Your fine noble countrymen, the only people in the whole world who do not acknowledge Gaius as a god, are now apparently courting death by disobedience. When I gave orders for a statue of Zeus to be set up in the Temple, they all collected in a body and trooped out of Jerusalem and the whole country, allegedly in order to make a petition, but in actual fact in order to oppose my commands." Before Gaius had time to add more, Agrippa's anguish of mind made him change color in every possible way; in one moment he became flushed, pale, and livid. He was already shivering from head to foot. Trembling and shuddering convulsed every limb and part of his body. His sinews became limp and slack, and he staggered and finally collapsed and would have fallen, had not some of the bystanders caught him. They carried him home as they were instructed. He was in a coma and conscious of none of the mass of troubles. . . . As a result, Gaius was even more exasperated, and intensified his hatred for Jews. He said, "If my closest and dearest friend, Agrippa, who is under great obligation to me, is such a slave of his national customs that he cannot bear to hear a word spoken against them but faints and almost dies, what must one expect of the other Jews, who have no powerful incentive for acting otherwise?"

In the course of describing Jewish resistance to offering divine honors to the emperor and to any idolatrous practice performed by the Roman state as it influenced Jews, Philo mentions the actions of the Roman ruler who figures most prominently in the narrative of the gospels: Pontius Pilate, who was procurator of Judea from A.D. 26 to 36. It was, of course, his ruthlessness in suppressing the beginning of a revolt, or even any action by Jews which might have led to a revolt, that brought about the execution of Jesus.

PP. 299–305

... Pilate[65] was an official who had been appointed procurator of Judea. With the intention of annoying the Jews rather than of honoring Tiberius,

[64]This Agrippa (not to be confused with Augustus's aide and son-in-law, who died in 12 B.C.) was Herod Agrippa I, grandson of Herod the Great. It is he who imprisoned Peter and executed James, the son of Zebedee, according to Acts 12. His own gruesome death by an avenging angel is reported in Acts 12:20–23. From other sources we know that he died in A.D. 44.

[65]Pontius Pilate was appointed procurator of Judea in A.D. 26 and held office until 36. As procurator, he was directly responsible to the emperor himself, rather than to the legate or governor of Syria, the larger province of which Judea was geographically a part. By both Philo and Josephus, Pilate is portrayed as arbitrary and ruthless in suppressing what he thought to be incipient revolts on the part of the Jews.

he set up gilded shields in Herod's palace in the Holy City. They bore no figure and nothing else that was forbidden, but only the briefest possible inscription, which stated two things—the name of the dedicator and that of the person in whose honor the dedication was made. But when the Jews at large learnt of his action, which was indeed already widely known, they chose as their spokesman the king's four sons, who enjoyed rank and prestige equal to that of kings, his other descendants, and their own officials, and besought Pilate to undo his innovation in the shape of the shields, and not to violate their native customs, which had hitherto been invariably preserved inviolate by kings and emperors alike. When Pilate, who was a man of inflexible, stubborn, and cruel disposition, obstinately refused, they shouted, "Do not cause a revolt! Do not cause a war! Do not break the peace! Disrespect done to our ancient laws brings no honor to the emperor. Do not make Tiberius an excuse for insulting our nation. He does not want any of our traditions done away with. If you say that he does, show us some decree or letter or something of the sort, so that we may cease troubling you and appeal to our master by means of an embassy." This last remark exasperated Pilate most of all, for he was afraid that if they really sent an embassy, they would bring accusations against the rest of his administration as well, specifying in detail his venality, his violence, his thefts, his assaults, his abusive behavior, his frequent executions of untried prisoners, and his endless savage ferocity. . . . When the Jewish officials . . . realized that Pilate was regretting what he had done, although he did not wish to show it, they wrote a letter to Tiberius, pleading their cause as forcibly as they could. What words, what threats Tiberius uttered against Pilate when he read it! It would be superfluous to describe his anger, since his reaction speaks for itself. For immediately, without even waiting until the next day, he wrote to Pilate, reproaching and rebuking him a thousand times for his new-fangled audacity and telling him to remove the shields at once and have them taken from the capital to the coastal city of Caesarea . . . to be dedicated in the Temple of Augustus. In this way both the honor of the Emperor and the traditional policy regarding Jerusalem were alike preserved.

CHRISTIANS IN CONFLICT WITH ROMAN POLICY

The Roman historians Suetonius and Tacitus refer in passing to the Christian movement in a few places. In his life of Claudius, Suetonius describes a disturbance that arose within the Jewish community at Rome. The central figure in the conflict is identified as "Chrestos." This common Greek name was almost certainly mistaken by the author for Christ(os), whose message had reached the Jews in Rome, with resultant controversy and division. Suetonius reports simply, "Since the Jews constantly made disturbances at the instigation of Chrestos, he Claudius expelled them from Rome." It was probably this event that brought Prisca and Aquila from Rome to Corinth, where they worked with Paul, and from which they returned to Rome (Acts 18:2, 18, 26; I Corinthians 16:19; Romans 16:3).

Pliny's Letter to the Emperor Trajan[66]

XCVI

It is a rule, Sir, which I inviolably observe, to refer myself to you in all my doubts; for who is more capable of guiding my uncertainty or informing my ignorance? Having never been present at any trials of the Christians, I am unacquainted with the method and limits to be observed either in examining or punishing them. Whether any difference is to be made on account of age, or no distinction allowed between the youngest and the adult; whether repentance admits to a pardon, or if a man has been once a Christian it avails him nothing to recant; whether the mere profession of Christianity, albeit without crimes, or only the crimes associated therewith are punishable—in all these points I am greatly doubtful.

Meanwhile, the method I have observed towards those who have been denounced to me as Christians is this: I interrogated them whether they were Christians; if they confessed it I repeated the question twice again, adding the threat of capital punishment; if they still persevered, I ordered them to be executed. For whatever the nature of their creed might be, I could at least feel no doubt that contumacy and inflexible obstinancy deserved chastisement. There were others also possessed with the same infatuation, but being citizens of Rome, I directed them to be carried thither.

These accusations spread (as is usually the case) from the mere fact of the matter being investigated and several forms of the mischief came to light. A placard was put up, without any signature, accusing a large number of persons by name. Those who denied they were, or had ever been, Christians, who repeated after me an invocation to the gods, and offered adoration, with wine and frankincense, to your image, which I had ordered to be brought for that purpose, together with those of the gods, and who finally cursed Christ—none of which acts, it is said, those who are really Christians can be forced into performing—these I thought it proper to discharge. Others who were named by that informer at first confessed themselves Christians, and then denied it; true, they had been of that persuasion but they had quitted it, some three years, others many years, and a few as much as twenty-five years ago. They all worshipped your statue and the images of the gods, and cursed Christ.

They affirmed, however, the whole of their guilt, or their error, was that they were in the habit of meeting on a certain fixed day before it was light, when they sang in alternate verses a hymn to Christ, as to a god, and bound themselves by a solemn oath, not to do any wicked deeds, but never to commit any fraud, theft or adultery, never to falsify their word, nor deny a trust when they should be called upon to deliver it up; after which it was their custom to separate, and then reassemble to partake of food—but food of an ordinary and innocent kind. Even this practice, however, they had abandoned after the publication of my edict, by which, according to your orders, I had forbidden political associations. I judged it so much the more necessary to extract the real truth, with the assistance of torture, from two female slaves, who were styled *deaconesses:* but I could discover nothing more than depraved and excessive superstition.

[66]Trajan was emperor from 98 to 117, during which time there were revolts among the Jews in Egypt and Cyrene, and the threat of invasion from the east by the Parthians was very real. Any suspicion of secret societies, especially with political overtones, would invite swift reprisals at the hand of the Roman authorities.

I therefore adjourned the proceedings, and betook myself at once to your counsel. For the matter seemed to me well worth referring to you—especially considering the numbers endangered. Persons of all ranks and ages, and of both sexes are, and will be, involved in the prosecution. For this contagious superstition is not confined to the cities only, but has spread through the villages and rural districts; it seems possible, however, to check and cure it. 'Tis certain at least that the temples, which had been almost deserted, began now to be frequented; and the sacred festivals, after a long general demand for sacrificial animals, which for some time past have met with but few purchasers. From hence it is easy to imagine what multitudes may be reclaimed from this error, if a door be left open to repentance.

Trajan's Response to Pliny

XCVII

The method you have pursued, my dear Pliny, in sifting the cases of those denounced to you as Christians is extremely proper. It is not possible to lay down any general rule which can be applied as the fixed standard in all cases of this nature.[67] No search should be made for these people; when they are denounced and found guilty they must be punished; with the restriction, however, that when the party denies himself to be a Christian, and shall give proof that he is not (that is, by adoring our Gods) he shall be pardoned on the ground of repentance, even though he may have formerly incurred suspicion. Information without the accuser's name subscribed must not be admitted in evidence against anyone, as it is introducing a very dangerous precedent, and by no means agreeable to the spirit of the age.

REFERENCES TO CHRISTIANS IN ROMAN HISTORIANS

Suetonius also makes mention in passing of the harassment of Christians under Nero: "Punishment was inflicted on the Christians, a class of men given to a new and mischievous superstition" (Life of Nero, XVI). But it is Tacitus who not only gives a fuller account of the brief persecution of Christians under Nero, but also gives some details about the origin of the movement. During his reign (A.D. 54–68), the city was set afire—by imperial order, as many believed. Nero sought to divert suspicion from himself:

Neither human help, nor imperial munificence, nor all the modes of placating heaven, could stifle scandal or dispel the belief that the fire had taken

[67]It is not clear from Trajan's response that the issue had actually arisen before; here he seems reluctant to appeal to precedent. But interpreters of Revelation have linked the words of the hymn in Rev. 4:11, "our Lord and God," with the reported insistence of Domitian (emperor from 81–96) that he be addressed a *dominus et deus* (lord and god), so that it is possible that the issue of divine honors to the emperor had arisen among the churches of Asia Minor decades earlier than the time of Pliny's governorship there.

> place by order, [*i.e.*, of Nero]. Therefore, to scotch the rumor, Nero substituted as culprits and punished with the utmost refinements of cruelty, a class of men, loathed for their vices, whom the crowd styled Christians. Christus, the founder of the name, had undergone the death penalty in the reign of Tiberius, by sentence of the procurator Pontius Pilate, and the pernicious superstition was checked for a moment, only to break out once more, not merely in Judea, the home of the disease, but in the capital itself, where all things horrible or shameful in the world collect and find a vogue. First, then, the confessed members of the sect were arrested; next, on their disclosures, vast numbers were convicted, not so much on the count of arson as for the hatred of the human race. And derision accompanied their end; they were covered with wild beasts' skins and torn to death by dogs; or they were fastened on crosses, and when daylight failed were burned to serve as lamps by night. Nero had offered his gardens for the spectacle, and gave an exhibition in his Circus, mixing with the crowd in the habit of a charioteer, or mounted on his car.[68]

Domitian, who reigned from 81–96, not only revived the custom of having his subjects address him as "lord" *(dominus)*,[69] but added to it the designation of "god" *(deus)*. He wrote a circular letter in the name of the regional governors, adding, "Our Master and our God bids this be done."[70]

The assassination of Domitian brought to an end the Flavian line of rulers, who were replaced by the Antonines, beginning with Trajan (98–117). Their epoch was a model of stability and consolidation for the empire. The threats of invasion of the empire from the east by the Parthians were very real, however. Any suspicion of secret societies raised the possibility of subversive activities.

[68]Nero's gardens were in the district of Rome known as Ager Vaticanus, which is famous as the traditional site of the death and burial of Peter.

[69]Suetonius tells us that Augustus cringed at being addressed as Lord (Life of Augustus LIII).

[70]Suetonius, Life of Domitian XIII.

2

The Religious Context

A. JUDAISM

All of our major sources for knowledge of the religious life of Jews in Palestine from the beginning of the Maccabean revolt (early second century B.C. to the middle of the second century A.D.) are beset with difficulties. Josephus, our chief historical source, shifted his attitudes toward the various factions within the Jewish community in reaction to the changing circumstances in which he found himself after the Fall of Jerusalem in A.D. 70, and the decision of Rome to support the Pharisees as the agents for the depoliticization of Judaism. The Mishnah and the Talmud claim to be the written version of the Oral Law, which is purported to go back to Moses and Mount Sinai, but the Mishnah can with certainty be reconstructed as a development within Judaism only from the end of the first to the end of the second century A.D., and the two Talmuds (from Palestine and Babylon) were developed around the Mishnah in the third and subsequent centuries.

The Dead Sea Scrolls certainly originated in the century before and the first two-thirds of the century after the birth of Jesus, but every indication confirms that these documents were written by and for a small sect within Judaism, so that the views represented in the scrolls cannot be seen as common features of Jewish religion in this period. Similarly, the large numbers of documents—admittedly of uncertain date—that are Jewish in origin but that were not included in the list of authoritative scriptures drawn up by the Jews at the end of the first century of our era may represent minority views rather than the mainstream of Palestinian Judaism.[1] These documents include apocalyptic, wisdom, and narrative writings, such as the Wisdom of Solomon, Wisdom of Sirach (Ben Sira), Jubilees, Testaments of the Twelve Patriarchs, Letter to Aristeas, and II Esdras. Excerpts from several of these documents follow. In addition to written documents for knowledge of the religion of Jews in this period, there have been some important archaeological discoveries that are relevant for our inquiry, but that run contrary to traditional depictions of this epoch.

ESSENES, PHARISEES, AND SADDUCEES

Josephus, Jewish War

The voluminous writings of this soldier-entrepreneur betray his own efforts to portray the religious movements within Judaism in nonpolitical terms, as well as his own ambivalence toward the Pharisees. In his earlier work, *Jewish War,* written in the years just after the Fall of Jerusalem and before he wrote his *Antiquities of the Jews,* Josephus described how, following the death of the Maccabean king Alexander Jannaeus (104–76 B.C.), the throne was occupied by his widow Alexandra. She sought to gain the allegiance of the populace by reversing her husband's brutal policies, and by encouraging stricter obedience to the Jewish laws. To aid her in her efforts, she sought and gained the support of the Pharisees, a party that took its stand over against the Sadducees, an aristocratic group linked with the priestly families.

JEWISH WAR I:110

Alongside Queen Alexandra, and gaining power with her, were the Pharisees, an important sector of the Jewish community who were considered more religious than the rest of the nation and stricter in observance and interpretation of the Laws. The pious Alexandra was so totally subservient to them that they gradually took advantage of the ingenuous and pious woman and in time became the real administrators of public affairs, free to banish and recall, to release or imprison whomever they pleased. In brief, they enjoyed the authority while Alexandra bore the responsibility and expenses. . . . While she ruled the nation, the Pharisees ruled her.

In *The Jewish War* II:120, Josephus begins a description of the "three
MK. schools of thought" found among the Jews in the time of Augustus, which
12:13 he wants to differentiate sharply from the other "sect," an extreme na-
–17 tionalist group that took the position that Jews should not pay taxes to

[1]Nowadays these writings are gathered in two collections: The Apocrypha (as they are called by Protestants) of the Old Testament, and the Pseudepigrapha, to be published as a supplement to the *Anchor Bible* (Garden City, N.Y.: Doubleday, 1983–84).

the Romans. Eventually that movement started the revolt against the Romans that led to the fall of the city in A.D. 70. Josephus takes care to show that there were other, nonpolitical movements within Judaism as well, and so represents these groups as philosophical schools devoid of political aims or ambitions.

The first "school" that he describes, the Essenes, do indeed appear to have been concerned solely with the internal affairs of their sect, and seemed free of political ambitions or activities. Josephus represents the Essenes as having conventicles in many cities, and that is probably accurate. From Philo of Alexandria, however, we hear of a similar sect he calls the *Therapeutae,* who live in a monastic-type community not far from Alexandria. But the discovery of the Dead Sea Scrolls, and the excavation of their community headquarters at Qumran overlooking the Dead Sea, has provided us with detailed information about the common life and the teachings of an Essene or Essene-type group. Before turning to examine some of that evidence (see chapter 2, pp. 62–75), we shall see what Josephus tells us about these three Jewish "philosophical schools." In the brief descriptions of the Pharisees and the Sadducees, however, there is no hint of political involvement. Rather, they differ on points of doctrine and lifestyle. The one hint of what Josephus will later write about the Pharisees is his description of them as "the leading sect."

The Essenes

JEWISH WAR II:120

Among the Jews there are three schools of thought. Their adherents are called Pharisees, Sadducees, and Essenes, respectively. The Essenes are known for their extreme piousness and saintliness. Jews by birth, they show a greater mutual attachment than do the other sects. They eschew pleasure as a vice and regard temperance and control of the passions as virtues. They disdain marriage, but adopt other people's children while still pliable and teachable, thus moulding them after their own ways. They do not, indeed, condemn wedlock in principle as a means of continuing the race, but they desire to protect themselves, since they are convinced that none of them keeps her pledged faithfulness to one man.

They hold wealth in contempt and maintain an admirable community of
ACTS goods, and none of them will be found to be any better off than the other.
2:44 Their rule is that new members admitted to the sect must surrender their
property to the order so that among them no humiliating poverty nor ex-
ACTS cessive wealth is ever seen, but each man's possessions become part of the
4:32 common resources and, as brothers, their entire patrimony belongs to them
all. They regard oil as polluting, and if a man intentionally comes in contact with it, he scrubs himself; for they regard it most desirable to keep the skin dry and always to wear white. They elect officers to supervise the affairs of the community, the particular services of each officer being determined by a general vote.

They populate no one city, but they are settled in great numbers in every

MK. 6:6–11 town. When adherents arrive from elsewhere, all local resources are put at their disposal as if they were their own, and they are entertained in the houses of men whom they have never known before as though they were the closest friends. And so when they travel, they carry no baggage with them, but only weapons to ward off brigands. In every town one of the order is appointed specially to look after strangers and provide them with clothing and provisions. In their dress and personal appearance they are like children in the care of a very stern tutor. They do not change garments nor shoes till they are torn to shreds or worn out with age. Among themselves nothing is bought or sold, but everyone gives what he has to anybody in need and receives from him in return something he himself can use; and even without giving anything in return they are freely permitted to share in the possessions of any of their brothers.

They show devotion to the Deity in a way all their own. Before the sun rises they do not utter a word on secular affairs, but offer to Him some traditional prayers as if beseeching Him to appear. They are then dismissed by those in charge to various crafts for which they have the best ability and are employed in strenuous activity until the fifth hour, when they again meet in one place, and donning linen loincloths, bathe their bodies in cold water. Thus purified, they assemble in a private hall of their own which none of the uninitiated is allowed to enter; pure now themselves, they go into the refectory, as to some sacred sanctuary. After taking their seats in silence, the baker serves them their loaves in turn, and the cook sets before each one of them a plate of one kind of food. The priest says grace before the meal and none may eat before his prayer. After breakfast he offers a sacred prayer, for both at the beginning and the end they give honor to God as the giver of life. Then, removing their sacred garments they again go back to their work until evening. On their return they eat in like manner and seat their guests beside them if any have arrived. No shouting or disorder ever desecrates their house; they speak in turn, each giving way to his neighbor. To people outside, the silence within seems like some awesome mystery; it is the result of their unfailing sobriety and the restriction of their allotted portions of meat and drink to a simple sufficiency.

In general they take no action without orders from their supervisors; but two things are left entirely to individual discretion: personal aid and compassion. They may, of their own accord, help any deserving person in need, or supply the destitute with food. However, presents to relatives are prohibited without official sanction from their supervisors. Showing indignation only when justified, they keep tempers under control; they champion good faith and serve the cause of peace. Every word they speak is more binding than an oath; they avoid swearing as something worse than perjury among other people, for they say a man is already condemned if he cannot be believed even without swearing by God.

They are wonderfully devoted to the study of the ancient writings, singling out mostly books that aim to benefit soul and body; from them, and with a view to curing diseases, they investigate medicinal roots and properties of different stones.

Persons desirous of joining the sect are not immediately admitted. Remaining outside the fraternity for a whole year, a man is required to observe the same rule of life as the members, receiving from them a hatchet, the loin-cloth mentioned above, and white garments. When he has given proof of his temperance during this probationary period, he is brought into closer touch with the rule and permitted to share the purer waters of sanctification, but is not yet received into the meetings of the community. For after having demonstrated his strength of purpose, his character is tested for two more years, and only then, if found worthy, is he accepted into the society. Yet, before he may touch the common food, he is made to swear great oaths first, that he will piously revere the Deity; secondly, that he will deal justly with men, will injure no one either of his own accord or at another's bidding; that he will forever hate the wicked and fight the battle of the just; that he will at all times keep faith with all men—especially with the powers that be, seeing no ruler attains his office except by the will of God. If he himself receives power, he will never abuse his authority nor, either by dress or additional ornament, outshine his subjects; he will love truth forever and expose liars; will keep his hands from stealing and his soul innocent of unholy gain; never hide anything from the members of the sect or reveal any of their secrets to others, even if he is tortured to death. He further swears to transmit their rules in no other manner than he himself received them; to take no part in armed robbery; and to preserve the scrolls of the sect and in the same way the names of the angels. Such are the oaths by which they bind their proselytes.

Men convicted of major offenses are expelled from the order; and the ejected individual often comes to a most miserable end; for being bound by their oaths and customs, he is not allowed to share other men's food and so he is forced to eat grass, his starved body wastes away and he dies of starvation. This has led them out of a compassion to take many offenders back at their last gasp, since they feel that men tortured to the point of death have paid a sufficient penalty for their misdeeds.

They are just and scrupulously careful in trying cases, never passing sentence in a tribunal of less than a hundred; their decisions thus reached are not subject to appeal. After God, they hold most in awe the name of the Lawgiver, and blasphemy against him is a capital offense. Obedience to older men and to the majority is a matter of principle; for instance, if ten sit down together one will not speak if the nine desire silence. They are careful not to spit within the midst of the company or to the right, and are stricter than all Jews in abstaining from work on the seventh day. For not only do they prepare food for themselves one day before so as not to kindle a fire on that day, but also they do not endeavor to remove any vessel or even to relieve themselves.

On other days they dig a trench a foot deep with a mattock—for such is the kind of hatchet they give to the novices—and wrapping their mantle around them, so as not to affront the rays of the sun, they squat over it: then they put the excavated soil back in the hole. On these occasions they select the more retired spots, and though the discharge of the bowels is quite natural, they make it a rule to wash after it, as if defiled.

They are divided into four grades, according to the duration of their training; and to such an extent are the juniors inferior to the seniors that if a senior is touched by a junior he must take a bath as though contaminated by an alien. They are long-lived, most of them passing the century, owing to the simplicity and regularity of their daily life, I imagine. They despise danger and conquer pain by will-power; death, if it comes with honor, they prefer to an easy death.

Their spirit was tested to the utmost by the war with the Romans. They racked, twisted, burnt and broke them, subjecting them to every instrument of torture in order to make them blaspheme their Lawgiver, or eat something forbidden. Yet they did not yield to either demand, nor ever once did they fawn on their tormentors or shed a tear. Smiling in their agony and gently mocking their torturers, they cheerfully resigned their souls, confident that they would receive them back again.

It is their unshakable conviction that bodies are corruptible and the material composing them impermanent, whereas the soul is immortal forever. Emanating from the most rarefied ether they are trapped, as it were, in the prison house of the body, as if drawn down by one of nature's spells. But when they are released from the bonds of the flesh, then, as though liberated from a long servitude, they rejoice and soar aloft. Holding, I believe, to the same conception as the Greeks, they declare that for the good souls there waits a home beyond the ocean, a place not troubled by rain or snow or heat, but refreshed by a gentle west wind blowing gently from the ocean, while they consign bad souls to a murky stormy abyss, full of punishments that know no end. I imagine the Greeks had the same notion when they assigned to their brave men, whom they called heroes and demigods, the isles of the blessed and to the souls of the wicked the place of the impious down in Hades, where, according to their mythology, certain people such as Sisyphus, Tantalus, Ixion and Tityus are undergoing punishment. Thus, they aimed, first, to establish that souls are immortal, and second, to promote virtue and discourage vice; since the good become better in their lifetime by the hope of a reward after death, and the ungovernable emotions of the wicked are restrained by the fear that, even though they escape detection in this life after their dissolution, they will undergo punishment. Such then are the theological views of the Essenes about the soul, providing an inescapable inducement to those who have once tested their philosophy.

Some of them claim to foretell the future as a result of a lifelong study of sacred writings, various forms of purification and the aphorisms of the prophets; rarely if ever do their predictions prove wrong.

There is yet a second order of Essenes, which agrees with the other in its way of life, customs and regulations, but differs only in its views on marriage. They think that the most important thing in life—the propagation of the race—is forfeited by men who do not marry, and further, if everyone would agree with them, mankind would disappear rapidly. However, they put their brides on probation for three years, and do not marry them till they have proven themselves capable of child-bearing after three periods of purification. They have no intercourse with them during pregnancy, thus showing that they marry not for pleasure but for the begetting of children. When the women bathe they wear a dress just as the men wear a loincloth. Such are the customs of this order.

The Pharisees

Of the two schools named first, the Pharisees are held to be the most accurate interpreters of the laws and are the leading sect. They attribute everything to fate and to God; they hold that to do right or otherwise rests mainly with men, but in every action fate has its share. Every soul, they maintain, is immortal, but the soul of the good alone passes into another body, while the souls of the wicked suffer eternal punishment.

The Sadducees

The Sadducees, the second order, deny fate altogether and hold that God is incapable of either committing sin or seeing it. They maintain that man has the choice of good and evil, and it rests with each individual to choose which he will follow. They deny the immortality of the soul after death and penalties in the underworld and rewards. The Pharisees are friendly to one another and cultivate harmonious relations with the community. The Sadducees, even towards each other, show a more disagreeable behavior, and in their relations with their peers are as rude as to aliens. This is all I have to say on the Jewish schools of thought.

Josephus, Antiquities of the Jews

In his *Antiquities of the Jews,* Josephus adopts a different attitude toward the Pharisees. In the second of two passages in which he describes the "schools," Josephus shifts his portrayal of the Pharisees so as to show how reasonable, powerful, and influential they are. It is no accident that at the very time he was changing his view of them, the Pharisees had been assigned the position of power by the Romans. Josephus knew well how to adjust to changes in the power structure.

> The Pharisees simplify their standard of living, making no concession to luxury. They follow the guidance of that which their doctrine has selected and transmitted as good, attaching the chief importance to the observance of those commandments which it has seen fit to dictate to them. They show respect and deference to their elders, nor do they rashly presume to contradict their proposals. Though they postulate that everything is brought about by fate, still they do not deprive the human will of the pursuit of what is in man's power, since it was God's good pleasure that there should be a fusion and that the will of man with his virtue and vice should be admitted to the council-chamber of fate. They believe that souls have power to survive death and that there are rewards and punishments under the earth for those who have led lives of virtue or vice: eternal imprisonment is the lot of evil souls, while the good souls receive an easy passage to a new life. Because of these views they are, as a matter of fact, extremely influential among the townsfolk; and all prayers and sacred rites of divine worship are performed according to their exposition. This is the great tribute that the inhabitants of the cities, by practising the highest ideals both in their way of living and in their discourse, have paid to the excellence of the Pharisees.
>
> The Sadducees hold that the soul perishes along with the body. They own no observance of any sort apart from the laws; in fact, they reckon it a virtue to dispute with the teachers of the path of wisdom that they pursue. There are but few men to whom this doctrine has been made known, but these are men of the highest standing. They accomplish practically nothing, however. For whenever they assume some office, though they submit unwillingly and perforce, yet submit they do to the formulas of the Pharisees, since otherwise the masses would not tolerate them.

Even in his recounting of incidents in the Maccabean period, Josephus now goes out of his way to assert the wide popular support enjoyed by the Pharisees. For example, in telling about the challenge raised by the Pharisees as to the legitimacy according to Jewish law of Hyrcanus's (reigned 134–104 B.C.) claim to the high priesthood, he reports the following:

> As for Hyrcanus, the envy of the Jews was aroused against him by his own successes and those of his sons; particularly hostile to him were the Pharisees, who are one of the Jewish schools, as we have related above. And so great is their influence with the masses that even when they speak against a king or high priest, they immediately gain credence. Hyrcanus too was a disciple of theirs, and was greatly loved by them. And once he invited them to a feast and entertained them hospitably, and when he saw that they were having a very good time, he began by saying that they knew he wished to be righteous and in everything he did tried to please God and them — for the Pharisees profess such beliefs; at the same time he begged them, if they observed him doing anything wrong or straying from the right path, to lead him back to it and correct him. But they testified to his being altogether virtuous, and he was delighted with their praise. However, one of the guests, named Eleazar, who had an evil nature and took pleasure in dissension, said, "Since you have asked to be told the truth, if you wish to be righteous, give up the high-priesthood and be content with governing the people." And when Hyrcanus asked him for what reason he should give up the high-priesthood, he replied, "Because we have heard from our elders that your mother was a captive in the reign of Antiochus Epiphanes." But the story was false, and Hyrcanus was furious with the man, while all the Pharisees were very indignant.
>
> Then a certain Jonathan, one of Hyrcanus's close friends, belonging to the school of Sadducees, who hold opinions opposed to those of the Pharisees, said that it had been with the general approval of all the Pharisees that Eleazar had made his slanderous statement; and this, he added, would be clear to Hyrcanus if he inquired of them what punishment Eleazar deserved for what he had said. And so Hyrcanus asked the Pharisees what penalty they thought he deserved—for, he said, he would be convinced that the slanderous statement had not been made with their approval if they fixed a penalty commensurate with the crime—, and they replied that Eleazar deserved stripes and chains; for they did not think it right to sentence a man to death for calumny, and anyway the Pharisees are naturally lenient in the matter of punishments. At this Hyrcanus became very angry and began to believe that the fellow had slandered him with their approval. And Jonathan in particular inflamed his anger, and so worked upon him that he brought him to join the Sadducaean party and desert the Pharisees, and to abrogate the regulations which they had established for the people, and punish those who observed them. Out of this, of course, grew the hatred of the masses for him and his sons, but of this we shall speak hereafter. For the present I wish merely to explain that the Pharisees had passed on to the people certain regulations handed down by former generations and not recorded in the Laws of Moses, for which reason they are rejected by the Sadducaean group, who hold that only those regulations should be considered valid which were written down [in Scripture], and that those which had been handed down by former generations need not be observed. And concerning these matters the two parties came to have controversies and serious differences, the Sadducees having the confidence of the wealthy alone but no following among the populace, while the Pharisees have the support of the masses. But of these two schools and of the Essenes a detailed account has been given in the second book of my *Judaica.*

> And so Hyrcanus quieted the outbreak, and lived happily thereafter; and when he died after administering the government excellently for thirty-one years, he left five sons.

Similarly, in *Antiquities* Josephus revises his attitude toward the Pharisees in relation to the accession to power of Alexandra, and implies that the dying Alexander Jannaeus had done so as well. When asked on his deathbed by Alexandra how she is to gain authority over the kingdom, Jannaeus counselled her what to do after capturing the fortress that he was besieging when he was fatally wounded.

> Thereupon he advised her to follow his suggestions for keeping the throne secure for herself and her children and to conceal his death from the soldiers until she had captured the fortress. And then, he said, on her return to Jerusalem as from a splendid victory, she should yield a certain amount of power to the Pharisees, for if they praised her in return for this sign of regard, they would dispose the nation favorably toward her.
>
> These men, he assured her, had so much influence with their fellow-Jews that they could injure those whom they hated and help those to whom they were friendly; when they spoke harshly of any person, even when they did so out of envy; and he himself, he added, had come into conflict with the nation because these men had been badly treated by him.
>
> "And so," he said, "when you come to Jerusalem, send for their partisans, and showing them my dead body, permit them, with every sign of sincerity, to treat me as they please, whether they wish to dishonor my corpse by leaving it unburied because of the many injuries that have suffered at my hands, or in their anger wish to offer my dead body any other form of indignity. Promise them also that you will not take any action, while you are on the throne, without their consent. If you speak to them in this manner, I shall receive from them a more splendid burial than I should from you; for once they have the power to do so, they will not choose to treat my corpse badly, and at the same time you will reign securely." With this exhortation to his wife he died, after reigning twenty-seven years, at the age of forty-nine.
>
> Thereupon Alexandra, after capturing the fortress, conferred with the Pharisees as her husband had suggested, and by placing in their hands all that concerned his corpse and the royal power, stilled their anger against Alexander, and made them her well-wishers and friends. And they in turn went to the people and made public speeches in which they recounted the deeds of Alexander, and said that in him they had lost a just king, and by their eulogies they so greatly moved the people to mourn and lament that they gave him a more splendid burial than had been given any of the kings before him.

Josephus goes on to show how completely deferential to the Pharisees Alexandra was, and what formidable powers they exercised among the people. The lesson for Josephus and his Roman readers was clear: The Pharisees have a long and impressive record of effective leadership backed by wide popular esteem. And in words that recall the more critical attitude Josephus expressed in the *Jewish War* but which are almost obsequious in their estimate of the Pharisees, Josephus now declares:

> Alexandra permitted the Pharisees to do as they like in all matters, and also commanded the people to obey them; and whatever regulations, introduced by the Pharisees in accordance with the tradition of their fathers, had been abolished by her father-in-law Hyrcanus, these she again restored. And so, while she had the title of sovereign, the Pharisees had the power.

As Morton Smith has noted, the aim of Josephus in *Antiquities* is to show that the Pharisees "have by far the greatest influence with the people. Any government which secures their support is accepted; any government which alienates them has trouble. . . . So any Roman government which wants peace in Palestine had better support and secure the support of the Pharisees."[2] From this evidence emerge two conclusions: that the Pharisees were deeply involved in political affairs during the Maccabean period; and that their interpretation of the Jewish Law had a broad and deep appeal to Jews living in Palestine down to and through the unsuccessful revolt against Rome in A.D. 66–70. The question for which Josephus provides no answer is, what was it about their understanding of the Law that had so powerful an effect?

FROM THE PHARISEES TO MISHNAH AND TALMUD

The traditional view of the interpretive process in which the Pharisees were engaged is that they were expounding and applying to contemporary life the Oral Law that was given at Sinai to Moses, along with the written law. The basic assumption is epitomized in the rabbinic exposition of Exodus (Ex.R. 47:1):

> When God revealed himself at Sinai to give the Torah to Israel, He communicated it to Moses in order: Scripture, Mishnah, Talmud, and Haggadah, as it says, "And God spoke all these words" (Ex. 20:1). Even the question a pupil asks his teacher, God told Moses at that time.

The Mishnah is a compilation of material that developed during the period from the Fall of Jerusalem until about A.D. 200. The central figure in its publication was Judah, called "the patriarch." He was the ruler of the Jewish community of the Land of Israel, or Palestine, and was regarded as a rabbi—that is, an authority on Torah, the Law of the Jews.

As the twin of the Written Law, the Mishnah was considered authoritative, and therefore in need of comment and interpretation. During

[2]Morton Smith, "Palestinian Judaism in the First Century," in *Israel: Its Role in Civilization,* ed. Moshe Davis (New York: Harper and Row, 1956), pp. 75–76.

the third and fourth centuries, sages in both Palestine and Babylon were engaged in expounding the Mishnah and in demonstrating its relationship to Scripture. To lend equal authority to the Mishnah and the Torah, the myth of their linked origins in time and place was important. There was in this connection the claim that the sages who transmitted and expounded the Oral Law had met in what was called "the Great Assembly," a kind of ongoing parliamentary body debating and modifying legal issues, which had preserved the oral tradition until it was finally set down in written form as the Mishnah and finally as the Talmud.[3] As a consequence of what is now known about the origins of this material, it can be used only with the greatest caution as a source of information about the pre-70 period in Jewish history. Nevertheless, the issues addressed between Jesus and the Pharisees in the first three gospels match well with what appear to be the older layers of tradition in the Mishnah: sabbath observance, divorce, fasting, cleanness laws pertaining to food and to those who are sick, and especially the issue of eating with Jews who do not observe the dietary laws. We shall examine some of these traditions below in the section on Jewish Interpretation of Scripture (pp. 95–130).

THE TEMPLE

As a source for knowledge of Judaism in his own time, Josephus is of supreme value for information about the temple and the worship of God carried out there.

Josephus, Jewish War

The following excerpt begins at the point where Titus is about to lay siege to Jerusalem. Josephus interrupts the narrative of the war, however, in order to give his reader a detailed picture of the city and its architectural and cultural prize: the temple on Zion.

V:47–53

(47) As Titus[4] advanced into enemy territory, his vanguard consisted of the contingents of the kings with the whole body of auxiliaries. Next to these were the pioneers and camp-measures, then the officers' baggage-train; behind the troops protecting these came the commander-in-chief, escorted by the lancers and other picked troops, (48) and followed by the legionary cavalry. These were succeeded by the engines, and these by the tri-

[3]For a detailed analysis of the modern theories about this ancient scholarly process see Jacob Neusner, *The Modern Study of the Mishnah* (Leiden: Brill, 1973).

[4]Titus was placed in command of the Roman troops attacking Jerusalem by his father, Vespasian, who had been called back to Rome in order to become emperor in A.D. 69. Marching by stages up the Palestinian coast as far as Caesarea, the Roman seat of power, Titus turned inland to Samaria, and from there marched south along the ridge of Judean hills toward Jerusalem.

bunes and prefects of cohorts with a picked escort; after them and surrounding the eagle came the ensigns preceded by their trumpeters, and behind them the solid column, six (49) abreast. The servants attached to each legion followed in a body, preceded by the baggage-train. Last of all came the mercenaries with a (50) rearguard to keep watch on them. Leading his army forward in this orderly array, according to Roman usage, Titus advanced through Samaria to Gophna,[5] previously captured by his father and now garrisoned. After resting here one night he set forward at dawn, and at the end of a full (51) day's march encamped in the valley which is called by the Jews in their native tongue "Valley of Thorns," close to a village named Gabath Saul,[6] which means "Saul's hill," at a distance of about thirty furlongs from Jerusalem. From here, with some six hundred picked (52) horsemen, he rode forward to reconnoitre the city's strength and to test the mettle of the Jews, whether, on seeing him, they would be terrified into surrender before any actual conflict; for he had learnt, (53) as indeed was the fact, that the people were longing for peace, but were overawed by the insurgents and brigands and remained quiet merely from inability to resist.

v:136–141

(136) The city was fortified by three walls, except where it was enclosed by impassable ravines, a single rampart there sufficing.[7] (137) It was built, in portions facing each other, on two hills separated by a central valley, in which the tiers of houses ended.

Of these hills, that on the upper city was far higher and had a straighter ridge than the other; consequently, owing to its strength it was called by King David—the father of Solomon the first builder of the temple—the Stronghold, but we called it the upper agora.[8] The second hill, which bore the name of Acra[9] and supported the lower city, (138) was a hog's back. Opposite this was a third hill, by nature lower than Acra, and once divided from it by another broad ravine. Afterwards, (139) however, the Hasmonaeans, during the period of their reign, both filled up the ravine, with the object of uniting the city to the temple, and also reduced the elevation of Acra by leveling its summit, in order that it might not block the view of the temple. The Valley of the (140) Cheesemakers,[10] as the ravine was called,

[5]A small city, now the Christian Arab village of Jiphna, some twenty miles north of Jerusalem.

[6]The site is clearly visible a few miles north of Jerusalem on the east side of the present main highway. The fortress built there by Saul, Israel's first king, has been excavated in recent years.

[7]The problem of fortifying the city was most difficult on the north side of the temple hill, since there alone the ground does not drop off precipitously. Heavy walls and a massive fortress-tower were erected there in an effort to prevent breaching the walls from that side.

[8]Excavations have shown that the oldest structures on the upper, western hill, including the citadel, go back only to Maccabean times. David's city was on the southern slope of the lower eastern hill. But local tradition very early transferred the name "Zion" to the higher western ridge and called the hellenistic fortress there "The Tower of David."

[9]Overlooking the temple enclosure from the north is the massive tower of Antonia, the present remains of which go back to Herod the Great.

[10]The *Tyropeon Valley* separating the eastern and western hills of Jerusalem has filled in considerably since the time that Josephus wrote, but it is still clearly visible as a long depression that begins southeast of the present Damascus Gate (actually built first by Hadrian), and slopes away to the south and east, running along below the western wall of the temple platform.

which, as we said, was lower, extends down to Siloam; for so we called that fountain of sweet and abundant water. On the exterior the two hills on which the city stood (141) were encompassed by deep ravines, and the precipitous cliffs on either side rendered the town nowhere accessible.

V:148–162

(148) This wall was built by Agrippa[11] to enclose the later additions to the city, which were quite unprotected; for the town, overflowing with inhabitants, had gradually crept beyond the ramparts. Indeed, the (149) population, uniting to the hill the district north of the temple, encroached so far that even a fourth hill was surrounded with houses. This hill, which is called Bezetha, lay opposite Antonia, but was cut off from it by a deep fosse, dug on purpose to sever the foundations of (150) Antonia from the hill and so to render them at once less easy of access and more elevated, the depth of the trench materially increasing (151) the height of the towers. The recently built quarter was called in the vernacular Bezetha, which might be translated into Greek as "New Town." Seeing then the residents of this district in need of defence, (152) Agrippa, the father and namesake of the present king, began the above-mentioned wall; but, fearing that Claudius Caesar might suspect from the vast scale of the structure that he had designs of revolution and revolt, he desisted after merely laying the foundations. Indeed (153) the city would have been impregnable, had the wall been continued as it began; for it was constructed of stones twenty cubits long and ten broad, so closely joined that they could scarcely have been undermined with tools of iron or shaken by engines.[12] The wall itself was ten (154) cubits broad, and it would doubtless have attained a greater height than it did, had not the ambition of its founder been frustrated. (155) Subsequently, although hurriedly erected by the Jews, it rose to a height of twenty cubits, besides having battlements of two cubits and bulwarks of three cubits high, bringing the total altitude up to twenty-five cubits.[13]

(156) Above the wall, however, rose towers, twenty cubits broad and twenty high, square and solid as the wall itself, and in the joining and beauty of the stones in no wise inferior to the temple. Over this solid masonry, twenty cubits in altitude, were magnificent apartments, (157) and above these, upper chambers and cisterns to receive the rain-water, each tower having broad spiral staircases. Of such towers the third (158) wall had ninety, disposed at intervals of two hundred cubits; the line of the middle wall was sixty. The whole circumference of the city was thirty-three furlongs.[14] But wonderful as was the third wall throughout, (159) still more so was the tower Psephinus, which rose at its northwest angle and opposite to which Titus encamped. For, being seventy (160) cubits high,[15] it afforded

[11]That is, Herod Agrippa, grandson of Herod the Great. Appointed king of an area north and east of the Sea of Galilee by the Emperor Caligula (37–41), he effectively interceded before the Roman Senate in behalf of Claudius's claim to be recognized as emperor. Claudius rewarded Agrippa by designating him as king over all the territories formerly ruled by his grandfather, but Agrippa's reign was brief (41–44 A.D.).

[12]Judging by the enormous stones still to be seen in the lower courses of the masonry platform on which Herod built the temple and its courts, these dimensions (approximately 67 by 7 by 9 feet) may not be exaggerated.

[13]The height would be about 10 yards.

[14]More than 4 miles.

[15]More than 100 feet high.

from sunrise a prospect embracing both Arabia and the utmost limits of Hebrew territory as far as the sea; (161) it was of octagonal form.

Over against this was the tower Hippicus, and close to it two others, all built by King Herod into the old wall, and for magnitude, beauty and strength without their equal in the world. For, apart from (162) his innate magnanimity and his pride in the city, the king sought, in the super-excellence of these works, to gratify his private feelings; dedicating them to the memory of three persons to whom he was most fondly attached, and after whom he named these towers—brother, friend, and wife. The last, as we have previously related, he had for love's sake actually slain; the others he had lost in war, after valiant fight.

v:176–194

(176) Adjoining and on the inner side of these towers, which lay to the north of it, was the king's palace, baffling all description: (177) indeed, in extravagance and equipment no building surpassed it. It was completely enclosed within a wall thirty cubits high,[16] broken at equal distances by ornamental towers, and contained immense banqueting-halls and bed-chambers for a hundred guests. The interior fittings (178) are indescribable—the variety of the stones (for species rare in every other country were here collected in abundance), ceilings wonderful (179) both for the length of the beams and the splendour of their surface decoration, the host of apartments with their infinite varieties of (180) design, all amply furnished, while most of the objects in each of them were of silver or gold. All around were many circular cloisters, (181) leading one into another, the columns in each being different, and their open courts all of greensward; there were groves of various trees intersected by long walks, which were bordered by deep canals, and ponds everywhere studded with bronze figures, through which the water was (182) discharged, and around the streams were numerous cotes for tame pigeons. However, it is impossible adequately to delineate the palace, and the memory of it is harrowing, recalling as it does the ravages of (183) the brigands' fire. For it was not the Romans who burnt it to the ground, but this was done, as we have said already, by conspirators within the walls at the opening of the revolt. The conflagration beginning at Antonia passed to the palace, and spread to the roofs of the three towers.

(184) Though the temple, as I said, was seated on a strong hill, the level area on its summit originally barely sufficed for shrine and altar, the ground around it being precipitous and steep. But king (185) Solomon, the actual founder of the temple, having walled up the eastern side, a single portico was reared on this made ground;[17] on its other sides the sanctuary remained exposed. In course of ages, however, through the constant additions of the people to the embankment, the hilltop by this process of levelling up was widened. They further broke (186) down the north wall and thus took in an area as large as the whole temple enclosure subsequently occupied. Then, after having enclosed (187) the hill from its base with a wall on three sides,

[16]About 45 feet.

[17]The portico on the southwest corner of the Herodian temple enclosure was named for Solomon, as is confirmed by the Gospel of John (10:23), but the entire structure, including the portico, dates from about 900 years after the time of Solomon. However costly Solomon's temple may have been, Herod's was far larger, far more complex, and probably much more costly.

and accomplished a task greater than they could ever have hoped to achieve—a task upon which long ages were spent by them as well as all their sacred treasures, though replenished by the tributes offered to God from every quarter (188) of the world—they built around the original block the upper courts and the lower temple enclosure. The latter, where its foundations were lowest, they built up from a depth of three hundred cubits; at some spots this figure was exceeded.[18] The whole depth of the foundations was, (189) however, not apparent; for they filled up a considerable part of the ravines, wishing to level the narrow alleys of the town. Blocks of stone were used in the building measuring forty cubits; for lavish funds and popular enthusiasm led to incredible enterprises, and a task seemingly interminable was through perseverance and in time actually achieved.

(190) Nor was the superstructure unworthy of such foundations. The porticoes, all in double rows, were supported by columns five and twenty (191) cubits high—each a single block of the purest white marble—and ceiled with panels of cedar. The natural magnificence of these columns, (192) their excellent polish and fine adjustment, presented a striking spectacle, without any adventitious embellishment of painting or sculpture. The porticoes were thirty cubits broad, and the complete circuit of them, embracing the tower of Antonia, measured six furlongs. The open court was from end to end variegated with paving of all manner of stones.

(193) Proceeding across this towards the second court of the temple, one found it surrounded by a stone balustrade, three cubits high and of (194) exquisite workmanship; in this at regular intervals stood slabs giving warning, some in Greek, others in Latin characters, of the law of purification, to wit that no foreigner was permitted to enter the holy place,[19] for so the second enclosure of the temple was called.

V:206–219

(206) Fifteen steps led up from the women's compartment to the greater gate, these steps being shallower than the five at each of the other gates.

(207) The sacred edifice itself, the holy temple, in the central position, was approached by a flight of twelve steps. The facade was of equal height and breadth, each being a hundred cubits;[20] but the building behind was narrower by forty cubits, for in front it had as it were shoulders extending twenty cubits on either side. The first gate was seventy cubits high and twenty-five broad and had no doors, displaying (208) unexcluded the void expanse of heaven; the entire face was covered with gold, and through it the first edifice was visible to a spectator without in all its grandeur and the surroundings of the inner gate (209) all gleaming with gold fell beneath his eye. But, whereas the sanctuary within consisted of two separate chambers, the first building alone stood exposed to view, from top to bottom, towering to a height of ninety cubits, its length being fifty and its breadth twenty. The gate (210) opening into the building was, as I said, completely overlaid with gold, as was the whole wall around it. It had, moreover, above it (211) those

[18]The retaining walls were explored to their foundations in the nineteenth century, and have been further excavated in recent years. Josephus does indulge in exaggeration as to the height of the walls, which are more like 150 feet than the 150 yards he describes.

[19]Several of the original examples of this inscription have been found. A translation of the inscription is given on p. 203.

[20]A cubit is usually considered to be about 18 inches.

golden vines, from which depended grape clusters as tall as a man; and it had golden doors fifty-five cubits high and sixteen broad. Before these hung a veil of equal length, of Babylonian tapestry, with (212) embroidery of blue and fine linen, of scarlet also and purple, wrought with marvellous skill. Nor was this mixture of materials without its mystic meaning: it typified the universe. For the scarlet (213) seemed emblematical of fire, the fine linen of the earth, the blue of the air, and the purple of the sea; the comparison in the two cases being suggested by their colour, and in that of the fine linen and purple by their origin, as the one is produced by the earth and the other by (214) the sea. On this tapestry was portrayed a panorama of the heavens, the signs of the Zodiac excepted.[21]

(215) Passing within one found oneself in the ground-floor of the sanctuary. This was sixty cubits in height, the same in length, and twenty cubits in breadth. But the sixty cubits of its length were (216) divided. The first portion, partitioned off at forty cubits, contained within it three most wonderful works of art, universally renowned: a (217) lampstand, a table, and an altar of incense. The seven lamps (such being the number of the branches from the lampstand) represented the planets; the loaves on the table, twelve in number, the circle of the Zodiac and the year; while the altar of incense, by the thirteen (218) fragrant spices from sea and from land, both desert and inhabited, with which it was replenished, signified that all things are of God and for God.

(219) The innermost recess measured twenty cubits, and was screened in like manner from the outer portion by a veil. In this stood nothing whatever: unapproachable, inviolable, invisible to all, it was called the Holy of Holies.

THE DEAD SEA COMMUNITY

The chance discovery of scrolls stored in a jar within a cave near the Dead Sea about 1950 has provided insight into a segment of Judaism in the time of Jesus of which there was no previous knowledge. The group that produced and preserved these writings has been given a name by scholars that derives from the deep ravine that flows below the plateau on which the sect had its community center, the Wadi Qumran. Although there were hints of earlier discoveries of scrolls in writings from the early centuries of the church's existence and from Jewish documents discovered in Cairo nearly a century ago, these documents provide detailed descriptions of the organization of the group, and of its beliefs and hopes. Although there are apparent similarities with what Josephus reports about the Essenes, the Qumran sect differed in that it withdrew completely from both pagan and Jewish society on the assumption that it could live in obedience to God only in isolation from all but its own adherents. It believed that its members had the true understanding of scripture and

[21]Josephus may be correct here, but the signs of the zodiac were the most popular decorative motif in Palestinian synagogues from the third century until at least 500 A.D., judging by excavated remains of mosaic pavements from ancient synagogues.

Dead Sea Caves. Natural caves, of which there are many in these cliffs overlooking the Dead Sea from the site of the ancient community of Qumran, provided the members of the community with what they considered to be safe places to keep the scrolls from their library. Apparently, they expected to return after the Roman troops had passed through the valley. They were, however, not able to do so, and the scrolls remained concealed for centuries. A few were found in the third century, but most remained until the middle of the present century, when they were discovered first by local herdsmen, and then by archaeologists. *(Courtesy of the Palestine Archaeological Museum)*

that they therefore would be designated by God to restore the pure and proper worship of God in a restored temple in Jerusalem.

The members considered themselves to be the elect people of the New Covenant, who had been called to repent and receive the insights into the divine purpose through the Teacher of Righteousness (or, One Who Teaches Rightly) who founded the movement. Copies of writings that describe his experiences and that set out the Community Rule have been preserved, as well as collections of hymns, predictions about the end of the age, and the group's own special interpretation of the Bible. Not least important are the recovery from Qumran of the oldest surviving copies of parts of the Hebrew Bible, especially the book of Isaiah. The picture of the group that comes through these writings is of a sect that insists on rigorous observance of laws of purity, that expects persecution at the hands of enemies, and that expects divine intervention to vindicate and reward the faithful members. In the two writings, the Temple Scroll and the War of the Children of Light and the Children of Darkness, these expectations are detailed.

Since the discovery of the scrolls, the suggestion has often been made that either Jesus or John the Baptist was a member of the Qumran community. John, while insisting on purity as the Qumran sect did, is convinced that he has been commissioned by God to go out and call others to repentance, rather than remain aloof from the rest of the world at Qumran. And Jesus was denounced by his contemporary Jews as being friendly toward and associating with persons who were morally and ritually impure: "a friend of tax collectors and sinners" (Mt. 11:19). What these two figures share with the Dead Sea sect, however, is the conviction that God is redefining the covenant community, and that there is an urgency in the enterprise, in light of the expectation of direct action by God to defeat the powers of evil and establish his rule on the earth.

The two writings from the Dead Sea caves that provide the most insight and information into the founding of the sect are the Damascus Document and the Rule of the Community. Copies of the former were found in the storage room of a synagogue in Cairo early in this century, but they remained a puzzling curiosity. With the finding of this document at Qumran, however, and with the additional light shed by the Rule of the Community, the broad outline of the rise of the leader of the Dead Sea sect can be traced.

THE DAMASCUS DOCUMENT

I. And now listen, all you who know righteousness and understand the works of God. For he has a controversy with all flesh, and will execute judgment upon all who despise him. For when those who forsook him trespassed, he hid his face from Israel and from his sanctuary, and gave them up to the sword; but when he remembered the covenant of the ancients, he left a remnant to Israel and did not give them up to destruction. And in the period of the wrath—three hundred and ninety years, when he gave them into the hand of Nebuchadnezzar, king of Babylon—he visited them and caused to sprout from Israel and Aaron a root of planting to inherit his land and to grow fat in the goodness of his soil. Then they perceived their iniquity and knew that they were guilty men; yet they were like men blind and groping for the way for twenty years. And God observed their works, that they sought him with a perfect heart; and he raised up for them a teacher of righteousness to lead them in the way of his heart. And he made known to later generations what he did to a later generation, to a congregation of treacherous men, those who turned aside out of the way.

This was the time concerning which it was written, "Like a stubborn heifer, Israel was stubborn," when arose the man of scorn, who preached to Israel lying words and led them astray in a trackless wilderness, so that he brought low their iniquitous pride, so that they turned aside from the paths of righteousness, and removed the landmark which the forefathers had fixed in their inheritance, so making the curses of his covenant cleave to them, delivering them to the sword that wreaks the vengeance of the covenant. For they sought smooth things, and chose illusions, and looked for breaches, and chose the fair neck; and they justified the wicked and condemned the righteous, transgressed the covenant, and violated the statute. And they banded together against the life of the righteous, and all who walked uprightly their soul abhorred, and they pursued them with the sword and exulted in the strife of the people. Then was kindled the wrath of God against their congregation, laying waste all their multitude; and their deeds were uncleanness before him.

II. And now listen to me, all you who have entered the covenant, and I will uncover your ears as to the ways of the wicked. God loves the knowledge of wisdom; and sound wisdom he has set before him; prudence and knowledge minister to him. Longsuffering is with him, and abundance of pardon to forgive those who turn from transgression, but power and might and great wrath with flames of fire by all the angels of destruction upon those who turn aside from the way and abhor the statute, so that they shall have no remnant of survival.

For God did not choose them from the beginning of the world, but before they were established he knew their works and abhorred their generations from of old, and he hid his face from the land and from his people until they were consumed; for he knew the years of abiding and the number and explanation of their periods for all who exist in the ages, and the things that come to pass even to what will come in their periods for all the years of eternity.

But in all of them he raised up for himself men called by name, in order to leave a remnant to the land, and to fill the face of the world with their seed. And he caused them to know by his anointed his Holy Spirit and a revelation of truth; and in the explanation of his name are their names. But those he hated he caused to go astray.

III. And now, my sons, listen to me, and I will uncover your eyes to see and understand the works of God, and to choose what he likes and reject what he hates; to walk perfectly in all his ways, and not to go about with thoughts of a guilty impulse and eyes of fornication; for many went astray in them, and mighty men of valor stumbled in them, formerly and until now. In their walking in the rebelliousness of their hearts the watchers of heaven fell; in it they were caught who did not keep the commandment of God, and their children, whose height was like the loftiness of the cedars, and whose bodies were like the mountains, fell thereby. Yea, all flesh that was on the dry land fell; yea, it perished; and they were as though they had not been, because they did their own will and did not keep the commandment of their Maker, until his anger was kindled against them.

IV. In it the sons of Noah and their families went astray; in it they were cut off. Abraham did not walk in it, and he was accounted as God's friend, because he kept the commandments of God and did not choose the will of his own spirit. And he passed on the commandment to Isaac and Jacob, and they kept it and were recorded as friends of God and possessors of the covenant forever.

The sons of Jacob went astray in them and were punished according to their error, and their sons in Egypt walked in the stubbornness of their hearts, taking counsel against the commandments of God and doing each what was right in his own eyes. They ate blood, and he cut off their males in the desert. And he said to them in Kadesh, "Go up and take possession of the land," but they hardened their spirit and did not listen to the voice of their Maker, the commandments of their Teacher, but murmured in their tents.

Then the anger of God was kindled against their congregation; their children perished by it, the kings were cut off by it, and their mighty men perished by it; and their land was made desolate by it. By it the first that entered the covenant became guilty, and they were delivered to the sword, because they forsook the covenant of God and chose their own will, and went about after the stubbornness of their heart, each doing his own will.

V. But with those who held fast to the commandments of God, those who were left of them, God established his covenant for Israel to eternity, revealing to them hidden things in which all Israel had gone astray. His holy Sabbaths and his glorious festivals, his righteous testimonies and his true ways, and the desires of his will, by which, if a man does them, he shall live, he opened up before them. And they dug a well for many waters, and he who despises them shall not live. But they defiled themselves with the transgression of man, and in the ways of the unclean woman, and they said,
"That is for us." But God in his wondrous mysteries forgave their iniquity
ACTS and pardoned their transgression, and he built for them a sure house in Is-
15:16 rael, the like of which has not existed from of old or until now. Those who
hold fast to it are for eternal life, and all the glory of man is theirs; as God
AMOS established it for them by the prophet Ezekiel, saying, "The priests and the
9:11–12 Levites and the sons of Zadok, who kept the charge of my sanctuary when
EZ. the sons of Israel went astray from me, they shall offer to me fat and
44:15 blood."

VI. The priests are the captivity of Israel who went forth from the land of Judah, and the Levites are those who joined them; and the sons of Zadok are the elect of Israel, those called by name, who will abide at the end of days. Behold the explanation of their names according to their generations, and the period of their abiding, and the number of their distresses, and the years of their sojourning, and the explanation of their works, the first saints whom God forgave, and who justified the righteous and condemned the wicked.

All who come after them must do according to the explanation of the law in which the forefathers were instructed until the completion of the period of these years. According to the covenant which God established with the forefathers to forgive their sins, so God will forgive them. And at the completion of the period to the number of these years they shall no more join themselves to the house of Judah, but everyone must stand up on his watchtower. The wall has been built; the decree is far away.

* * *

VIII. In the period of the destruction of the land arose the removers of the landmark and led Israel astray. And the land became desolate, because they spoke rebellion against the commandments of God by Moses, and also by the holy anointed ones; and they prophesied falsehood to turn away Israel from following God.

But God remembered the covenant of the forefathers, and raised up from Aaron men of understanding, and from Israel wise men. And he made them listen, and they dug the well. "A well which princes dug, which the nobles of the people delved with the staff." The well is the law, and those who dug it are the captivity of Israel, who went out from the land of Judah and sojourned in the land of Damascus, all of whom God called princes, because they sought him, and their glory was not rejected in the mouth of anyone. And the staff [or legislator] is he who studies the law, as Isaiah said, "He produces an instrument for his work." And the nobles of the people are those who come to dig the well with the staves [or rules] which the staff [or legislator] prescribed to walk in during the whole period of wickedness; and without them they shall not attain to the arising of him who will teach righteousness at the end of days.

And all who have been brought into the covenant not to come into the sanctuary to kindle fire on his altar in vain shall become those who shut the door, as God said, "Who among you will shut his door, so that you will not kindle fire on my altar in vain?"—unless they observe to do according to the explanation of the law for the period of wickedness; and to separate from the sons of the pit; and to keep away from the unclean wealth of wickedness acquired by vowing and devoting and by appropriating the wealth of the sanctuary; and not to rob the poor of his people, so that widows become their spoil, and they murder the fatherless; and to make a separation between the unclean and the clean, and to make men know the difference between the holy and the common; and to keep the Sabbath day according to its explanation, and the festivals and the day of the fast, according to the decision of those who entered the new covenant in the land of Damascus;
JN. to contribute their holy things according to their explanation; to love each
13:35 his brother as himself; and to hold fast the hand of the poor and the needy
and the proselyte; and to seek everyone the peace of his brother; for a man shall not trespass against his next of kin; and to keep away from harlots according to the ordinance; to rebuke each his brother according to the commandment, and not to bear a grudge from day to day; and to separate from all uncleanness according to their ordinances; for a man shall not make abominable his holy spirit, as God separated for them.

For all who walk in these things in perfection of holiness, according to all his teaching, God's covenant stands fast, to make them live to a thousand generations.

* * *

When the two houses of Israel separated, Ephraim departed from Judah; and all who turned back were given over to the sword, but those who stood firm escaped to the land of the north, as it says, "And I will exile the *sikkuth* of your king and the *kiyyun* of your images from the tents of Damascus." The books of the law are the booth of the king, as it says, "And I will raise up the booth of David that is fallen"; the king is the assembly; and the
AMOS *kiyyun* of the images are the books of the prophets, whose words Israel de-
9:11 spised; and the star is the interpreter of the law who came to Damascus, as
it is written, "A star shall come forth out of Jacob, and a sceptre shall rise
NUM. out of Israel." The sceptre is the prince of the whole congregation. And
24:17 when he arises, he "shall break down all the sons of Seth."

And such shall be the judgment of everyone who rejects the former ones and the latter ones; those who have taken idols into their hearts and walked in the stubbornness of their hearts. They have no share in the house of the law. According to the judgment of their fellows who turned back with the men of scorn shall they be judged, for they spoke error against the statutes of righteousness and rejected the firm covenant which they had established in the land of Damascus, that is, the new covenant. And neither they nor their families shall have a share in the house of the law.

From the day of the gathering in of the unique teacher until the annihilation of all the men of war who returned with the man of the lie will be about forty years; and in that period will be kindled the anger of God against Israel, as it says, "There is no king and no prince and no judge, and none who rebuke in righteousness." Those who repented of the transgressions of Jacob have kept the covenant of God.

Then each will speak to his neighbor, to strengthen one another, that their steps may hold fast to the way of God; and God will listen to their words and hear, and a book of remembrance will be written before him for those who fear God and think of his name, until salvation and righteousness are revealed for those who fear God. Then you shall again discern between the righteous and the wicked, between him who serves God and him who does not serve him. And he will show kindness to thousands, to those who love him and keep his commandments, to a thousand generations, after the manner of the house of Peleg, who went out from the holy city and leaned upon God during the period when Israel transgressed and polluted the sanctuary; but they turned to God. And he smote the people with few words. All of them, each according to his spirit, shall be judged in the holy council. And all who have broken through the boundary of the law, of those who entered the covenant, at the appearing of the glory of God to Israel shall be cut off from the midst of the camp, and with them all who condemn Judah in the days of its trials.

But all who hold fast to these ordinances, going out and coming in according to the law, and who listen to the voice of a teacher and confess before God, "We have sinned, we have done wickedly, both we and our fathers, in walking contrary to the statutes of the covenant; right and true are thy judgments against us"; all who do not lift a hand against his holy statutes and his righteous judgments and his true testimonies; who are instructed in the former judgments with which the men of the community were judged; who give ear to the voice of a Teacher of Righteousness and do not reject the statutes of righteousness when they hear them—they shall rejoice and be glad, and their hearts shall be strong, and they shall prevail over all the sons of the world, and God will forgive them, and they shall see his salvation, because they have taken refuge in his holy name.

THE RULE OF THE COMMUNITY

. . . the order of the community; to seek God . . . ; to do what is good and upright before him as he commanded through Moses and through all his servants the prophets; to love all that he has chosen and hate all that he has rejected; to be far from all evil and cleave to all good works; to do truth and righteousness and justice in the land; to walk no longer in the stubbornness of a guilty heart and eyes of fornication, doing all evil; to bring all those who have offered themselves to do God's statutes into a covenant of steadfast love; to be united in the counsel of God and to walk before him perfectly with regard to all the things that have been revealed for the appointed times of their testimonies; to love all the sons of light, each according to his lot in the counsel of God, and to hate all the sons of darkness, each according to his guilt in vengeance of God.

And all who have offered themselves for his truth shall bring all their knowledge and strength and wealth into the community of God, to purify their knowledge in the truth of God's statutes, and to distribute their strength according to the perfection of his ways and all their property according to his righteous counsel; not to transgress in any one of all the words of God in their periods; not to advance their times or postpone any of their appointed festivals; not to turn aside from his true statutes, going to the right or to the left.

And all who come into the order of the community shall pass over into the covenant before God, to do according to all that he has commanded, and not to turn away from following him because of any dread or terror or trial or fright in the dominion of Belial. And when they pass into the covenant, the priests and the Levites shall bless the God of salvation and all his works of truth; and all those who are passing into the covenant shall say after them, "Amen! Amen!"

The priests shall recount the righteous acts of God in his mighty works and tell all the acts of steadfast love and mercy upon Israel; and the Levites shall recount the iniquities of the sons of Israel and all their guilty transgressions and sin in the dominion of Belial. Then all those who are passing into the covenant shall confess after them, saying, "We have committed iniquity, we have transgressed, we have sinned, we have done evil, we and our fathers before us, in walking contrary to the statutes of truth; but righteous is God, and true is his judgment on us and on our fathers; and the mercy of his steadfast love he has bestowed upon us from everlasting to everlasting."

PSA. 106:2 FF. Then the priests shall bless all the men of God's lot, who walk perfectly in all his ways, and shall say: "May he bless you with all good and keep you from all evil; may he enlighten your heart with life-giving prudence and be gracious to you with eternal knowledge; may he lift up his loving countenance to you for eternal peace." And the Levites shall curse all the men of Belial's lot and shall answer and say: "Accursed may you be in all your wicked, guilty works; may God make you a horror through all those that wreak vengeance and send after you destruction through all those that pay recompense; accursed may you be without mercy according to the darkness of your works, and may you suffer wrath in the deep darkness of eternal fire. May God not be gracious to you when you call, and may he not pardon, forgiving your iniquities; may he lift up his angry countenance for vengeance upon you, and may there be no peace for you at the mouth of all those that hold enmity!" And all who are passing over into the covenant shall say after those who bless and those who curse, "Amen! Amen!"

And the priests and Levites shall continue and say: "Accursed for passing over with the idols of his heart may he be who comes into this covenant and sets the stumbling block of his iniquity before him, turning back with it, and when he hears the words of this covenant blesses himself in his heart, saying, 'May I have peace, because I walk in the stubbornness of my heart!' But his spirit will be swept away, the thirsty together with the sated, without pardon. The wrath of God and the jealousy of his judgments will burn in him to eternal destruction; and all the curses of this covenant will cleave to him; and God will set him apart for evil; and he will be cut off from the midst of all the sons of light, when he turns away from following God with his idols and the stumbling-block of his iniquity. He will put his lot in the midst of those accursed forever." And all who are coming into the covenant shall an-
II COR. 4:4 swer and say after them, "Amen! Amen!"

So shall they do year by year all the days of the dominion of Belial. The priests shall pass over first in order, according to their spirits, one after an-
II THESS. 2:7–10 other; and the Levites shall pass over after them, and all the people shall pass over third in order, one after another, by thousands and hundreds and fifties and tens, so that every man of Israel may know his appointed position in the community of God for the eternal council. And none shall be abased below his appointed position or exalted above his allotted place; for they shall all be in true community and good humility and loyal love and righteous thought, each for his fellow in the holy council, and they shall be sons of the eternal assembly.

Everyone who refuses to enter God's covenant, walking in the stubbornness of his heart, shall not attain to his true community. For his soul has abhorred the discipline of knowledge, the judgments of righteousness he has not confirmed because of his apostasies; and with the upright he will not be reckoned. His knowledge and his strength and his wealth shall not come into the council of community, because in the traffic of wickedness is his devising, and there is pollution in his plans. He will not be justified while giving free rein to the stubbornness of his heart. In darkness he looks at the ways of light, and with the perfect he will not be reckoned. He will not be purified by atonement offerings, and he will not be made clean with the water for impurity; he will not sanctify himself with seas and rivers or be made clean with any water for washing. Unclean, unclean he will be all the days that he rejects the ordinances of God, not being instructed in the community of his counsel.

* * *

The instructor's duty is to make all the sons of light understand and to teach them in the history of all the sons of man as to all their kinds of spirits with their signs, as to their works in their generations, and as to the visitation of their afflictions together with the periods of their recompense. From the God of knowledge is all that is and that is to be; and before they came into being he established all their designing. And when they come into being for their testimony according to his glorious design, they fulfill their

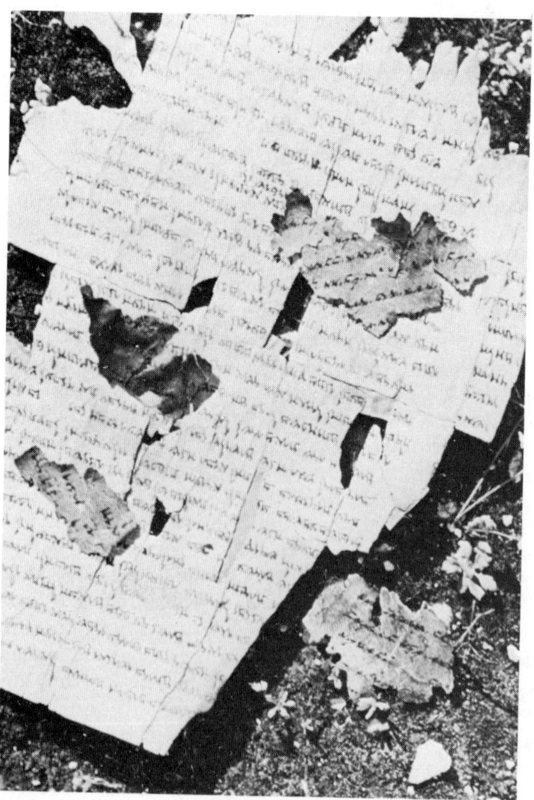

Dead Sea Scroll. Written on parchment made from animal skins, this document has been remarkably well preserved from the first century A.D. or possibly earlier. The combination of a relatively uniform heat and a low level of humidity in the caves in which they were stored for centuries, which are nearly 1,000 feet below sea level, were the major factors in their remarkable preservation. The documents included copies of the Hebrew scriptures, as well as original documents prepared by and for the community itself. *(Courtesy of the Palestine Archaeological Museum)*

work; and nothing is to be changed. In his hand are the ordinances of all; and he provides for them in all their affairs.

He created man to have dominion over the world and made for him two spirits, that he might walk by them until the appointed time of his visitation; they are the spirits of truth and of error. In the abode of light are the origins of truth, and from the source of darkness are the origins of error. In the hand of the prince of lights is dominion over all sons of righteousness; in the ways of light they walk. And in the hand of the angel of darkness is all dominion over the sons of error; and in the ways of darkness they walk. And by the angel of darkness is the straying of all the sons of righteousness, and all their sins and their iniquities and their guilt, and the transgressions of their works in his dominion, according to the mysteries of God, until his time, and all their afflictions and the appointed times of their distress in the dominion of his enmity. And all the spirits of his lot try to make the sons of light stumble; but the God of Israel and his angel of truth have helped all the sons of light. For he created the spirits of light and of darkness, and upon them he founded every work and upon their ways every service. One of the spirits God loves for all the ages of eternity, and with all its deeds he is pleased forever; as for the other, he abhors its company, and all its ways he hates forever.

And these are their ways in the world: to shine in the heart of man, and to make straight before him all the ways of true righteousness, and to make his heart be in dread of the judgments of God, and to induce a spirit of humility, and slowness to anger, and great compassion, and eternal goodness, and understanding and insight, and mighty wisdom, which is supported by all the works of God and leans upon the abundance of his steadfast love, and a spirit of knowledge in every thought of action, and zeal for righteous judgments, and holy thought with sustained purpose, and abundance of steadfast love for all the sons of truth, and glorious purity, abhorring all unclean idols, and walking humbly with prudence in all things, and concealing the truth of the mysteries of knowledge.

COL. These are the counsels of the Spirit for the sons of the truth of the world
2:2–3 and the visitation of all who walk by it, for healing and abundance of peace
in length of days, and bringing forth seed, with all eternal blessings and everlasting joy in the life of eternity, and a crown of glory with raiment of majesty in everlasting light.

I JN. But to the spirit of error belong greediness, slackness of hands in the
4:1–6 service of righteousness, wickedness and falsehood, pride and haughtiness,
lying and deceit, cruelty and great impiety, quickness to anger and abundance of folly and proud jealousy, abominable works in a spirit of fornication and ways of defilement in the service of uncleanness, and a blasphemous tongue, blindness of eyes and dullness of ears, stiffness of neck and hardness of heart, walking in all the ways of darkness and evil cunning. And the visitation of all who walk by it is for abundance of afflictions by all destroying angels, to eternal perdition in the fury of the God of vengeance, to eternal trembling and everlasting dishonor, with destroying disgrace in the fire of dark places. And all their periods to their generations will be in sorrowful mourning and bitter calamity, in dark disasters until they are destroyed, having no remnant or any that escape.

In these two spirits are the origins of all the sons of man, and in their divisions all the hosts of men have their inheritance in their generations. In the ways of the two spirits men walk. And all the performance of their works is in their two divisions, according to each man's inheritance, whether much or little, for all the periods of eternity. For God has established the two spirits in equal measure until the last period, and has put eternal enmity between their divisions. An abomination to truth are deeds of error, and an abomination to error are all ways of truth. And contentious jealousy is on all their judgments, for they do not walk together.

But God in the mysteries of his understanding and in his glorious wisdom has ordained a period for the ruin of error, and in the appointed time
I COR. of punishment he will destroy it forever. And then shall come out forever
15:23– the truth of the world, for it has wallowed in the ways of wickedness in the
28 dominion of error until the appointed time of judgment which has been decreed. And then God will refine in his truth all the deeds of a man, and will purify for himself the frame of man, consuming every spirit of error hidden in his flesh, and cleansing him with a holy spirit from all wicked deeds. And he will sprinkle upon him a spirit of truth, like water for impurity, from all abominations of falsehood and wallowing in a spirit of impurity, to make the upright perceive the knowledge of the Most High and the wisdom of the sons of heaven, to instruct those whose conduct is blameless. For God has chosen them for an eternal covenant, and theirs is all the glory of man; and there shall be no error, to the shame of all works of deceit.

MT. 10:1 There shall be in the council of the community twelve men, and there shall be three priests who are perfect in all that has been revealed of the
ACTS whole law, to practice truth and righteousness and justice and loyal love and
5:21 walking humbly each with his neighbor, to preserve faithfulness in the land with sustained purpose and a broken spirit, and to make amends for iniquity by the practice of justice and the distress of tribulation, and to walk with all by the standard of truth and by the regulation of the time.

When these things come to pass in Israel, the council of the community will be established in the truth for an eternal planting, a holy house for Is-
I PET. rael, a foundation of the holy of holies for Aaron, true witnesses for justice
2:4–8 and the elect by God's will, to make atonement for the land and to render to the wicked their recompense—this is the tested wall, a precious cornerstone; its foundations will not tremble or flee from their place—a most holy dwelling for Aaron with eternal knowledge for a covenant of justice and to offer a pleasing fragrance, and a house of perfection and truth in Israel to establish a covenant for eternal statutes. And they shall be accepted to make atonement for the land and to decide the judgment of wickedness, and there shall be no error. When these men have been prepared in the foundation of the community for two years with blameless conduct, they shall be separated in holiness in the midst of the council of the men of the community; and when anything which has been hidden from Israel is found by the man who is searching, it shall not be hidden from these men out of fear of an apostate spirit.

When these things come to pass for the community in Israel, by these
ISA. 40:3 regulations they shall be separated from the midst of the session of the men of error to go to the wilderness to prepare there the way of the LORD; as
MK. 1:3 it is written, "In the wilderness prepare the way of the LORD; make straight in the desert a highway for our God." This is the study of the law, as he commanded through Moses, to do according to all that has been revealed from time to time, and as the prophets revealed by his Holy Spirit.

Any man of the men of the community, of the covenant of the community, who wilfully takes away a word from the whole commandment shall not touch the sacred food of the holy men; he shall not know any of their counsel until his works are cleansed from all error, so that he conducts himself blamelessly. Then he shall be admitted to the council as directed by the masters, and afterward he shall be registered in his position. According to this law shall it be done for everyone who is added to the community.

These are the ordinances by which the men of perfect holiness shall walk, each with his neighbor, everyone who enters the holy council, those who conduct themselves blamelessly as he commanded. Any man of them who transgresses a word of the law of Moses overtly or with deceit shall be dismissed from the council of the community and shall not come back again; and none of the holy men shall participate in his wealth or in his counsel concerning anything. But if he acts unintentionally, he shall be separated from the sacred food and the council; and they shall interpret the ordinance that he shall not judge a man or be asked concerning any counsel for two years. If his conduct is perfect in the meeting, in interpretation, and in counsel as directed by the masters; if he has not again sinned unintentionally by the completion of his two years—because for one unintentional sin he shall be punished for two years—as for him who acts deliberately, he shall not come back again; only he who sins unintentionally shall be tested for two years, that his conduct and his counsel may be perfected under the direction of the masters—after that he shall be registered in his position for the holy community.

When these things come to pass in Israel according to all these regulations, for a foundation of a holy spirit, for eternal truth, for a ransom for the guilt of transgression and sinful faithlessness, and for acceptance for the land more than the flesh of whole burnt offerings and the fats of sacrifice, and an offering of the lips for justice like the pleasing quality of righteousness, and perfect conduct like a willing gift of an acceptable offering; at that time the men of the community shall be set apart, a house of holiness for Aaron, to be united as a holy of holies and a house of community for Israel, those who conduct themselves blamelessly.

THANKSGIVING PSALM (1)

MT. Blessed art thou, O my God,
11:25 who openest to knowledge the heart of thy servant.
Direct in righteousness all his works
and establish the son of thy handmaid,
as thou didst accept the elect of mankind
to stand before thee forever.
For without thee conduct will not be blameless,
and apart from thy will nothing will be done.
It is thou that hast taught all knowledge;
and everything that has come to pass has been by thy will.
And there is no other beside thee
to oppose thy counsel,
to understand all thy holy purpose,
to gaze into the depth of thy mysteries,
or to comprehend all thy marvels,
together with the strength of thy power.
Who is able to bear thy glory,
and what then is he,
the son of man, among thy marvelous works;
what shall one born of woman be accounted before thee?
As for him, he was kneaded from dust,

and the food of worms is his portion.
He is an emission of spittle, a cut-off bit of clay,
and his desire is for the dust.
What will clay reply, a thing formed by hand?
What counsel will it understand?
ROM. But as for me, my justification belongs to God,
3:23–26 and in his hand is the blamelessness of my conduct
together with the uprightness of my heart;
and in his righteousness my transgression will be wiped out.
For from the source of his knowledge he has opened up my light;
my eye has gazed into his wonders
and the light of my heart penetrates the mystery that is to be.
That which is eternal is the staff of my right hand;
on a strong rock is the way I tread;
before nothing will it be shaken.
For the faithfulness of God is the rock I tread,
and his strength is the staff of my right hand.
From the source of his righteousness is my judgment.
MT. A light is in my heart from his marvelous mysteries;
11:27 my eye has gazed on that which is eternal,
sound wisdom which is hidden from the man of knowledge,
II COR. and prudent discretion from the sons of man,
4:6 a source of righteousness and reservoir of strength
together with a spring of glory hidden from the company of flesh.
MK. 4:11 To those whom God has chosen he has given them for an eternal
possession;
he has given them an inheritance in the lot of the holy ones
and with the sons of heaven has associated their company
for a council of unity and a company of a holy building,
for an eternal planting
through every period that is to be.

THANKSGIVING PSALM (2)

I thank thee, O Lord,
because thou hast redeemed my soul from the pit;
from the Sheol of Abaddon
thou hast brought me up to an eternal height,
and I walk in an unsearchable plain.
I know that there is hope
for him whom thou hast formed from the dust
for an eternal company.
Thou hast purified the perverse spirit of a great sin,
to stand in his place with the army of the holy ones,
and to come together with the congregation of the sons of heaven.
Thou hast cast for man an eternal lot
with the spirits of knowledge,
to praise thy name together in joyful song
and to recount thy wonders in the presence of all thy works.
But I, a thing formed of clay, what am I?
A thing kneaded with water, for whom have I value,
and what strength have I?
For I took my stand in the border of wickedness,

and with the hapless in their lot;
but the poor man's soul was in dread, with great confusion;
engulfing destruction accompanied my steps;
when all the snares of the pit were opened,
and all the nets of wickedness were spread,
the seine of the hapless also on the face of the water;
when all the arrows of the pit flew, not turning aside,
and were loosed beyond hope;
when the line fell on judgment,
and the lot of anger on those who were forsaken;
a molten mass of wrath on dissemblers,
and a period of wrath for all worthlessness.
The cords of death surrounded me inescapably;
the torrents of Belial flowed over all the high banks.
Like a fire eating into all their springs,
destroying every green or dry tree in their channels,
it rushes about with flashes of flame,
until all who drink of them are no more;
into the walls of clay it eats,
and into the platform of the dry land.
The foundations of the mountains are given to the flames;
the roots of flint become torrents of pitch.
It devours to the great abyss;
the torrents of Belial burst into Abaddon;
the sentient beings of the abyss roar
with the noise of the eruptions of mire.
The earth cries aloud at the ruin
which has been wrought in the world;
all its sentient beings shout;
all who are upon it go mad
and melt in utter ruin.
For God thunders with the noise of his might,
and his holy dwelling re-echoes with his glorious truth;
the host of heaven utter their voice;
the eternal foundations melt and shake;
and the war of the mighty ones of heaven
rushes about in the world and turns not back
until the full end decreed forever;
and there is nothing like it.

WISDOM AND ITS MEDIATORS

In the hellenistic period the exposure of Jews to Greek culture produced an ambivalence within the Jewish community. On the one hand there was an enormous appeal of both the intellectual and the more superficial aspects of the hellenistic world, which led some Jews to adopt Greek modes of dress and recreation in defiance of the Law of Moses, and induced others to study Greek philosophy in order to discover how it might be correlated with the revealed truths of Mosaic Law. But on the other hand, many Jews stiffened their opposition to hellenistic ways, and concentrated their attention on the study of the Law. In the so-called wisdom literature of Judaism from this period, both tendencies are evident.

The *Wisdom of Jesus Ben Sira* (or Jesus Sirach, but usually known simply as *Ecclesiasticus,* from the title given in Latin versions of the collection of late, post-biblical Jewish writings commonly called *The Apocrypha*), is the oldest surviving, and perhaps the very first documentation we have for the scribal movement, members of which devoted themselves to the study of the Law of Moses and to interpreting its truths for their contemporaries. Ben Sira was a teacher, and it has been conjectured that his book is a poeticized transcript of some of his lectures.[22] For him wisdom consists in devotion to the teachings of the scriptures—the books of Moses, as well as the prophetic writings, the psalms, and the proverbs—and the appropriation of their truths in the light of a commonsense assessment of life based on experience itself. Thus Ben Sira comes down on the side of Jewish distinctiveness, though without dogmatically narrow limitation to the words of the Law, on which the Sadducees were later to insist. The excerpts from the *Wisdom of Jesus Ben Sira* given here include the wisdom of pursuing wisdom, the place of man in the creation, the preferential nature of the scribe's place in society, and finally the praise of men of the past, ranging from obscure artisans whose work binds society together to the recently deceased Simon the High Priest (ca. 200 B.C.), whose splendor Ben Sira depicts.

The *Wisdom of Solomon* affirms the uniqueness of Jewish knowledge of truth, even while showing the correlation between the revealed wisdom of God of which "Solomon" speaks and the truth as perceived by the great philosophers of the Greek tradition. The book implies that its author is the historical Solomon (the King of Israel who built the temple in Jerusalem) addressing his fellow kings, but it was composed in Greek, depends on the Greek translation of the Bible rather than on the Hebrew text, and utilizes many of the technical terms of Greek philosophy for which there would be no exact equivalents in Hebrew. Building on a theme that appears in the canonical book of Proverbs (8:22–31), which was also traditionally assigned to Solomon, the author describes wisdom in a personified form as the agent of God in creating and ordering the world. What is distinctive about the development of this idea in the excerpt from *Wisdom of Solomon* is that some of the technical terms of the Platonic doctrine of the creation of the world are used there, although in keeping with the Jewish tradition, the relationship with wisdom is allegorized on the analogy of a lover and his beloved. The mood of the work, then, is one of Jewish piety, rational striving for understanding of metaphysical problems about the creation of the world and the origin of evil, and a mystical religious longing.

[22]Proposed by R. H. Pfeiffer, *History of New Testament Times* (New York: Harper and Row, 1949), p. 367.

Wisdom of Ben Sira

15:1–20

The man who fears the Lord will do this,
and he who holds to the law will obtain wisdom.
She will come to meet him like a mother,
and like the wife of his youth she will welcome him.
She will feed him with the bread of understanding,
and give him the water of wisdom to drink.
He will lean on her and will not fall,
and he will rely on her and will not be put to shame.
She will exalt him above his neighbors,
and will open his mouth in the midst of the assembly.
He will find gladness and a crown of rejoicing,
and will acquire an everlasting name.
Foolish men will not obtain her,
and sinful men will not see her.
She is far from men of pride,
and liars will never think of her.

A hymn of praise is not fitting on the lips of a sinner,
for it has not been sent from the Lord.
For a hymn of praise should be uttered in wisdom,
and the Lord will prosper it.

Do not say, "Because of the Lord I left the right way";
for he will not do what he hates.
Do not say, "It was he who led me astray";
for he has no need of a sinful man.
The Lord hates all abominations,
and they are not loved by those who fear him.
It was he who created man in the beginning,
and he left him in the power of his own inclination.
If you will, you can keep the commandments,
and to act faithfully is a matter of your own choice.
He has placed before you fire and water:
stretch out your hand for whichever you wish.
Before a man are life and death,
and whichever he chooses will be given to him.
For great is the wisdom of the Lord;
he is mighty in power and sees everything;
His eyes are on those who fear him,
and he knows every deed of man.
He has not commanded anyone to be ungodly,
and he has not given anyone permission to sin.

16:26–17:32

The works of the Lord have existed from the beginning by his creation,
and when he made them, he determined their divisions.
He arranged his works in an eternal order,
and their dominion for all generations;

they neither hunger nor grow weary,
    and they do not cease from their labors.
They do not crowd one another aside,
    and they will never disobey his word.
After this the Lord looked upon the earth,
    and filled it with his good things;
with all kinds of living beings he covered its surface,
    and to it they return.

(17) The Lord created man out of earth,
    and turned him back to it again.
He gave to men few days, a limited time,
    but granted them authority over the things upon the earth.
He endowed them with strength like his own,
    and made them in his own image.
He placed the fear of them in all living beings,
    and granted them dominion over beasts and birds.
He made for them tongue and eyes;
    he gave them ears and a mind for thinking.
He filled them with knowledge and understanding,
    and showed them good and evil.
He set his eye upon their hearts
    to show them the majesty of his works.
And they will praise his holy name,
    to proclaim the grandeur of his works.
He bestowed knowledge upon them,
    and allotted to them the law of life.
He established with them an eternal covenant,
    and showed them his judgments.
Their eyes saw his glorious majesty,
    and their ears heard the glory of his voice.
And he said to them, "Beware of all unrighteousness."
And he gave commandments to each of them concerning his
    neighbor.
Their ways are always before him,
    they will not be hid from his eyes.
He appointed a ruler for every nation,
    but Israel is the Lord's own portion.
All their works are as the sun before him,
    and his eyes are continually upon their ways.
Their iniquities are not hidden from him,
    and all their sins are before the Lord.
A man's almsgiving is like a signet with the Lord,
    and he will keep a person's kindness like the apple of his eye.
Afterward he will arise and requite them,
    and he will bring their recompense on their heads.
Yet to those who repent he grants a return,
    and he encourages those whose endurance is failing.
Turn to the Lord and forsake your sins;
    pray in his presence and lessen your offenses.
Return to the Most High and turn away from iniquity,
    and hate abominations intensely.

Who will sing praises to the Most High in Hades,
as do those who are alive and give thanks?
From the dead, as from one who does not exist, thanksgiving has ceased;
he who is alive and well sings the Lord's praises.
How great is the mercy of the Lord,
and his forgiveness for those who turn to him!
For all things cannot be in men,
since a son of man is not immortal.
What is brighter than the sun? Yet its light fails.
So flesh and blood devise evil.
He marshals the host of the height of heaven;
but all men are dust and ashes.

38:24–39:11

The wisdom of the scribe depends on the opportunity of leisure;
and he who has little business may become wise.
How can he become wise who handles the plow,
and who glories in the shaft of a goad,
who drives oxen and is occupied with their work,
and whose talk is about bulls?
He sets his heart on plowing furrows,
and he is careful about fodder for the heifers.
So too is every craftsman and master workman
who labors by night as well as by day;
those who cut the signets of seals,
each is diligent in making a great variety;
he sets his heart on painting a lifelike image,
and he is careful to finish his work.
So too is the smith sitting by the anvil,
intent upon his handiwork in iron;
the breath of the fire melts his flesh,
and he wastes away in the heat of the furnace;
he inclines his ear to the sound of the hammer,
and his eyes are on the pattern of the object.
He sets his heart on finishing his handiwork,
and he is careful to complete its decoration.
So too is the potter sitting at his work
and turning the wheel with his feet;
he is always deeply concerned over his work,
and all his output is by number.
He moulds the clay with his arm
and makes it pliable with his feet;
he sets his heart to finish the glazing,
and he is careful to clean the furnace.

All these rely upon their hands,
and each is skilful in his own work.
Without them a city cannot be established,
and men can neither sojourn nor live there.

Yet they are not sought out for the council of the people,
nor do they attain eminence in the public assembly.
They do not sit in the judge's seat,
nor do they understand the sentence of judgment;
they cannot expound discipline or judgment,
and they are not found using proverbs.
But they keep stable the fabric of the world,
and their prayer is in the practice of their trade.
(39) On the other hand he who devotes himself
to the study of the law of the Most High
will seek out the wisdom of all the ancients,
and will be concerned with prophecies;
he will preserve the discourse of notable men
and penetrate the subtleties of parables;
he will seek out the hidden meanings of proverbs
and be at home with the obscurities of parables.
He will serve among great men
and appear before rulers;
he will travel through the lands of foreign nations,
for he tests the good and the evil among men.
He will set his heart to rise early to seek the Lord who made him,
and will make supplication before the Most High;
he will open his mouth in prayer
and make supplication for his sins.

If the great Lord is willing,
he will be filled with the spirit of understanding;
he will pour forth words of wisdom
and give thanks to the Lord in prayer.
He will direct his counsel and knowledge aright,
and meditate on his secrets.
He will reveal instruction in his teaching,
and will glory in the law of the Lord's covenant.
Many will praise his understanding,
and it will never be blotted out;
his memory will not disappear,
and his name will live through all generations.
Nations will declare his wisdom,
and the congregation will proclaim his praise;
if he lives long, he will leave a name greater than a thousand,
and if he goes to rest, it is enough for him.

44:1–15

Let us now praise famous men,
and our fathers in their generations.
The Lord apportioned to them great glory,
his majesty from the beginning.
There were those who ruled in their kingdoms,
and were men renowned for their power,
giving counsel by their understanding,
and proclaiming prophecies;
leaders of the people in their deliberations

and in understanding of learning for the people,
wise in their words of instruction;
those who composed musical tunes,
and set forth verses in writing;
rich men furnished with resources,
living peaceably in their habitations—
all these were honored in their generations,
and were the glory of their times.
There are some of them who have left a name,
so that men declare their praise.
And there are some who have no memorial,
who have perished as though they had not lived;
they have become as though they had not been born,
and so have their children after them.
But these were men of mercy,
whose righteous deeds have not been forgotten;
their prosperity will remain with their descendants,
and their inheritance to their children's children.
Their descendants stand by the covenants;
their children also, for their sake.
Their posterity will continue forever,
and their glory will not be blotted out.
Their bodies were buried in peace,
and their name lives to all generations.
Peoples will declare their wisdom,
and the congregation proclaims their praise.

50:1–17

The leader of his brethren and the pride of his people
was Simon the high priest, son of Onias,
who in his life repaired the house
and in his time fortified the temple.
He laid the foundations for the high double walls,
the high retaining walls for the temple enclosure.
In his days a cistern for water was quarried out,
a reservoir like the sea in circumference.
He considered how to save his people from ruin,
and fortified the city to withstand a siege.
How glorious he was when the people gathered round him
as he came out of the inner sanctuary!
Like the morning star among the clouds,
like the moon when it is full;
like the sun shining upon the temple of the Most High,
and like the rainbow gleaming in glorious clouds;
like roses in the days of the first fruits,
like lilies by a spring of water,
like a green shoot on Lebanon on a summer day;
like fire and incense in the censer,
like a vessel of hammered gold adorned with all kinds of precious stones;
like an olive tree putting forth its fruit,
and like a cypress towering in the clouds.

When he put on his glorious robe
    and clothed himself with superb perfection
and went up to the holy altar,
    he made the court of the sanctuary glorious.
And when he received the portions from the hands of the priests,
    as he stood by the hearth of the altar
with a garland of brethren around him,
    he was like a young cedar on Lebanon;
and they surrounded him like the trunks of palm trees,
    all the sons of Aaron in their splendor,
with the Lord's offering in their hands,
    before the whole congregation of Israel.
Finishing the service at the altars,
    and arranging the offering to the Most High, the Almighty,
he reached out his hand to the cup
    and poured a libation of the blood of the grape;
he poured it out at the foot of the altar,
    a pleasing odor to the Most High, the King of all.
Then the sons of Aaron shouted,
    they sounded the trumpets of hammered work,
they made a great noise to be heard
    for remembrance before the Most High.
Then all the people together made haste
    and fell to the ground upon their faces
to worship their Lord,
    the Almighty, God Most High.

Wisdom of Solomon

7:15–8:16

May God grant that I speak with judgment
and have thoughts worthy of what I have received,
for he is the guide even of wisdom
and the corrector of the wise.
For both we and our words are in his hand,
as are all understanding and skill in crafts.
For it is he who gave me unerring knowledge of what exists,
to know the structure of the world and the activity of the elements;
the beginning and end and middle of times,
the alternations of the solstices and the changes of the seasons,
the cycles of the year and the constellations of the stars,
the natures of animals and the tempers of wild beasts,
the powers of spirits and the reasonings of men,
the varieties of plants and the virtues of roots;
I learned both what is secret and what is manifest,
for wisdom, the fashioner of all things, taught me.

For in her there is a spirit that is intelligent, holy,
unique, manifold, subtle,
mobile, clear, unpolluted,
distinct, invulnerable, loving the good, keen,

irresistible, beneficent, humane,
steadfast, sure, free from anxiety,
all-powerful, overseeing all,
and penetrating through all spirits
that are intelligent and pure and most subtle.
For wisdom is more mobile than any motion;
because of her pureness she pervades and penetrates all things.
For she is a breath of the power of God,
and a pure emanation of the glory of the Almighty;
therefore nothing defiled gains entrance into her.
For she is a reflection of eternal light,
a spotless mirror of the working of God,
and an image of his goodness.
Though she is but one, she can do all things,
and while remaining in herself, she renews all things;
in every generation she passes into holy souls
and makes them friends of God, and prophets;
for God loves nothing so much as the man who lives with wisdom.
For she is more beautiful than the sun,
and excels every constellation of the stars.
Compared with the light she is found to be superior,
for it is succeeded by the night,
but against wisdom evil does not prevail.

(8) She reaches mightily from one end of the earth to the other,
and she orders all things well.

I loved her and sought her from my youth,
and I desired to take her for my bride,
and I became enamored of her beauty.
She glorifies her noble birth by living with God,
and the Lord of all loves her.
For she is an initiate in the knowledge of God,
and an associate in his works.
If riches are a desirable possession in life,
what is richer than wisdom who effects all things?
And if understanding is effective,
who more than she is fashioner of what exists?
And if anyone loves righteousness,
her labors are virtues;
for she teaches self-control and prudence,
justice and courage;
nothing in life is more profitable for men than these.
And if any one longs for wide experience,
she knows the things of old, and infers the things to come;
she understands turns of speech and the solutions of riddles;
she has foreknowledge of signs and wonders
and of the outcome of seasons and times.
Therefore I determined to take her to live with me,
knowing that she would give me good counsel
and encouragement in cares and grief.
Because of her I shall have glory among the multitudes
and honor in the presence of the elders, though I am young.
I shall be found keen in judgment,

and in the sight of rulers I shall be admired.
When I am silent they will wait for me,
and when I speak they will give heed;
and when I speak at greater length
they will put their hands on their mouths.
Because of her I shall have immortality,
and leave an everlasting remembrance to those who come after me.
I shall govern peoples,
and nations will be subject to me;
dread monarchs will be afraid of me when they hear of me;
among the people I shall show myself capable, and courageous in war.
When I enter my house, I shall find rest with her,
for companionship with her has no bitterness,
and life with her has no pain, but gladness and joy.
When I considered these things inwardly,
and thought upon them in my mind,
that in kinship with wisdom there is immortality,
and in friendship with her pure delight,
and in the labors of her hand unfailing wealth,
and in experience of her company, understanding,
and renown in sharing her words,
I went about seeking how to get her for myself.
As a child I was by nature well endowed,
and a good soul fell to my lot;
or rather, being good, I entered an undefiled body.
But I perceived that I would not possess wisdom unless God
gave her to me—
and it was a mark of insight to know whose gift she was—
so I appealed to the Lord and besought him . . .

ESCHATOLOGICAL TEXTS

After the shock of the fall of Jerusalem to the Babylonians and the subsequent captivity of the Jewish people, the return to the land and the reestablishment of the Jewish commonwealth there did not bring about the establishment of the universal rule of God through the Scion of David that the prophets Isaiah and Micah had foretold. The Maccabean revolt established the Hasmonean family on the throne of Palestine for a century, but it became hopelessly corrupt and worldly in the final decades. In reaction to these disillusioning national experiences, the faith of the covenant people, if it was to survive at all, had two lines of development open to it: It could repeat the hopes of the ancient prophets, and leave to God the time and circumstances under which the promises would be fulfilled, or it could assess the national calamities as the work of a demonic power opposed to God and shift the sphere of the final triumph of God from the chronological future to the cosmic realms.

The Pharisees in the first century B.C. took the first of these options.

Documentation of their outlook has survived in a pseudonymous work known as the *Psalms of Solomon.* But other groups—chiefly the Essenes—adopted a dualistic view. They taught that God had revealed to them the secret schedule for the outworking of His plan, by which the evil powers would be overcome and His rule established. They did not expect the restoration of the whole of the Jewish people, but rather the vindication of a small faithful remnant, which was of course identical with the sect of Jews that produced this literature. The second of these points of view found expression in a distinctive type of literature, highly figurative and even enigmatic in style, filled with veiled references to historical events, structured around a series of events that would lead up to the final conflict that would usher in the New Age. All was predetermined, but only those within the group were able to decipher the revelations (in Greek, *Apocalypse*) and to interpret the scriptures in the appropriate way so as to discern there the movement of the divine purpose. The oldest of the apocalypses is the Book of Daniel, although there are apocalyptic passages in Zechariah, Isaiah, and Ezekiel.

The mainstream of Judaism largely repudiated the apocalytic tradition after it was adapted for its own purposes by the Christian community. The language of the gospels and Paul, not to mention the book of Revelations, is filled with apocalyptic concepts and expressions. But the church preserved many of the originally Jewish apocalyptic writings, translating them into various languages. Then when the Dead Sea Scrolls began to come to light in the 1950s, fragments of known apocalyptic writings appeared among the scrolls, and previously unknown apocalypses were found as well. The following excerpts include portions of three long-known writings—The Testaments of the Twelve Patriarchs, Enoch, and IV Ezra—in addition to parts of several of the Dead Sea Scrolls.

The Psalms of Solomon

The Psalms of Solomon seem to have been written by Pharisees, who longed for the establishment of the Davidic ruler as God's anointed vicegerent over Israel but who did not see in the Hasmonean dynasty the hand of God. The Psalms allude to the death of Pompey, who took over Palestine for the Romans in 63 B.C., and therefore probably were written about the middle of the first century B.C. There are no predictions about the trials that the faithful will undergo before the messianic era comes, nor are there any cryptic chronological clues as to when that event will occur, so the Psalms entirely lack the characteristic features of apocalyptic writings. There is instead unswerving confidence that God will establish the Davidic Messiah (no mention is made, as at Qumran, of an anointed priest as well), and through him God will exercise authority over all the nations. This will occur, the Psalmist declares (17:24), "At the time in the which thou seest, O God . . ."

17:1–38

(17:1) Lord, Thou art our King forever and ever,
For in Thee, O God, doth our soul glory.
(2) How long are the days of man's life upon the earth?
As are his days, so is the hope [set] upon him.
(3) But we hope in God, our deliverer;
For the might of our God is forever with mercy,
(4) And the kingdom of our God is forever over the nations in judgement.
(5) Thou, O Lord, didst choose David [to be] king over Israel,
And didst swear to him concerning his seed that never should his kingdom fail before thee.
(6) But, for our sins, sinners rose up against us;
They assailed us and thrust us out;
What Thou hadst not promised to them, they took away [from us] with violence.
(7) They in no wise glorified Thy honourable name;
They set a [worldly] monarchy in place of [that which was] their excellency;
(8) They laid waste the throne of David in tumultuous arrogance.
But Thou, O God, didst cast them down, and remove their seed from the earth,
(9) In that there rose up against them a man that was alien to our race.
(10) According to their sins didst Thou recompense them, O God;
So that it befell them according to their deeds.
(11) God showed them no pity;
He sought out their seed and let not one of them go free.
(12) Faithful is the Lord in all His judgements
Which He doeth upon the earth.
(13) The lawless one laid waste our land so that none inhabited it,
They destroyed young and old and their children together.
(14) In the heat of His anger He sent them away even unto the west,
And [He exposed] the rulers of the land unsparingly to derision.
(15) Being an alien the enemy acted proudly,
And his heart was alien from our God.
(16) And all . . . Jerusalem,
As also the nations . . .
(17) And the children of the convenant in the midst of the mingled peoples . . .
There was not among them one that wrought in the midst of Jerusalem mercy and truth.
(18) They that loved the synagogues of the pious fled from them,
As sparrows that fly from their nest.
(19) They wandered in deserts that their lives might be saved from harm,
And precious in the eyes of them that lived abroad was any that escaped alive from them.
(20) Over the whole earth were they scattered by lawless [men].
(21) For the heavens withheld the rain from dropping upon the earth,

Springs were stopped [that sprang] perennial[ly] out of the deeps,
[that ran down] from lofty mountains.
For there was none among them that wrought righteousness, and
justice;
From the chief of them to the least [of them] all were sinful;
(22) The king was a transgressor, and the judge disobedient, and the
people sinful.
MK. (23) Behold, O Lord, and raise up unto them their king, the son of
11:10 David,
At the time in the which Thou seest, O God, that he may reign
MT. 21:9 over Israel Thy servant.
(24) And gird him with strength, that he may shatter unrighteous
rulers,
MK. (25) And that he may purge Jerusalem from nations that trample [her]
11:15–17 down to destruction.
Wisely, righteously (26) he shall thrust out sinners from [the]
inheritance,
He shall destroy the pride of the sinner as a potter's vessel.
With a rod of iron he shall break in pieces all their substance,
(27) He shall destroy the godless nations with the word of his mouth;
At his rebuke nations shall flee before him,
And he shall reprove sinners for the thoughts of their heart.
MT. (28) And he shall gather together a holy people, whom he shall lead
24:31 in righteousness,
And he shall judge the tribes of the people that has been sanctified
by the Lord his God.
(29) And he shall not suffer unrighteousness to lodge anymore in their
midst,
Nor shall there dwell with them any man that knoweth wickedness,
(30) For he shall know them, that they are all sons of their God.
And he shall divide them according to their tribes upon the land,
(31) And neither sojourner nor alien shall sojourn with them anymore.
He shall judge peoples and nations in the wisdom of his righteousness.

SELAH

(32) And he shall have the heathen nations to serve him under his
yoke;
And he shall glorify the Lord in a place to be seen of [?] all the
earth;
(33) And he shall purge Jerusalem, making it holy as of old:
MK. (34) So that nations shall come from the ends of the earth to see his
11:17 glory,
Bringing as gifts her sons who had fainted,
MT. (35) And to see the glory of the Lord, wherewith God hath glorified
28:19 her.
And he [shall be] a righteous king, taught of God, over them.
LK. (36) And there shall be no unrighteousness in his days in their midst,
24:37 For all shall be holy and their king the anointed of the Lord.
(37) For he shall not put his trust in horse and rider and bow,
MT. Nor shall he multiply for himself gold and silver for war,
21:1–9 Nor shall he gather confidence from [?] a multitude [?] for the day
of battle.
JN. (38) The Lord Himself is his king, the hope of him that is mighty
12:13 through [his] hope in God.

Testaments of the Twelve Patriarchs

These writings have long been known and widely read in the eastern churches. Based on Genesis 49, in which the dying Jacob makes specific pronouncements and predictions concerning each of his twelve sons, this writing purports to be the last will and testament of each of his sons. Some scholars think that it received its present form considerably later, and there do seem to be some specifically Christian interpolations in the text. But at Qumran fragments of several parts of this writing have been found, including the Testaments of Naphtali and Levi. Of special importance is the belief expressed in the Testament of the XII that there will be in the End Time *two* anointed ones (Messiahs): The king, from the tribe of Judah, and the priest, from the tribe of Levi. Of the two, the priest has precedence.

TESTAMENT OF LEVI 4:1–5:7

(4:1) Now, therefore, know that the Lord shall execute judgement upon the sons of men.
Because when the rocks are being rent,
And the sun quenched,
And the waters dried up,
And the fire cowering,
And all creation troubled,
And the invisible spirits melting away,
And Hades taketh spoils through the visitations of the Most High,
Men will be unbelieving and persist in their iniquity.
On this account with punishment shall they be judged.
(2) [Therefore] the Most High hath heard thy prayer,
MK. 1:11 To separate thee from iniquity, and that thou shouldst become to Him a son,
MK. And a servant, and a minister of His presence.
10:45 (3) The light of knowledge shalt thou light up in Jacob,
And as the sun shalt thou be to all the seed of Israel.
MK. Until the Lord shall visit all the Gentiles in His tender mercies forever.
11:17 (4) And there shall be given to thee a blessing, and to all thy seed,
(5) [And] therefore there have been given to thee counsel and
MT. understanding,
24:14 That thou mightst instruct thy sons concerning this;
(6) Because they that bless Him shall be blessed,
And they that curse Him shall perish.

(5:1) And thereupon the angel opened to me the gates of heaven, and I saw the holy temple, and upon (2) a throne of glory the Most High. And He said to me: Levi, I have given thee the blessings of the (3) priesthood until I come and sojourn in the midst of Israel. Then the angel brought me down to the earth, and gave me a shield and a sword, and said to me: Execute vengeance on Shechem because (4) of Dinah, thy sister, and I will be with thee because the Lord hath sent me. And I destroyed at (5) that time the sons of Hamor, as it is written in the heavenly tables. And I said to him: I pray (6) thee, O Lord, tell me Thy name, that I may call upon Thee in a day of tribulation. And he said: I am the angel who intercedeth for the nation of Israel that they may not be smitten utterly, (7) for every evil spirit attacketh it. And after these things I awakened; and blessed the Most High, and the angel who intercedeth for the nation of Israel and for all the righteous.

9:1–10:5

(9:1, 2) And after two days I and Judah[23] went up with our father Jacob to Isaac our father's father. And my father's father blessed me according to all the words of the visions which I had seen. And (3) he would not come with us to Bethel. [And when we came to Bethel], my father saw a vision (4) concerning me, that I should be their priest unto God. And he rose up early in the morning, (5) and paid tithes of all [to the Lord] through me. And [so] we came to Hebron to dwell there. (6) And Isaac called me continually to put me in remembrance of the law of the Lord, even as the (7) angel of the Lord showed unto me. And he taught me the law of the priesthood, of sacrifices, (8) whole burnt-offerings, first-fruits, freewill-offerings, peace-offerings. And each day he was instructing (9) me, and was busied on my behalf before the Lord, and said to me: Beware of the spirit of (10) fornication; for this shall continue and shall by thy seed pollute the holy place. Take, therefore, to thyself a wife without blemish or pollution, while yet thou art young, and not of the race of (11) strange nations. And before entering into the holy place, bathe; and when thou offerest the (12) sacrifice, wash; and again, when thou finishest the sacrifice, wash. Of twelve trees having leaves (13) offer to the Lord, as Abraham taught me also. And of every clean beast [and bird] offer a (14) sacrifice to the Lord. And of all thy first-fruits and of wine offer the first, as a sacrifice to the Lord God; and every sacrifice thou shalt salt with salt.

(10:1) Now, therefore, observe whatsoever I command you, children; for whatsoever things I have (2) heard from my fathers [I have declared unto you. And behold] I am clear from your ungodliness and transgression, which ye shall commit in the end of the ages [—against the Saviour of the world, Christ, acting godlessly—],[24] deceiving Israel, and stirring up against it great evils from the (3) Lord. And ye shall deal lawlessly together with
MK. Israel, so He shall not bear with Jerusalem because of your wickedness; but
15:38 the veil of the temple shall be rent, so as not to cover your (4) shame. And ye shall be scattered as captives among the Gentiles, and shall be for a reproach (5) and for a curse there. For the house which the Lord shall choose shall be called Jerusalem, as is contained in the book of Enoch[25] the righteous.

15:1–16:5

(15:1) Therefore the temple, which the Lord shall choose, shall be laid
MK. 13:2 waste through your uncleanness, (2) and ye shall be captives throughout all

[23]Throughout, there is special prominence given to the two sons Levi and Judah, from whom the two messiahs are to come.

[24]Probably a Christian interpolation, although the present wording may replace an original reference to the two anointed ones (in Greek, *christoi*).

[25]The reference indicates that the Testaments of the XII and Enoch likely originated in the same circles.

nations. And ye shall be an abomination unto them, and ye (3) shall receive reproach and everlasting shame from the righteous judgement of God. And all who hate (4) you shall rejoice at your destruction. And if you were not to receive mercy through Abraham, Isaac, and Jacob, our fathers, not one of our seed should be left upon the earth.

(16:1) And now I have learnt that for seventy weeks[26] ye shall go astray,
and profane the priesthood, and (2) pollute the sacrifices. And ye shall
make void the law, and set at nought the words of the prophets by evil per-
verseness. And ye shall persecute righteous men, and hate the godly; the
words of the (3) faithful shall ye abhor. And a man who reneweth the law
in the power of the Most High, ye shall call a deceiver; and at last ye shall
MT. rush upon him—to slay him, not knowing his dignity, taking (4) innocent
27:19, blood through wickedness upon your heads. And your holy places shall be
24 laid waste (5) even to the ground because of him. And ye shall have no place
that is clean; but ye shall be among the Gentiles a curse and a dispersion
until He shall again visit you, and in pity shall receive you through faith and
water.

18:1–14

(18:1) And after their punishment shall have come from the Lord,
the priesthood shall fail.
(2) Then shall the Lord praise up a new priest.[27]
And to him all the words of the Lord shall be revealed;
And he shall execute a righteous judgement upon the earth for a
multitude of days.
(3) And his star shall arise in heaven as of a king.
Lighting up the light of knowledge as the sun the day,
And he shall be magnified in the world.
(4) He shall shine forth as the sun on the earth,
And shall remove all darkness from under heaven,
And there shall be peace in all the earth.
(5) The heavens shall exult in his days,
And the earth shall be glad,
And the clouds shall rejoice;
(And the knowledge of the Lord shall be poured forth upon the
earth, as the water of the seas);
And the angels of the glory of the presence of the Lord shall
be glad in him.
(6) The heavens shall be opened.
And from the temple of glory shall come upon him sanctification,
With the Father's voice as from Abraham to Isaac.

[26]This reference goes back to Jeremiah 25:12, where the interval between the punishment of the nation and its deliverance is seventy years. In Daniel 9:24, however, the predicted period has been expanded to seventy "weeks" of years ($70 \times 7 = 490$). Probably this allusion to the corruption of the nation and its priesthood was written in the declining decades of the Hasmonean era, that is, after 100 B.C.

[27]The new priest refers to the Zadokite priesthood, as they styled themselves, who were established by the Teacher of Righteousness—or more accurately, the One who Teaches Rightly—the founder of the Qumran community that settled on the shores of the Dead Sea. They were awaiting the fulfillment of God's time before He would restore them to the true and pure priestly service of God in Jerusalem.

(7) And the glory of the Most High shall be uttered over him,
And the spirit of understanding and sanctification shall rest upon him [in the water].
(8) For he shall give the majesty of the Lord to His sons in truth for evermore;
And there shall none succeed him for all generations forever.
(9) And in his priesthood the Gentiles shall be multiplied in knowledge upon the earth,
And enlightened through the grace of the Lord:
In his priesthood shall sin come to an end,
And the lawless shall cease to do evil.
[And the just shall rest in him.]
(10) And he shall open the gates of paradise,
And shall remove the threatening sword against Adam.
(11) And he shall give to the saints to eat from the tree of life,
And the spirit of holiness shall be on them.
(12) And Beliar[28] shall be bound by him,
And he shall give power to His children to tread upon the evil spirits.
(13) And the Lord shall rejoice in His children,
And be well pleased in His beloved ones forever.
(14) Then shall Abraham and Isaac and Jacob exult,
And I will be glad,
And all the saints shall clothe themselves with joy.

TESTAMENT OF JUDAH 1:1–6

(1:1, 2) The copy of the words of Judah, what things he spake to his sons before he died. They gathered (3) themselves together, therefore, and came to him, and he said to them: Hearken, my children, to Judah your father. I was the fourth son born to my father Jacob; and Leah my mother named (4) me Judah, saying, I give thanks to the Lord, because He hath given me a fourth son also. I was (5) swift in my youth, and obedient to my father in everything. And I honoured my mother and my (6) mother's sister. And it came to pass, when I became a man, that my father blessed me, saying, Thou shalt be a king, prospering in all things.

21:1–22:3

(21:1) And now, my children, I command you, love Levi,[29] that ye may
abide, and exalt not yourselves (2) against him, lest ye be utterly destroyed.
HEB. For to me the Lord gave the kingdom, and to him the (3) priesthood, and
9:11, He set the kingdom beneath the priesthood. To me He gave the things
23–26 upon the (4) earth; to him the things in the heavens. As the heaven is
higher than the earth, so is the priesthood of God higher than the earthly
kingdom, unless it falls away through sin from the Lord and is (5) dominated by the earthly kingdom—. For the angel of the Lord said unto me:
The Lord chose him rather than thee, to draw near to Him, and to eat of

[28]Beliar (sometimes spelled Belial) was the chief opponent of God, the ruler of the demonic powers, roughly equivalent to Satan (meaning Adversary). The creation was to be under the sway of Beliar until the Rule of God was reestablished in the End Time.

[29]Judah, the king-designate, is to cooperate with the priestly son of Levi.

His table and to offer Him the first-fruits of the choice things of the sons of Israel; but thou shalt be king of Jacob.

(6) And thou shalt be amongst them as the sea. For as, on the sea, just and unjust are tossed about, some taken into captivity while some are enriched, so also shall every race of men be in thee: some shall be impoverished, being taken captive, and others grow rich by plundering the possessions of others.

(7) For the kings shall be as sea-monsters.
They shall swallow men like fishes:
The sons and daughters of freemen shall they enslave;
Houses, lands, flocks, money shall they plunder:
(8) And with the flesh of many shall they wrongfully feed the ravens and the cranes;
—And they shall advance in evil, in covetousness uplifted,—
(9) And there shall be false prophets like tempests,
And they shall persecute all righteous men.

(22:1) And the Lord shall bring upon them divisions one against another
MK. And there shall be continual wars in Israel;
13:7–8 (2) And among men of another race[30] shall my kingdom be brought to an end,
Until the salvation of Israel shall come,
ROM. Until the appearing of the God of righteousness,
11:25– That Jacob and all the Gentiles may rest in peace.
27 (3) And he shall guard the might of my kingdom forever;
For the Lord sware to me with an oath that He would not destroy the kingdom from my seed forever.

TESTAMENT OF NAPHTALI 8:1–10

(8:1) And lo! my children, I have shown unto you the last times, how everything shall come to pass in (2) Israel. Do ye also, therefore, charge your children that they be united to Levi and to Judah;
For through them shall salvation arise unto Israel,
And in them shall Jacob be blessed.
MK. 1: (3) For through their tribes shall God appear [dwelling among men][31]
2–3 on earth,
To save the race of Israel,
(CF. And to gather together the righteous from amongst the Gentiles.
MAL. (4) If ye work that which is good, my children,
3:1) Both men and angels shall bless you;
And God shall be glorified among the Gentiles through you,
MT. 1:23 And the devil shall flee from you,
And the wild beasts shall fear you—,
And the Lord shall love you,
[And the angels shall cleave to you].
(5) As a man who has trained a child well is kept in kindly remembrance;
So also for a good work there is a good remembrance before God.

[30]Possibly a reference to the Romans, who seized control of Jerusalem in 63 B.C.

[31]Probably a Christian interpolation.

(6) But him that doeth not that which is good,
Both angels and men shall curse,
And God shall be dishonoured among the Gentiles through him,
And the devil shall make him as his own peculiar instrument,
And every wild beast shall master him,
And the Lord shall hate him.
(7) For the commandments of the law are two-fold,
And through prudence must they be fulfilled.
I COR. (8) For there is a season for a man to embrace his wife,
7:5 And a season to abstain therefrom for his prayer.
(9) So, then, there are two commandments; and, unless they be done in due order, they bring (10) very great sin upon men. So also is it with the other commandments. Be ye therefore wise in God, my children, and prudent, understanding the order of His commandments, and the laws of every word, that the Lord may love you.

The War Scroll

Discovered in the caves at Qumran in a nearly complete copy, as well as in some fragmentary copies, the War Scroll consists of an elaborate set of military preparations for the final battle at the end of the age between the evil forces of Belial and the elect community. Included in the work are prayers and praise for the eschatological fulfillment of God's promises to his chosen people. At stake is not merely the fate of the land of Palestine and the Jerusalem temple—although these are central to the values of the community—but the destiny of the whole cosmos, including the powers of good and evil. Since the visible manifestation of "the enemy" seems to be the Romans, who came to Palestine in force in 63 B.C., the writing must have originated after that date. Its main importance for the study of Christian origins is to demonstrate the apocalyptic view of history, which saw the historical forces as divided into two sharply differentiated groups (Sons of Light; Sons of Darkness); the course of history as filled with conflict and headed toward catastrophe; the goal of history as achieved through a coalition of human and divine forces (the elect and the angels), whose joint efforts would establish the divine rule in the cosmos.

WAR SCROLL XI:4–XII:15

Truly the battle is Thine and the power from Thee! It is not ours. Our strength and the power of our hands accomplish no mighty deeds except by Thy power and by the might of Thy great valour. This Thou hast taught us from ancient times, saying, *A star shall come out of Jacob, and a sceptre shall rise out of Israel. He shall smite the temples of Moab and destroy all the children of Sheth. He shall rule out of Jacob and shall cause the survivors of the city to perish. The enemy shall be his possession and Israel shall accomplish mighty deeds* (Num. XXIV, 17–19).

By the hand of Thine anointed, who discerned Thy testimonies, Thou hast revealed to us the [times] of the battles of Thy hands that Thou mayest glorify Thyself in our enemies by levelling the hordes of Satan, the seven nations of vanity, by the hand of Thy poor whom Thou hast redeemed [by Thy might] and by the fulness of Thy marvelous power. (Thou hast opened) the door of hope to the melting heart: Thou wilt do to them as Thou didst to Pharaoh, and to the captains of his chariots in the Red Sea. Thou wilt kindle the downcast of spirit and they shall be a flaming torch in the straw to consume ungodliness and never to cease till iniquity is destroyed.

From ancient times Thou hast fore[told the hour] when the might of Thy hand (would be raised) against the Kittim, saying, *Assyria shall fall by the sword of no man, the sword of no mere man shall devour him* (Isa. XXXI, 8). For Thou wilt deliver into the hands of the poor the enemies from all the lands, to humble the mighty of the peoples by the hand of those bent to the dust, to bring upon the [head of Thine enemies] the reward of the wicked, and to justify Thy true judgement in the midst of all the sons of men, and to make for Thyself an everlasting Name among the people [whom Thou hast redeemed] . . . of battles to be magnified and sanctified in the eyes of the remnant of the peoples, that they may know . . . when Thou chastisest Gog and all his assembly gathered about him . . .

For Thou wilt fight with them from heaven . . . **XII** For the multitude of the Holy Ones [is with Thee] in heaven, and the host of the Angels is in Thy holy abode, praising Thy Name. And Thou hast established in [a community] for Thyself the elect of Thy holy people. [The list] of the names of all their host is with Thee in the abode of Thy holiness; [the reckoning of the saints] is in Thy glorious dwelling-place. Thou hast recorded for them, with the graving-tool of life, the favours of [Thy] blessings and the Covenant of Thy peace, that Thou mayest reign [over them] for ever and ever and throughout all the eternal ages. Thou wilt muster the [hosts of] Thine [el]ect, in their Thousands and Myriads, with Thy Holy Ones [and with all] Thine Angels, that they may be mighty in battle, [and may smite] the rebels of the earth by Thy great judgements, and that [they may triumph] together with the elect of heaven.

For Thou art [terrible], O God, in the glory of Thy kingdom, and the congregation of Thy Holy Ones is among us for everlasting succour. We will despise kings, we will mock and scorn the mighty; for our Lord is holy, and the King of Glory is with us together with the Holy Ones. Valiant [warriors] of the angelic host are among our numbered men, and the Hero of war is with our congregation; the host of His spirits is with our foot-soldiers and horsemen. [They are as] clouds, as clouds of dew (covering) the earth, as a shower of rain shedding righteousness on all that grows on the earth.

Rise up, O Hero!
Lead off Thy captives, O Glorious One!
Gather up Thy spoils, O Author of mighty deeds!
Lay Thy hand on the neck of Thine enemies
    and Thy feet on the pile of the slain!

Smite the nations, Thine adversaries,
    and devour the flesh of the sinner with Thy sword!
Fill Thy land with glory
    and Thine inheritance with blessing!
Let there be a multitude of cattle in Thy fields,
    and in Thy palaces silver and gold and precious stones!

O Zion, rejoice greatly!
O Jerusalem, show thyself amidst jubilation!
Rejoice, all you cities of Judah;
keep your gates ever open
  that the hosts of the nations
  may be brought in!

Their kings shall serve you
  and all your oppressors shall bow down before you;
  [they shall lick] the dust [of your feet].
Shout for joy, [O daughters of] my people!
Deck yourselves with glorious jewels
  and rule over [the kingdoms of the nations!
Sovereignty shall be to the Lord]
  and everlasting dominion to Israel.
. . .

JEWISH INTERPRETATION OF SCRIPTURE

With the administration of the temple in increasingly secularized priestly hands, and the enormous power of Rome as an insurmountable barrier to establishment of an independent Jewish state, the focus of Jewish piety was focused increasingly on the scriptures. The questions were, how to understand these documents, written as they were in the archaic language of Hebrew? And how might one go about appropriating the meaning and claims of these documents in the present situation?

A range of answers was offered to these problems by Jewish thinkers and writers of the period. To assure comprehension of the Bible, it was paraphrased in Aramaic, the Semitic language that had long before the hellenistic period replaced Hebrew as the dominant tongue of Jews, as well as of most dwellers in the Middle East. These Aramaic documents, which combined elements of translation and paraphrase, were known as *targums.* Others prepared detailed expansions of scripture called *midrash,* which served to interpret the ancient writings and to show their relevance for the interpreter's own time. Still others used *allegorical* methods in the effort to show that the biblical narratives and laws were not to be taken literally, but were to be understood as expressing philosophical truths. Chief among such interpreters was Philo of Alexandria. And then there were those who wanted simply to retell the biblical stories or to rehearse the ancient laws in such a way as to give the hearer a sense of the personal stake he or she had in the events or regulations being described. This procedure, when based on legal traditions, was known as *halakah,* and furnished the basis for the development of the Talmud in the second and subsequent centuries. The reappropriation of the narrative materials was known as *haggadah.* In what follows we shall consider in greater detail what each of these interpretive efforts involves, and we shall examine samples of each type.

Targum

Because the ordinary spoken language of Palestine was Aramaic—although Hebrew was used for religious ceremonial purposes and Greek for public and commercial communication—it was necessary to provide for the mass of worshipping Jews interpretive translations of the Hebrew scriptures into Aramaic. Such a translation was known as a *targum* (plural, *targumim*). Although the targum followed the Hebrew text verse by verse, it was more often a paraphrase than a translation. This interpretive process probably took formal shape in connection with the synagogue, where the public reading of the Hebrew scripture in the synagogue was followed by an impromptu interpretation in the Aramaic vernacular. The targumic tradition survives, therefore, in several different written traditions, each of which aims to preserve a particular oral interpretation of scripture. Like all the other forms of rabbinic interpretation of scripture, the targumim developed along different lines in Babylon and in Jerusalem, although the relative ease of movement between these two widely separated centers of Jewish life resulted in considerable mutual influence. The surviving targumic materials are of late date (after the sixth century A.D.), but they incorporate older material that reaches back to the first century A.D. One such complete targum on the entire Pentateuch (the first five books of the Hebrew Bible, often referred to as the Torah) is called *pseudo-Jonathan,* as a result of its having been wrongly attributed to a certain Jonathan ben Uzziel, a pupil of Hillel (the most important of the liberal teachers, fl. after 30 B.C.).

Midrash

Midrash is a general term for the exposition of Jewish scripture. It is written on the basis of the biblical text itself, verse by verse, and hence differs significantly from the Mishnah, which is free interpretation of biblical ideas. Mishnah is sometimes based on specific texts or phrases, but it elaborates on them in order to provide detailed instructions as to how to apply the texts to the situation of the interpreter. Some midrashim are devoted almost entirely to the exposition of the legal portions of scripture; others are hortatory, or merely entertaining. The legal type is called *halakah;* the latter variety is *haggadah.* Two examples are given here, one of each type. Midrash Sifre on Numbers has been traditionally attributed to the School of Ishmael (second century A.D.) and is mostly halakhic. The other sections are from the Mechilta, a midrash on Exodus, which has also been linked to the School of Ishmael. Both are probably from a later time, however. The Mechilta is mostly haggadic. Its attempt to trace its claim to authority in interpretation back through generations of teachers stands in sharp contrast to Jesus's words, "You have heard it said of old . . . but I say to you . . ." (Mt. 5:21 ff.).

Exposition of scripture was also carried on around the beginning of our era by interpreters who were not included among the rabbis. Only rabbinic interpretations were later recognized by or included in the official body of oral law and scriptural exposition. Two quite different examples of the nonrabbinic exposition will be given. The first is a curious document, unknown until a copy was found among the first of the Dead Sea Scrolls to be discovered, consisting of a midrashic expansion of the book of Genesis. It retells the story, elaborating details of human interest, such as Sarah's beauty, and explaining supernatural events in terms that were meaningful in the writer's own time, such as the demonic origin of the plagues that fell upon Egypt when Pharaoh took Abraham's wife, Sarah, into his household. The details of the elaborated narrative resemble closely those of such apocalyptic writings as the Book of Enoch, so that it is extremely likely that the *Genesis Apocryphon,* as scholars call this midrash, was written (together with the books of Enoch and Jubilees) by Essenes.

The Biblical Antiquities of Pseudo-Philo, which was wrongly attributed to Philo of Alexandria, recounts Israel's history from creation to the time of David, although the original may have carried the story even further. Some of the details are an expansion of scripture; others have no basis in the scriptural account. *The Biblical Antiquities of Pseudo-Philo* is therefore a partly targumic and partly haggadic midrash, developing its own expansion of scripture. Although it was attributed to Philo, it was written in Greek (or possibly translated from a Hebrew original into Greek) sometime in the first century A.D. It represents, therefore, a very early exegetical tradition.

PARAPHRASES AND EXPANSION OF THE SCRIPTURAL NARRATIVES

The four excerpts following are from the Targum of Pseudo-Jonathan, which includes early material even though it assumed its present form in the seventh century or later. The first excerpt is a slight expansion of the creation story of Genesis 3; the second is chiefly significant because it mentions Enoch as a personal mediator of the will of God, similar to Christian conceptions of Jesus; the third has some legendary touches, as in the mention of Abraham's using the altar earlier employed for worship by Adam and Noah, and in the enlargement on the role of angels; the fourth manifests the strong messianic interests of the period, with the explicit expectations of the kingly son of Judah who is to establish the divine rule. The basic biblical text is printed here in italics.

Targum of Pseudo-Jonathan

GENESIS 3:1–24

(3:1) *Now the serpent was* wiser for evil *than any beast of the field which the Lord God had made. And he said unto the woman,* "Is it in truth that the Lord *God hath said, Ye shall not eat of any tree of the garden?"*

(2) *And the woman said unto the serpent, "Of the* other *fruit of the trees of the garden we may eat:*

(3) *but of the fruit of the tree which is in the midst of the garden,* the Lord *God hath said, Ye shall not eat of it, neither shall ye touch it, lest ye die."*

(4) *And the serpent* acting as an informer to its creator *said unto the woman:* "You will not die at all for every craftsman hates his fellow-craftsman.

(5) It is revealed before the Lord that *in the day* on which you eat of it, *your eyes shall be* enlightened, *and ye shall be as* the mighty angels who are wise (enough) to distinguish between *good and evil."*

(6) *And the woman saw* Sammael, the angel of death, and she was afraid, and she knew *that the tree was good for food, and that* it was a remedy for the enlightenment of *the eyes, and that the tree was to be desired to make one wise, she took of the fruit thereof, and did eat; and she gave also unto her husband with her, and he did eat.*

(7) *And the eyes of them both were opened, and they knew that they were naked,* stripped of the clothing of onyx in which they had been created, and they saw their shame; *and they sewed fig leaves together, and made themselves aprons.*

(8) *And they heard the voice of* the word of *the Lord God walking in the garden in the* resting-time *of the day. And* Adam *and his wife hid themselves from the presence of the Lord God amongst the trees of the garden.*

(9) *And the Lord God called unto* Adam *and said unto him:* "Is not all the world which I have created open before me, the darkness the same as the light? So how can you think in your heart to hide yourself from before me? Can I not see the place in which you are hiding? And where are the commandments which I commanded you?"

(10) *And he said, "I heard* the voice of your word *in the garden, and I was afraid, because I was naked,* and the laws which you commanded me I have transgressed, *and I hid myself* for shame."

(11) *And he said, "Who told thee that thou wast naked,* except *thou hast eaten of* the fruit of *the tree, whereof I commanded thee that thou shouldest not eat?"*

(12) *And* Adam *said "The woman whom thou gavest to be with me, she gave me of* the fruit of *the tree, and I did eat."*

(13) *And the Lord God said unto the woman, "What is this thou hast done?" And the woman said, "The serpent beguiled me* with his cleverness and deceived me with his wickedness, *and I did eat."*

(14) *And the Lord God* brought the three of them to judgment, and he *said unto the serpent, "Because thou hast done this, cursed art thou above all cattle, and above every beast of the field; upon thy belly shalt thou go,* and your feet will be cut off, and your skin you will cast off once in every seven years, and the poison of death will be in your mouth, *and dust shalt thou eat all the days of thy life:*

(15) *and I will put enmity between thee and the woman, and between* the seed of your offspring and the seed of her offspring; and it shall be that when the offspring of the woman keep the commandments of the Law, they will aim right [at you] and they will smite you on the *head*; but when they abandon the commandments of the Law, you will aim right [at them], and you

will wound them in the *heel*. However, for them there will be a remedy, but for you there will be none, and in the future they will make peace with the heel in the days of the king, Messiah."

(16) *Unto the woman he said, "I will greatly multiply thy sorrow* by the blood of your virginity *and thy conception; in sorrow thou shalt bring forth children; and thy desire shall be to thy husband, and he shall rule over thee* for good and for ill."

(17) *And unto Adam he said, "Because thou hast hearkened unto the* word *of thy wife, and hast eaten of* the fruit of *the tree, of which I commanded thee, saying, Thou shalt not eat of it; cursed is the ground* because it did not show forth your guilt; *in toil shalt thou eat of it all the days of thy life; thorns also and thistles shall it bring forth* and increase on account of you; *and thou shalt eat the herb* which is on the face *of the field."*

(18) Adam answered and said, "I pray by the mercies which are before you, O Lord, that we may not be reckoned as cattle to eat grass in the open field. Let us stand up and labour with the labour of the hands, and eat food from the food of the earth, and in this way let there be a distinction before you between the children of men and the cattle."

(19) *"In the sweat of* the palm of your hands *shalt thou eat* food *till thou return unto the* dust from which you were created. *For dust thou art, and unto dust shalt thou return,* and from the dust you will arise in the future to render reckoning and account for all that you have done, on the day of the great judgment."

(20) *And* Adam *called his wife's name Eve, because she was the mother of all the sons of men.*

(21) *And the Lord God made for Adam and for his wife* glorious garments from the skin cast off by the serpent on the skin of their flesh, instead of their onyx which had been cast away; and he *clothed them.*

(22) *And the Lord God said* to the angels who minister before him, "Behold, Adam is unique in the world as I am in the heavens above; and in the future there will arise from him men who know how to distinguish between *good and evil.* If he had kept the commandments which I commanded him he would have lived and flourished as the tree of life forever; but in fact he has not kept what I commanded him, so we are going to decree against him and we forbid him the garden of Eden before he stretches out his hand and takes for himself from the fruit of the tree of life. For if he eats from it he will *live* and flourish *forever."*

(23) *So the Lord God* took him out of *the garden of Eden,* and he went and dwelt on mount Moriah, *to till the ground from whence he was created.*

(24) *So he drove* Adam *out and he* set the glory of his Shekina[32] to *the east of the garden of Eden* between the two Cherubim. Before God created the world he created the Law, he prepared the garden of Eden for the righteous that they might eat and be satisfied with the fruit of the tree, because they would have observed in their lives the instruction of the Law (in this world) and would have maintained the commandments; and he prepared Gehinnom for the wicked which is like the sharp sword devouring with two edges, and he prepared within flashing sparks of fire and burning coals for

[32]In order to bridge the gap between the created world and Yahweh, who was increasingly conceived in post-exilic Judaism as utterly transcendent, the rabbis spoke of the manifestations of God as quasi-personified agents created to accomplish God's will. One such agent was the *shekinah* (lit., "dwelling place") or divine presence. Often identified with the cloud of glory that filled the innermost court of the temple built by Solomon (I Kings 8: 10–11), *shekinah* was often used as a circumlocution for the divine name, which was considered by the rabbis as too holy to be pronounced or written.

the judgment of the wicked who rebelled in their lives against the instruction of the Law. Better is the Law to one who observed it and walks in the paths of the way of life, than the fruit of the tree of life; for the word of the Lord prepared it for man to keep it, that he may be established in the world to come.

GENESIS 5:1–3; 22–24

(5:1) *This is the book of the* genealogy of the *generations of Adam. In the day that* the Lord *created* Adam, *in the likeness of* the Lord *made he him;*

(2) *male* with female parts *created he them; and blessed them* in the name of his word, *and called their name Adam, in the day when they were created.*

(3) *And Adam lived an hundred and thirty years, and begat* Seth who resembled his likeness and his appearance. For before that time, Eve had borne Cain who was not from him [Adam] and did not resemble him, and Abel was killed at the hands of Cain, and Cain was cast out, and his descendants were not recorded in the book of the geneaology of Adam. And after that there was born one who resembled him, and he *called his name Seth.*

(22) *And Enoch* served before the Lord in uprightness *after he begat Methuselah three hundred years, and begat sons and daughters:*

(23) *and all the days of Enoch* with the dwellers on earth *were three hundred sixty and five years:*

(24) *and Enoch* served before the Lord in uprightness, and, behold, *he was not* with the dwellers on earth, for he was withdrawn and went up to the firmament by the word before the Lord, and his name was called Metatron[33] the great scribe.

GENESIS 22:1–21

(22:1) *And it came to pass after these things, that* Isaac and Ishmael were disputing. Ishmael said: "It is right for me to be the heir of my father, since I am his first-born son." But Isaac said: "It is right for me to be the heir of my father, since I am the son of Sarah his wife, but you are the son of Hagar, the handmaid of my mother." Ishmael answered and said: "I am more righteous than you because I was circumcised when thirteen years old; and if it had been my wish to refuse I would not have handed myself over to be circumcised." Isaac answered and said: "Am I not now thirty-seven years old? If the Holy One, blessed be he, demanded all my members I would not hesitate." Immediately, these words were heard before the Lord of the universe, and immediately, the word of the Lord tested *Abraham, and said unto him, "Abraham"; and he said, "Here am I."*

(2) *And he said, "Take now thy son, thine only son, whom thou lovest, even Isaac, and get thee into the land of* worship; *and offer him there for a burnt offering upon one of the mountains which I will tell thee of."*

(3) *And Abraham rose early in the morning and he saddled his ass, and took two of his young men,* Eliezer and Ishmael, *with him, and Isaac his son; and he clave the wood* of the olive and the fig and the palm which are proper *for the burnt offering, and rose up, and went unto the place of which* the Lord *had told him.*

[33]Metatron figures frequently in later Jewish speculation about the communication and intrepretation of the divine will.

(4) *On the third day Abraham lifted up his eyes, and saw* the cloud of glory smoking on the mountain, and he recognised it *afar off.*

(5) *And Abraham said unto his young men, "Abide ye here with the ass, and I and the lad will go yonder* to find if what I was assured—'so shall thy seed be'—will be established; *and we will worship* the Lord of the universe, *and come again to you."*

(6) *And Abraham took the wood of the burnt offering, and laid it upon Isaac his son; and he took in his hand the fire and the knife; and they went both of them together.*

(7) *And Isaac spake unto Abraham his father, and said, "My father": and he said, "Here am I, my son." And he said, "Behold the fire and the wood: but where is the lamb for a burnt offering?"*

(8) *And Abraham said:* "The Lord will choose for himself *the lamb for a* burnt offering, my son." *So they went both of them* with a single heart *together.*

(9) *And they came to the place which God had told him of; and Abraham built the altar there* which Adam had built, which had been destroyed by the waters of the flood and which Noah had rebuilt. It had been destroyed in the generation of the division. And he *laid the wood in order, and bound Isaac his son, and laid him on the altar, upon the wood.*

(10) *And Abraham stretched forth his hand, and took the knife to slay his son.* Isaac answered and said to his father: "Bind me well that I may not struggle at the anguish of my soul, and that a blemish may not be found in your offering, and that I may not be cast into the depth of destruction." The eyes of Abraham looked at the eyes of Isaac, but the eyes of Isaac looked at the angels on high: Isaac saw them but Abraham did not see them. The angels on high answered, "Come and see these two unique men in the earth; the one slaughters and the other is slaughtered. The one who slaughters does not hesitate, the one to be slaughtered stretches out his neck."

(11) *And the angel of the Lord called unto him out of heaven, and said* to him, *"Abraham, Abraham": and he said, "Here am I."*

(12) *And he said, "Lay not thine hand upon the lad, neither do thou anything evil unto him: for now* it is revealed before me *that thou fearest the Lord, seeing thou has not withheld thy son, thine only son, from me."*

(13) *And Abraham lifted up his eyes, and looked, and behold,* that one ram which created in the evening of the completion of the world *caught in the thicket* of a tree *by his horns: and Abraham went and took the ram, and offered him up for a burnt offering in the stead of his son.*

(14) *And Abraham* gave thanks and prayed there in *that place,* and said: "When I prayed for mercy from before you, O Lord, it was revealed before you that there was no deviousness in my heart, and I sought to perform your decree with joy, that when the descendants of Isaac, my son, shall come to the hour of distress, you may remember them, and answer them, and deliver them; and that all generations to come may say, In this mountain Abraham bound Isaac, his son, and there the Shekina *of the Lord* was revealed to him."

(15) *And the angel of the Lord called unto Abraham a second time out of heaven*

(16) *and said, "By* my word *have I sworn, saith the Lord, because thou hast done this thing, and hast not withheld thy son, thine only son:*

(17) *that in blessing I will bless thee, and in multiplying I will multiply thy seed as the stars of the heaven, and as the sand which is upon the seashore; and thy* sons *shall possess the* cities of their *enemies;*

(18) *and* because of the merit of your sons *shall all the nations of the earth be blessed; because thou hast obeyed my voice."*

(19) And the angels on high led Isaac and brought him to the school of Shem the great, and he was there three years. And on the same day *Abraham returned unto his young men, and they rose up and went together to Beer-sheba; and Abraham dwelt at Beer-sheba.*

(20) *And it came to pass after these things,* after Abraham had bound Isaac, that Satan came and told Sarah that Abraham had slaughtered Isaac; and Sarah rose up and cried out and was choked and died because of the anguish. And Abraham came and rested on the way, and *it was told Abraham, saying, Behold, Milcah, she also hath borne children;* she is granted easement through the merit of her sister to bear sons *unto thy brother Nahor;*

(21) *Uz his firstborn, and Buz his brother, and Kemuel* the master of the Aramaean diviners.

GENESIS 49:1–28

(49:1) *And Jacob called unto his sons, and said:* "Purify yourselves from uncleanness, and I will show you hidden secrets and unknown ends, the recompense of the reward of the just, and the retribution of the wicked, and the security of Eden, what it is." The twelve tribes of Israel gathered themselves as one around the golden bed on which he lay: and after the glory of the Shekina of the Lord had been revealed to him, the time when the king, Messiah, was going to come was concealed from him; and then he said, "Come, *that I may tell you that which shall befall you in the latter days.*

(2) *Assemble yourselves, and hear, ye sons of Jacob; and* receive instruction from *Israel your father.*

(3) *Reuben, thou art my first-born,* the *beginning* of the *might* of my generation and the first outpouring of my imagination full of desire. To you belonged the birthright and the chief priesthood and the kingdom, but because you sinned, my son, the birthright has been given to Joseph, the kingdom of Judah, and the priesthood to Levi.

(4) I will liken you to a small garden into which enter torrents rushing and strong, and it is not able to endure them, and it is swamped. So you have been carried away, Reuben, my son; in that you have sinned, do not do so again, and your sin will be forgiven you; for it is reckoned to you as though you went to the woman with whom your father had lain, at the time when you disturbed *my* bed, when you went to it.

(5) *Simeon and Levi are brethren* alike in every way. Sharp weapons for violence, it is this by which they may be recognised.

(6) In their counsel *my soul* has taken no pleasure, and in their gathering to destroy Shechem my honour was not involved; *for in their anger they* killed the king and rulers, and of their own freewill they split open the fortified wall of their enemy."

(7) Jacob said, "The stronghold of Shechem was cursed when they entered it to destroy[34] it in their anger which was relentless, and (cursed) their hatred against Joseph, because it was adamant." Jacob said, "If both of them dwell together as one, there is no king or ruler who can stand before them. *I will divide* the inheritance of the sons of Simeon into two parts. One part shall come from the inheritance of the sons of Judah, one part shall be among the rest of the tribes of *Jacob,* and I will scatter the tribe of Levi among all the tribes of *Israel.*

(8) *Judah,* you acknowledged what happened with Tamar, therefore your

[34]The warfare of Simeon and Levi against Shechem to avenge the abuse of their sister Dinah is described in Genesis 34.

brothers shall acknowledge you, and they shall be called Jehudain after your name. Your hands will take revenge for you on your enemies, shooting arrows at them when they turn their necks before you. And *thy father's sons* will be ever quick to give you their greeting in advance of your own.

(9) I will liken you, Judah my son, to a *whelp,* the young one of lions, because from the killing of Joseph my son your soul departed, and in the judgment of Tamar you spared her. He is at ease and rests in confidence *as a lion,* and like a strong lion when he is resting *who shall rouse him up?*

(10) Kings and rulers shall not cease *from* the house of *Judah,* nor scribes teaching the law from his seed, until the time when the king, Messiah,[35] shall *come,* the youngest of his sons; and because of him *the peoples* shall flow together.

(11) How noble is the king, Messiah, who is going to rise from the house of Judah. He has girded his loins and come down, setting in order the order of battle with his enemies and killing kings with their rulers (and there is not a king or a ruler who shall stand before him), reddening the mountains with the blood of their slain. With his garments dipped in blood, he is like one who treads grapes in the press.

(12) More noble are the eyes of the king, Messiah, like sparkling *wine,* than to see the uncovering of nakedness and the shedding of innocent blood, his *teeth* are cleaner than *milk,* not for eating the torn or the stolen. And thus his mountains are red, and his press red from wine, and his hills are white from the corn and from the tents of the flocks.

(13) *Zebulun shall dwell* on the shores *of the sea,* and he will have authority over the harbours, subduing the domains of the sea with *ships; and his border* will extend as far as *Zidon.*

(14) *Issachar* longs for the law. He is a strong tribe knowing the determined times, and he lies down *between the* borders of his brothers.

(15) *And he saw the resting place* of the world to come, *that it is good,* and the portion of the land of Israel, that it is pleasant, therefore he bent his shoulders to labour in the law, and to him shall his brothers offer gifts.

(16) From the house of *Dan* there is going to arise a man who will judge his people with the judgment of truth; *as one* the tribes of Israel will listen to him.

(17) He will be a chosen man, and he will arise from the house of *Dan,* being like the venomous snake which lies at the parting of *the way,* and like the head of the *serpent* which hides on *the path* and *biteth the horse* in its *heel,* and it falls. And in his terror *his rider* is thrown off *backward* on his back. So will Samson the son of Manoah kill all the mighty men of the Philistines, both horsemen and men on foot, and he will hamstring their horses and throw their riders on to their backs."

(18) Jacob, when he saw Gideon the son of Joash, and Samson the son of Manoah, who were established to be deliverers, said: "I do not await the deliverance of Gideon, and I do not look out for the deliverance of Samson, because their salvation, being temporal, will not last. But I wait for your *salvation,* and look out for it, O Lord, because your salvation is eternal.

(19) The tribes of *Gad,* well-armed, will cross, with the rest of the tribes,

[35]Although some texts from this period (e.g., some of the Dead Sea Scrolls and the Testaments of the Twelve Patriarchs) expect an anointed king as well as an anointed priest in the end time, this targum envisions only the descendant of Judah as the messianic king. See K. G. Kuhn, "The Two Messiahs of Aaron and Israel," in *The Scrolls and the New Testament,* K. Stendhahl, ed. (New York: Harper and Row, 1956), pp. 54–64.

the streams of Arnon, and they will subdue before them the inhabitants of the land. And they will return armed at the end with great riches, and they will dwell securely beyond the crossing of the Jordan. For as they desire, so will it be to them, and they will receive their possession.

(20) Happy is *Asher,* how rich are his fruits! His land produces spices and the roots of frankincense, and his border will produce the delicacies of kings, and he utters thanks and praises for them before the Lord of the universe.

(21) *Naphtali* is a swift messenger, like *a hind* which runs on the tops of the mountains, bringing good news. He brought the news that Joseph was still alive. He went at speed to Egypt and brought the title deed of the field of the double cave, in which Esau has no part. And when he opens his mouth in the company of Israel, his voice will be chosen out of all voices.

(22) My son, whom I brought up, *Joseph,* you my son who became great and strong: the end was upon you to be strong and to subdue your inclination in the case of your mistress and in the case of your brothers. I will liken you to a vine planted by streams of water which sends out its roots and splits the sharp rocks, and with her branches subdues all the barren trees. Even so, Joseph my son, you subdued by your wisdom and your good deeds all the sorcerers of Egypt. And when praises were sung before you, the daughters of the rulers walked on the walls and threw before you rings and necklaces of gold to make you raise your eyes to them, but you did not raise your eyes to [any] one of them to be united with them in the day of great judgment.

(23) And all the sorcerers of Egypt were bitter and angry against him, so they brought information to Pharaoh hoping to bring him down from [his place of] honour. They spoke against him slanderously, which is as wounding as arrows.

(24) And the strength of his member reverted [through penitence] to its former state so as not to lie with his mistress, and *his hands* were strengthened from the imagining of seed, and he subdued his inclination because of the firm training which he received from *Jacob.* And for that reason he became worthy to be a leader and to have his name engraved with theirs on the stones *of Israel.*

(25) From the word of the *God of thy father* will be your *help,* and he who is called *'Almighty' shall bless thee, with blessings* which come down from the dew of heaven from above, and from the good *blessings* of the streams *of the deep* which come up and make the plant grow from below. Blessed are *the breasts* from which you were suckled and *the womb* in which you lay.

(26) *The blessings of thy father* will be added to *the blessings* by which my fathers Abraham and Isaac blessed me, which the princes of this world, Ishmael and Esau and all the sons of Qeturah, desired. All these blessings will be united and be made a diadem of majesty for *the head of Joseph, and on the crown* of the man who became a chief man and a ruler in Egypt, and attentive to in the glory of his *brethren.*

(27) *Benjamin is* a strong tribe like *a wolf* with his prey. In his land the Shekina of the ruler of the world will dwell, and in his possession will be built the house of the sanctuary. *In the morning* the priests will offer the lamb regularly until the fourth hour *and at even* they will offer the second lamb and in the evening they will *divide* what is left, the remainder of the offerings, and they will eat each man his own part."

(28) *All these are the twelve tribes of Israel,* all of them righteous as one: *and this is it that their father spake unto them and blessed them; everyone according to his blessing he blessed them.*

Midrash Sifre on Numbers 113

THE SABBATH-BREAKER (NUM. 15:32–36)

And while the children of Israel were in the wilderness they found a man gathering sticks upon the Sabbath Day. Scripture relates this incident to show up Israel's lack of piety: they kept only one Sabbath, the second they profaned. *And they who found him gathering sticks, brought him unto Moses* [5:33]. Why is it repeated? It implies that the man has been warned beforehand concerning works of this kind that are prohibited on the Sabbath. Hence the rule concerning all those chief works, which, according to the Torah, are not to be done on the Sabbath, that a warning must be given first /if the person breaking them is to be punished/.

R. Isaac says: "It is not at all necessary [to deduce it from this passage]. It stands to reason [we can deduce it by inference]: if idolatry, which is such a grave sin, is only punished after due warning, much more so must it be with other transgressions."

[The rest of the text is defective.]

And they put him in ward. This suggests that all criminals who are to be executed must first be put in ward.

Because it had not been declared what should be done to him. But does it not say "all those who profane the Sabbath should surely die" [Ex. 31:14]? The meaning is: Moses did not know by what *manner of death* he should die, until he was told directly by the mouth of Holiness.

And the Lord said to Moses: The man shall surely be put to death. This is a law for all generations.

All the congregation shall stone him. This means: he should be stoned in the *presence* of the whole congregation. Thou sayest that it means in their presence, but perhaps it is to be understood literally [that they should all stone him]? It says: "The hand of THE WITNESSES shall be on him first to kill him."

And the whole congregation brought him without the camp and stoned him to death with stones. From here it can be inferred that criminals who are to be executed should be put to death outside the court.

And stoned him to death with stones. Here is says "with *stones*," and in another passage it says, "and they stoned him with *a stone*" [Lev. 24:23]; how should these passages be reconciled? The house of stoning [the stoning-place] was twice the height of a man. One of the witnesses pushed him [the criminal] from behind, so he fell face downward. He was then turned on his back. If he died from this fall, it was sufficient; if not, the second witness took the stone and dropped it on his heart. If this caused death, it was sufficient; if not, he was stoned by the whole congregation of Israel, as it is said: *"The hand of the witnesses should be the first to kill him and the hand of the whole people last"* [Deut. 13:10]. Thus *both* passages are in harmony with one another.

As the Lord commanded Moses. He [Moses] said to them: "Stone him!" and they stoned him. "Hang him!" and they hanged him. Concerning the hanging, we should know nothing, were it not for Deut. 21:22: *"If there be found in man a sin which causes death, and he is executed, then he shall be hanged on a tree."* Thus R. Eliezer. R. Hidka said: "I had a fellow student, one of the disciples of R. Akiba, and he said: 'Moses knew that the penalty for him who gathers wood on the Sabbath was to be death, but he did not know what manner of death he should die.' "

AND WHEN YE GO TO WAR IN YOUR LAND AGAINST THE ADVERSARY THAT OPPRESSES YOU [Num. 10:9]. Both offensive and defensive warfare are meant [lit., "whether they come against you or ye come against them"].

AGAINST THE ADVERSARY THAT OPPRESSES YOU. This refers to the war of Gog and Magog [i.e., the future Messianic war, Ezek. 38]. Thou sayest, it refers to the war of Gog and Magog, but perhaps it refers to all other wars mentioned in Torah? It goes on to say here: "And ye shall be saved from your enemies." Come and see: which war is it [of which it can be said] that it will result in Israel's victory and which will not be followed by a renewed subjection [to the empires]? It can only be the war of Gog and Magog. Again it says: "And Yahweh will go out and fight against those nations" [Zech. 14:3]. What follows? "And the Lord will be king over the whole earth" [9].

PROPITIATION FOR SINS OF IGNORANCE

And when ye shall err and not observe all these commandments [Num. 15:22–31].

This refers to idolatry. Thou sayest, "to idolatry," but maybe it refers to any Commandment of the Law? When it says [5:24]: "That if *it* has been hidden from the eyes of the community, and done unwittingly;" Scripture singles out one Commandment as being something unique, so it must be idolatry. When, also, it says here: "When ye shall err and not observe *all these Commandments,*" a comparison is made between *all* the Commandments and the *one Commandment,* namely, as he who transgresses against all the Commandments of the Torah, throws off the yoke /of God/, and destroys the covenant /of God with Israel, or with Abraham/, and "uncovers faces in the Torah," so the transgressor of *the one Commandment* referred to in the passage is also one who breaks the yoke, and destroys the covenant, and treats the Torah irreverently; and this must refer to an idolater, as it is said in connexion with idolatry, "to break his *covenant*"; and "covenant" is always "words of the *covenant*" [Deut. 28:69]. Rabbi says: "The 'all' here and the 'all' there are akin to one another: as there it is connected with idolatry, so also here."

Which the Lord spoke to Moses. How can it be inferred that he who is given over to idolatry, denies all the Ten Words? Because it says /here, in connexion with idolatry/: *"which the Lord spoke to Moses,"* and in connexion with the Decalogue it also says [Ex. 21:1]: *"And the Lord spoke* all these words, saying; 'I am the Lord thy God, thou shalt have none other Gods but Me.' "

Whence is it further to be inferred that he who worships idols denies all that was commanded to Moses [not only the Decalogue, which God spoke directly]? Because it says: *"All that the Lord God has commanded through Moses."* He also breaks that which was commanded to the prophets, because it says: *"From the day when the Lord commanded"* [i.e., all Commandments are included]. Also that which was commanded to the Patriarchs, because it says: "For your generations." And when did the Holy One, blessed be He, begin to give Commandments to the Patriarchs? Since the time when it is said concerning Adam: "And the Lord *commanded* Adam." Thus, Scripture intimates that he who professes idolatry denies the Ten Words; the Commandments given through Moses; the Commandments given through the Prophets; and the Commandments given to the Patriarchs. And he who *denies* idolatry, professes the whole Torah.

If it be done unwittingly, etc., the priest shall make atonement for all the congregation of the house of Israel. How is it to be inferred from this that if one of the twelve tribes was prevented from bringing the Sacrifice it frustrated the Atonement? Because it says: "and the priest shall make atonement *for all the congregation of Israel, then shall they be forgiven.*" Are we to understand that sacrifice as a means of atonement is efficacious for sins committed *wilfully* as well as unintentionally? /No,/ because it says: "For it was in *error*" [a sin-offering is brought only for sins committed in ignorance, *not for wilful sins*]. R. Eliezer says: "*/On the contrary/,* this passage implies that the sins of the community *as a whole* [in contrast to the sins of the individual], even when done wilfully, are as if they were done unintentionally /and are atoned for by sacrifice/."

And it shall be forgiven. This [the masculine verb] implies only men. How then do we know that it refers to women also? Because it says: *"And it shall be forgiven to the whole congregation of the children of Israel."*

And to the stranger [proselyte]. As Israel is specified, the proselytes must be specially mentioned. It is always the case in Scripture when Israel is specified, the proselytes must be expressly included (otherwise *we* would exclude them].

And if one person sin unwittingly [Num. 15:27]. This is to exclude intentional sin /from sacrificial atonement/.

And the priest shall make atonement for the soul that erreth. The sins in his hand [i.e., his sins] have caused him to come to the "house of sin-offering" [unintentional sin is a revelation of sub-conscious sinfulness].

When he sinneth unwittingly. This [the repetition] is to exclude [from the necessity of a sacrifice] the "niceties" of idolatry [i.e., acquiescence in contemporary heathen customs, not directly idolatrous]. For otherwise we might have deduced by inference that those should also be included; for if the niceties of other Commandments, which, compared with idolatry, are "light," man is obliged [to bring a sacrifice in case of unintentional transgression], much more so should it be the case in connexion with idolatry.

And it shall be forgiven him. Perfect forgiveness, like all forgiveness [mentioned] in the Torah.

Ye shall have one law for him that is home born among the sons of Israel and for the stranger. Why this repetition? Since we should otherwise have inferred that as Gentiles are put upon equal terms with the Israelites with regard to idolatry, they are also their equals in cases of unintentional idol worship; but now we learn that only the Israelites bring [a sacrifice] in such a case.

That doth aught unwittingly. R. Judah ben Bethyra says: "[This additional expression is to include] any sin which, if committed intentionally, is punished by 'Karet,' and if done in ignorance requires a sin-offering, as in the case of the sin of idolatry."

But the soul that doeth aught with a high hand [intentionally]; this is he who treats the Torah irreverently, like Manasseh the son of Hezekiah.

The same blasphemeth the Lord. For he [Manasseh] used to sit and discuss scandalous homilies before God. Said he: "He (God) had nothing else to write in the Torah than, 'And Reuben went in the days of harvest and found mandrakes in the field, etc.' [Gen. 30:14]; and He had nothing else to write than 'And the children of Lotan were Kor and Herman'!" [Gen. 36:22]. Concerning him it is clearly stated in tradition: *"Thou sittest and speakest against thy brother, thou slanderest thine own mother's son: these things hast thou done and I kept silence, thou thoughtest that I was as thyself"* [Ps. 1:20,21]. God said unto him: "Dost thou think that the ways of God are like the ways of man? I will reprove thee."

Isaiah [also] came and explicitly stated in tradition: "*Woe* unto them that draw iniquity with cords of vanity, and sin as it were with a cart rope" [Isa. 5:18]; [which means]: the beginning of sin is like one strand of a spider's web, but its end is like unto a cart rope, [meaning, either that the will is weakened by small offences, or that *one* sin is followed by many]. Rabbi says: "He who fulfills *one* Commandment for its own sake [not from selfish motives] should not rejoice merely because of that particular Commandment, for the end will be that this *one* good deed will be followed by many others; and he who breaks *one* Commandment, should not merely be perturbed because of that sin, for the end will be that *one* sin will be followed by many others. *One* good deed will bring forth another.

He blasphemeth [*megaddeph*] *the Lord.* R. El'azar ben Azaryah says: "It is like unto a man saying to his neighbour: 'thou hast scooped out [the first meaning of *gadef*] the dish and lessened it [the dish itself].' " Isi ben Akabya says: "It is like unto a man who says to his neighbour: 'Thou hast scratched out the whole dish and left nothing in it.' "

The soul shall be utterly cut off. "Cut off" means ceasing to be [total annihilation is implied].

From among his people. But the people will be at peace [the whole people is not responsible for the *intentional* idolatry of the individual].

Because he has despised the word of the Lord and has broken His Commandment. "Despised the word of the Lord" refers to a Sadducee; "and has broken His Commandment"—to an Epicurean. Another explanation:— *"Because he has despised the word of the Lord,"*—is he who treats the Torah irreverently; *"And hath broken His Commandment"* is he who breaks the covenant of the flesh [i.e., who opposes circumcision]. Hence R. El'azar of Modi'im says: "He who profanes the holy things [the Sanctuary], and despises the *festivals,* and breaks the covenant of Abraham our father [*circumcision*], even if he has in his hand many good deeds, is worthy to be thrust out of the world" [i.e., of the world to come]. If he says: "I accept the whole Torah, with the exception of *this* word," of him it is said: "For he despised the word of the Lord." If he says, "The whole Torah was spoken by the mouth of Holiness, and this word Moses himself said," he despises the word of the Lord.

Another interpretation: *"For he has despised the word of the Lord."* R. Meir says: "This is he who studies [the word of God], but does not teach others." [He "despises" the word in not being eager to spread it.] R. Nathan says: "It is he who does not consider the words of the Torah at all" [the indifferent]. R. Ishamel says: "This passage speaks of idolatry, because it says, 'he despises *the word* of the Lord,' which means, he despises the *first word* [Commandment] which was spoken to Moses direct, by the Mouth of the Power, namely, 'I am the Lord thy God, thou shalt have no other gods before me' " [Ex. 20:2].

That soul shall utterly be cut off [hikareth tikareth, infinitive with imperfect]. The first word refers to this world, and the second to *the world to come.* Thus R. Akiba. R. Ishmael said to him: "[Do you deduce from hikareth tikareth]? You might as well add the words in the preceding verse: 'and that soul shall be cut off,' and say that there are three 'cuttings off' from three worlds!" [It is a fanciful exegesis], for the Torah speaks in the tongues of men.

His iniquity shall be upon him. Death atones for all sinners, except idolaters. It is similar to the expression [Ezek. 32:27] "their iniquities shall be upon their bones." Perchance this also refers to an idolater who repents? It says

> were asked and they refused to accept it, for it is said, AND HE SAID, "THE LORD CAME FROM SINAI" etc. [Deut. 33:2]. He appeared to the children of Esau the wicked and said to them: Will you accept the Torah? They said to Him: What is written in it? He said to them: THOU SHALT NOT MURDER [Deut. 5:17]. They then said to Him: The very heritage which our father left us was: AND BY THY SWORD SHALT THOU LIVE [Gen. 27:40]. He then appeared to the children of Amon and Moab. He said to them: Will you accept the Torah? They said to Him: What is written in it? He said to them: THOU SHALT NOT COMMIT ADULTERY [Deut. 5:17]. They, however, said to Him that they were all of them children of adulterers, as it is said THUS WERE BOTH THE DAUGHTERS OF LOT WITH CHILD BY THEIR FATHER [Gen. 19:36]. Then He appeared to the children of Ishmael. He said to them: Will you accept the Torah? They said to Him: What is written in it? He said to them: THOU SHALT NOT STEAL [Deut. 5:17]. They then said to Him: The very blessing that had been pronounced upon our father was: AND HE SHALL BE AS A WILD ASS OF A MAN: HIS HAND SHALL BE UPON EVERYTHING [Gen. 16:12]. . . . But when He came to the Israelites and AT HIS RIGHT HAND WAS A FIERY LAW UNTO THEM [Deut. 33:22], they all opened their mouths and said ALL THAT THE LORD HAS SPOKEN WILL WE DO AND OBEY [Ex. 24:7]. . . . Rabbi Simon ben Eleazar says: If the sons of Noah could not endure the seven commandments enjoined upon them, how much less could they have endured all the commandments of the Torah! To give a parable: A king had appointed two administrators. One was appointed over the store of straw and the other was appointed over the treasure of silver and gold. The one appointed over the store of straw was held in suspicion. But he used to complain about the fact that they had not appointed him over the treasure of silver and gold. The people then said to him: "Reka!"[39] If you were under suspicion in connection with the store of straw how could they trust you with the treasure of silver
> MT. 5:22 and gold! Behold, it is a matter of reasoning by the method of *kai vachomer* [a logical rule: from light to heavy]: If the sons of Noah could not endure the seven commandments enjoined upon them, how much less could they have endured all the commandments of the Torah!
>
> Why was the Torah not given in the land of Israel? In order that the nations of the world should not have the excuse for saying: Because it was given in Israel's land, therefore we have not accepted it. Another reason: To avoid causing dissension among the tribes. Else one might have said: In my territory the Torah was given. And the other might have said: In my territory the Torah was given. Therefore, the Torah was given in the desert, publicly and openly, in a place belonging to no one. To three things the Torah is likened: To the desert, to fire, and to water. This is to tell you that just as these three things are free to all who come into the world, so also are the words of the Torah free to all who come into the world.

The Genesis Apocryphon

Among the Dead Sea Scrolls was found a paraphrase on and expansion of the book of Genesis, of which Column XX of the scroll, based on

[39] *Reka,* from a root found in Hebrew and Aramaic meaning "empty," and used therefore as an epithet, "empty-headed." It occurs in Mt. 5:22 as a term of insult.

Genesis 12:10–20, is given here in the translation of Geza Vermes. The story recounts how Abraham and Sarah took refuge in Egypt during a famine in Palestine and dwells at length on the beauty of Sarah, a fact that is simply stated without elaboration in the biblical account. More significant is the dualistic element that the expositor has introduced by attributing the plague to an evil spirit.

> And I, Abram, wept aloud that night, I and my nephew Lot, because Sarai had been taken from me by force. I prayed that night and I begged and implored, and I said in my sorrow while my tears ran down: "Blessed art Thou, O Most High God, Lord of all the worlds, Thou who art Lord and King of all things and who rulest over all the kings of the earth and judgest them all! I cry now before Thee, my Lord, against Pharaoh of Zoan the king of Egypt, because of my wife who has been taken from me by force. Judge him for me that I may see Thy mighty hand raised against him and against all his household, and that he may not be able to defile my wife this night (separating her) from me, and that they may know Thee, my Lord, that Thou art Lord of all the kings of the earth." And I wept and was sorrowful.
>
> And during that night the Most High God sent a spirit to scourge him, an evil spirit to all his household; and it scourged him and all his household. And he was unable to approach her, and although he was with her for two years he knew her not.
>
> At the end of those two years the scourges and afflictions grew greater and more grievous upon him and all his household, so he sent for all [the sages] of Egypt, for all the magicians, together with all the healers of Egypt, that they might heal him and all his household of this scourge. But not one healer or magician or sage could stay to cure him, for the spirit scourged them all and they fled.
>
> The Harkenosh came to me, beseeching me to go to the king and to pray for him and to lay my hands upon him that he might live, for the king had dreamt a dream . . . But Lot said to him, "Abram my uncle cannot pray for the king while Sarai his wife is with him. Go, therefore, and tell the king to restore his wife to her husband; then he will pray for him and he shall live."
>
> When Harkenosh had heard the words of Lot, he went to the king and said, "all these scourges and afflictions with which my lord the king is scourged and afflicted are because of Sarai the wife of Abram. Let Sarai be restored to Abram her husband, and this scourge and the spirit of festering shall vanish from you."
>
> And he called me and said, "What have you done to me with regard to [Sarai]? You said to me, She is my sister, whereas she is your wife; and I took her to be my wife. Behold your wife who is with me; depart and go hence from all the land of Egypt! And now pray for me and my house that this evil spirit may be expelled from it."
>
> So I prayed [for him] . . . and I laid my hands on his [head]; and the scourge departed from him and the evil [spirit] was expelled [from him], and he lived. And the king rose to tell me . . . and the king swore an oath to me that . . . and the king gave her much [silver and gold] and much raiment of fine linen and purple . . . And Hagar also . . . and he appointed men to lead [me] out [of all the land of Egypt]. And I, Abram, departed with very great flocks and with silver and gold, and I went up from [Egypt] together with my nephew [Lot]. Lot had great flocks also, and he took a wife for himself from among [the daughters of Egypt].

Midrash Pesher

A distinctive type of midrashic exposition of scripture was found among the Dead Sea Scrolls. Most of the interpretive passages begin with the term, "its interpretation is" (*peshru,* in Hebrew). The meaning that is set forth is not that intended by the original writer, but a special hidden meaning, intended for the elect community that believes itself to be living in the End Time and to whom the secrets of the divine plan have alone been vouchsafed. To accomplish this interpretive process the expositor feels free to alter the text, to redistribute the letters so as to give other meanings than those usually understood, and to supply different vowels to the consonantal Hebrew text where the resultant meaning is more to the interpreter's purpose. The orientation of the interpretation is overwhelmingly eschatological in bent, and the community can read its own history from the words of scripture. The similarities of this method to the interpretation of scripture by the New Testament writers are evident.

COMMENTARY ON HABAKKUK 1–6 (FROM DEAD SEA SCROLLS)

(1) And God told Habakkuk to write the things that were to come upon the last generation,[40] but the consummation of the period he did not make known to him. (2) And as for what it says, *that he may run who reads it,* this means the teacher of righteousness,[41] to whom God made known all the mysteries of the words of his servants the prophets.

(3) *For still the vision is for an appointed time; it hastens to the period and does not lie.* This means that the last period extends over and above all that the prophets said; for the mysteries of God are marvelous. *If it tarries, wait for it, for it will surely come; it will not delay.* This means the men of truth, the doers of the law, whose hands do not grow slack from the service of the truth, when the last period is stretched out over them. For all the periods of God will come to their fixed term, as he decreed for them in the mysteries of his wisdom.

(4) *Behold, puffed up, not upright is his soul in him.* This means that they make double the judgment upon themselves; they do not win acceptance when they are judged, for their souls are not upright. *But the righteous shall live by his faith.* This means all the doers of the law in the house of Judah, whom God will rescue from the house of judgment because of their labor and their faith in the teacher of righteousness.

(5) *Moreover wealth is treacherous, an arrogant man, and will not abide. His greed is as wide as Sheol; and he like death has never enough. To him are gathered all the nations, and to him are assembled all the people.* (6) *Shall not all of them take up their taunt against him, in scoffing derision of him, and say, "Woe to him who heaps up, but it is not his own! How long will he load himself with pledges?"*

[40]The community is convinced that it is living in the last generation of the present age and that it alone will survive into the Age to Come.

[41]Better, the One Who Teaches Rightly. See the Rule of the Community for the sect's account of his role in founding the community. He was the one who gave them the clues to understand the scriptures.

This means the wicked priest,[42] who was named according to the truth when he first took office; but when he had begun to rule in Israel, his heart was lifted up, and he forsook God and betrayed the statutes because of wealth. He plundered and assembled the wealth of men of violence who rebelled against God. He took the wealth of peoples, adding to himself iniquity and guilt; and ways of abominations he wrought, in all impurity of uncleanness.

Biblical Antiquities of Pseudo-Philo

The next excerpt is a continuous expansion of the text of Torah, written for narrative and homiletical rather than for legal purposes, and is hence haggadic in nature. It was probably composed in Hebrew or Aramaic, but was translated into Greek and then into the Latin version in which it is alone extant. Although the date cannot be determined with certainty, it was likely written in the first century A.D., sometime after the fall of Jerusalem.

The first selection is a slightly expanded version of the flood in the days of Noah. The second narrative is based on the story of the Tower of Babel (Gen. 11), to which have been added elements from the story of Abraham but also from the account (Dan. 3) of God's delivering from the fiery furnace the faithful Hebrews who risked death rather than accede to the pagan king's demand that they participate in idolatrous practices. That issue would be a live one during the period between the first and second Jewish revolts against the Romans.

Even though there is no hint of a doctrine of the resurrection of the dead in the book of Genesis, Pseudo-Philo finds it there in his expanded version of Genesis (3:10), just as the early Christians found support for the doctrine in their reading of the Old Testament. The advice to stand firm for the faith in the face of impending persecution (6:1–18) sounds like the apocalyptic sections of the gospels (Mk. 13) and Revelation.

III:1–11

(1) And it happened when men had begun to multiply on the earth, that beautiful daughters were born to them. And the sons of God saw the daughters of men, that they were very beautiful; they took wives for themselves of all that they had chosen.

(2) And God said: "My spirit will not judge among all these men forever, because they are flesh; but their years will be 120"; at which he set the limits of life; "and in their hands the law will not be extinguished."

(3) And God saw that among all the dwellers on earth evil works were put into effect, and since they thought about wickedness all their days, he said, "I will destroy man and everything which has come to life in the earth, because it repents me that I have made him."

[42] Various conjectures have been advanced as to who the Wicked Priest is, but it was presumably one of the Hasmonean King-Priests of the period around 100 B.C.

(4) But Noe found favour and pity before the Lord; and these are his generations. Noe, who was a just man and undefiled in his own generation, was pleasing to God. To him God said, "The time of all men living on the earth has come, because their works are very evil. And now, make for yourself an ark of cedar wood, and thus shall you make it: its length shall be 300 cubits, and its width 50 cubits, and its height 30 cubits. And you shall enter into the ark, yourself and your wife and your sons and your sons' wives with you, and I will make my covenant with you, that I will destroy all the dwellers on earth. But of the clean animals and of the clean birds of the sky you shall take them seven by seven, male and female, that their seed may be able to bring life to the earth. Of the unclean animals and of the unclean birds you shall take them for yourself two by two, male and female. You shall take provision for yourself and for them."

(5) So Noe did what God commanded him, and he entered into the ark, himself and all his sons with him. And it happened after seven days that the water of the flood began to be on the earth. And in that day all the depths were opened and the great fountain and the cataracts of heaven, and there was rain on the earth for forty days and forty nights.

(6) It was then 1652 years since God had made heaven and earth, on the day when the earth was destroyed together with its inhabitants because of the wickedness of their works.

(7) And with the flood continuing 150 days on the earth, Noe alone was left, and those who were with him in the ark. And when God remembered Noe, he made the water diminish.

(8) And it happened on the ninetieth day that God dried the earth and said to Noe: "Go out of the ark, you and all who are with you, and increase and multiply in the earth." So Noe went out of the ark, himself and his sons and his sons' wives, and all the beasts and reptiles and birds and cattle he brought out with him, just as God had commanded him. Then Noe built an altar to the Lord, and he took of all the clean animals and birds, and offered burnt offerings on the altar, and it was acceptable to the Lord as an odour of rest.

(9) And God said, "I will not again curse the earth for man, since the image of man's heart has left him from his youth; and therefore I will not again destroy all living things as I have done. But it will be that when the dwellers on earth have sinned, I will judge them by famine or sword or fire or death, and there will be earthquakes, and they will be scattered to uninhabited parts. But I will not again destroy the earth with a flood of water, and in all the days of the earth seed-time and harvest, cold and heat, summer and autumn, day and night will not cease, as long as I remember those who dwell on the earth, until the times are complete.

(10) But when the years of the world are complete, then will light cease and darkness be extinguished, and I will give life to the dead, and I will raise up those who sleep from the earth. The nether world will pay its debt, and destruction make good its part, that I may pay to each one according to his works and according to the fruit of his imaginings, as I judge between soul and body. And the world shall cease and death shall be extinguished, and the nether world shall close his mouth. And the earth will not be without birth, nor barren for those dwelling in it. And none shall be defiled once they have been justified in me. And there will be another earth and another heaven, and everlasting habitation."

(11) And the Lord again spoke to Noe and his sons: "Behold, I will make my covenant with you and with your seed after you, and I will not add again

to destroy the earth with the water of a flood. And everything which moves and lives shall be for you as food. Nevertheless flesh with the blood of life you shall not eat. For he who sheds the blood of man, at the hand of God his blood shall be shed, since God made man in his own image. But as for you, increase and multiply and fill the earth, as the multitude of fishes multiplying themselves in the waves."

VI:1–18

(1) Then those who had been divided, all the dwellers on earth, assembled after that and dwelt together. And they set forth from the East and found a plain in the land of Babylon, and, dwelling there, they said each to his neighbour: "See, it is going to come about that we shall be scattered, each from his own brother, and in the last days we will be fighting one against another. Now, therefore, come, and let us build for ourselves a tower, whose top shall reach to heaven, and we shall make for ourselves a name and a glory on earth."

(2) And they said each one to his neighbour: "Let us take bricks and write each of us our own names on the bricks and burn them with fire; and it will be that they will be thoroughly baked into clay and brick."

(3) So they took, each of them, their bricks, except for twelve men who refused to do so; and these are their names: Abraham, Nachor, Loth, Ruge, Tenute, Zaba, Armodat, Jobab, Esar, Abimahel, Saba, Ausin.

(4) And the people of the land seized them, and brought them to their rulers and said to them: "These are the men who have transgressed our plans and refuse to walk in our ways." So the leaders said to them: "Why have you refused to set out each one of you his brick with the people of the land?" Then they answered saying to them, "We do not set out bricks with you, nor do we join our intentions with yours. One God we know and him do we worship. Even if you set us in the fire with your bricks we will not consent to you."

(5) Then the angered leaders said, "As they have spoken so do to them: it shall be that unless they consent with you in setting forth bricks, you shall consume them in fire with your bricks."

(6) Then Jectan, who was the first ruler of the leaders, replied: "Not so; there shall be given them a space of seven days, and it shall be that if they turn away from their most evil decisions and are willing to set forth bricks with you, they shall live. But if not, they shall be burned according to your decision." But he sought how he might save them from the hands of the people, since he was of their tribe, and served God.

(7) With these words he took them and shut them up in the king's house. And when evening was come he ordered fifty men, mighty in courage, to be called to him, and said to them: "Go, and take those men tonight who are shut up in my house, and put provisions for them from my house on ten pack-animals, and bring those men to me; and take their provisions with the pack-animals to the mountains, and wait with them there. And understand that if anyone knows what I have said to you, I will burn you with fire."

(8) So the men went and did everything which their leader had commanded them. And they brought the men to his house by night, and taking their provisions they put them on pack-animals and led them to the mountains as he had ordered them.

(9) Then the ruler called those twelve men to himself and said to them:

"Be of good courage and fear not, for you are not going to die. For God is strong in whom you trust, and therefore be firm in him, who will set you free and save you. And now understand, I have given orders to fifty men to lead you out, with provisions taken from my house. Go to the mountains and hide yourselves in a valley, and I will give you fifty other men to lead you out thither. So go and hide yourselves there in the valley, having water to drink flowing down from the rock, and keep yourselves there for thirty days, until the hatred of the people of the land abates and until God sends his wrath upon them and shatters them. For I know that the plan of wickedness which they have plotted to do will not endure, since their thinking is empty. And it shall be, when seven days have passed and they look for you, that I shall say to them: 'The door of the prison, in which they were shut up, was broken, so they have gone out and have fled in the night, and I have sent a hundred men to look for them.' And I will turn them away from their present fury."

(10) Then eleven of the men replied to him saying, "Your servants have found favour in your eyes, because we have been set free from the hands of these proud men."

(11) But Abraham alone was silent, so the leader said to him: "Why do you not reply to me, Abraham, servant of God?" Abraham replied and said: "Suppose I flee today to the mountains: if I escape the fire, wild animals may emerge from the mountains and come and devour us, or our food may run out and we shall die of hunger; and we shall be found fleeing before the people of the earth and falling in our sins. And now, as he lives in whom I trust, I will not move from my place in which they have put me. And if there be any sin of mine so that I am utterly consumed [in the fire], God's will be done." Then the leader said to him: "Your blood be on your own head if you are unwilling to go with them. But if you are willing to go you will be free. So if you wish to stay, stay as you will." Then Abraham said, "I will not go, here I will stay."

(12) Then the leader took the eleven men and sent fifty others with them, and gave them orders saying, "Wait as well in the mountains for fifteen days with those fifty who have been sent on ahead, and when you come back, say, We did not find them, just as I have told the earlier men. And know that if anyone disobeys any of these words which I have spoken to you he shall be burned with fire." So when the men had gone, he took Abraham alone and shut him up where he had been imprisoned before.

(13) After seven days had gone by the people assembled and spoke to their leader saying, "Hand over to us the men who refused to join in our plans and we will burn them with fire." And they sent authorities to bring them, and they found none except Abraham. And the whole assembly said to their leaders, "The men whom you imprisoned have fled, eluding our intention."

(14) Then Fenech and Nembroth said to Jectan: "Where are the men whom you imprisioned?" He said: "They completely broke their bonds in the night. But I have sent a hundred men to look for them, not only shall they burn them with fire but they shall give their bodies to the birds of the air, and thus shall they destroy them."

(15) At that they said to him, "Then let us burn this one who was found." And they took Abraham, and led him to their leaders; and they said to him, "Where are those who were with you?" And he said, "I was sleeping soundly one night; when I woke I could not find them."

(16) So they took him and built a furnace and set it alight. And they put

bricks burnt with fire into the furnace. Then Jectan, stupefied, took Abraham and put him with the bricks in the fire of the furnace.

(17) But God caused a great earthquake, and the fire, leaping up from the furnace, burst into flames and sparks of flame, and it burnt up all those standing around in sight of the furnace. And all those who were burnt up in that day were 83,500. But on Abraham there was not any sign of hurt in the burning of the fire.

(18) So Abraham arose from the furnace and the fiery furnace fell down; and Abraham was saved, and he went to the eleven men who had hidden themselves in the mountains, and he told them everything that had happened to him. And they came down with him from the mountains rejoicing in the name of the Lord, and no one met them to terrify them that day. And they called that place by the name of Abraham, and in the Chaldaean language Deli, which means God.

Allegorical Interpretation of Scripture: Philo

Although there are allegorical passages in the rabbinic sources, it was Philo of Alexandria whose exposition of the Jewish scriptures was almost wholly allegorical in method. Philo's religious views were dominated by the hybrid philosophical views that prevailed in Alexandria: The metaphysical views were Platonic in origin; the views of the natural world as ruled by Reason were Stoic, as were the main ethical virtues. But the whole of his religious outlook and therefore of his allegorical method of interpretation was placed in a mystical-religious framework. In this way, for example, it was possible for Philo to equate the Ultimate Unity behind the manifold world of appearances with the One God affirmed in the Shema: "Hear, O Israel, Yahweh our God is one" (Deut. 6:4).

Philo of Alexandria: On the Cherubim

In the tractate here excerpted, Philo is explaining by his allegorical method the "real" significance of the biblical description of the ark of the covenant, the sacred box in which the stone tablets of the Mosaic Law were kept, and atop which were the winged sphinxes known as Cherubim. Understood literally, a pious Jew might have had difficulty in accepting the biblical condoning of representational art work, which conflicted with the prohibition against "graven images," but Philo saw in the Cherubim as prescribed in the Law of Moses profound philosophical and mystical meaning.

SEC. VII, VIII, AND IX PHILO OF ALEXANDRIA (ON THE CHERUBIM)

VII. We must now examine what is symbolized by (21) the Cherubim and the sword of flame which turns every way. I suggest that they are an allegorical figure of the revolution of the whole heaven. For the movements assigned to the heavenly spheres are of two opposite kinds, in the one case an unvarying course, embodying the principle of sameness, to the right, in the other a variable course, embodying the principle of otherness, to the left. The outermost (22) sphere, which contains what are called the fixed stars, is a single one and always makes the same revolution from east to west. But the inner spheres, seven in number, contain the planets and each has two motions of opposite nature, one voluntary, the other under a compelling force. Their involuntary motion is similar to that of the fixed stars, for we see them pass every day from east to west, but their own proper motion is from west to east, and it is in this that we find the revolutions of the seven governed also by certain lengths of time. (23) These lengths are the same in the case of three whose course is equal, and these three which have the same rate of speed are known as the Sun, the Morning-star, and the Sparkler [Mercury]. The others have unequal courses and different lengths of time in revolution, though these too preserve a definite proportion to each other and to the above-named three.

(24) One of the Cherubim then symbolizes the outermost sphere of the fixed stars. It is the final heaven of all, the vault in which the choir of those who wander not move in a truly divine unchanging rhythm, never leaving the post which the Father who begat them has appointed them in the universe. The other of the Cherubim is the inner contained sphere, which through a sixfold division He has made into seven zones of regular proportion and fitted each planet into one of them. He has set each star in its proper zone as a driver in a chariot, and yet He has in no case trusted the reins to the driver, fearing that their rule might be one of discord, but He has made them all dependent on Himself, holding that thus would their march be orderly and harmonious. For when God is with us all we do is worthy of praise; all that is done without Him merits blame.

VIII. This then is one interpretation of the (25) allegory of the Cherubim, and the flaming turning sword represents, we must suppose, their movement and the eternal revolution of the whole heaven. But perhaps on another interpretation the two Cherubim represent the two hemispheres. For we read that the Cherubim stand face to face with their wings inclining to the mercy-seat [Exod. 30:19]. And so, too, the hemispheres are opposite to each other and stretch out to the earth, the centre of all things, which actually parts them. And as this alone in all the universe stands firm, it has been rightly named by men of old the standing-place, and it stands thus, that the revolution of each of the hemispheres may circle round one fixed centre and thus be wholly harmonious. The flaming sword on this interpretation is the Sun, that packed mass of flame, which is the swiftest of all existing things and whirls round the whole universe in a single day.

IX. But there is a higher thought than these. It comes from a voice in my own soul, which oftentimes is God-possessed and divines where it does not know. This thought I will record in words if I can. The voice told me that while God is indeed one, His highest and chiefest powers are two, even goodness and sovereignty. Through His goodness He begat all that is, through His sovereignty He rules what He has begotten. And in the midst between the two there is a third which unites them, Reason, for it is through reason that God is both ruler and good. Of these two potencies, sovereignty and goodness, the Cherubim are symbols, and the fiery sword is the symbol of reason. For exceeding swift and of burning heat is reason and chiefly so the reason of the [Great] Cause, for it alone preceded and outran all things, conceived before them all, manifest above them all.

O then, my mind, admit the image unalloyed of the two Cherubim, that having learnt its clear lesson of the sovereignty and beneficence of the

> Cause, thou mayest reap the fruits of a happy lot. For straightway thou shalt understand how these unmixed potencies are mingled and united, how, where God is good, yet the glory of His sovereignty is seen amid the beneficence, how, where He is sovereign, through the sovereignty the beneficence still appears. Thus thou mayest gain the virtues begotten of these potencies, a cheerful courage and a reverent awe towards God. When things are well with thee, the majesty of the sovereign king will keep thee from high thoughts. When thou sufferest what thou wouldest not, thou wilt not despair of betterment, remembering the loving-kindness of the great and bountiful God. And for this cause is the sword a sword of flame, because in their company reason the measure of things must follow, reason with its fierce and burning heat, reason that ever moves with unswerving zeal, teaching thee to choose the good and eschew the evil.

Halakah and Haggadah

The process of expounding the scripture, and especially of appropriating its teachings for the profoundly changed situation of Jews living under Roman rule, was given the authority of alleged antiquity by the legend of the Oral Law, as we have noted. Exposition of scripture took the form of direct interpretation of legal precepts, which was called *halakah,* and attention to stories or themes more concerned with general moral truths, instructions about worship, or simply human interest, which is *haggadah.*

The Mishnah

Mishnah is the end product of a process that began formally and systematically in the late first century A.D., following the destruction of the Temple. The final form of Mishnah was achieved under Judah the Patriarch at the end of the second century. It has been characterized by Jacob Neusner as

> . . . a collection of exquisitely composed philosophical essays on various legal problems. Framed in carefully formalized and patterned sentences, put together within a nearly uniform set of literary conventions and redactional patterns, the Mishnah was established, from its time onward, as the principal source of Jewish law and mediator of the law of scripture. In form it is a construction in six divisions, themselves comprised of sixty-three tractates. All divisions take up the issue of the sanctification of Israel, the Jewish nation, through provisions of the laws of holiness as they touch these six successive dimensions of the national life: [the agricultural] economy, the divisions of time and season, the conduct of the life of the family, with special attention to women and their rights, the construction of the government and the conduct of civil law, the correct conduct of the service of God through the cult, and the protection of the life of the cult and the bed and the table of the ordinary Israelite from the contagions of uncleanness and for the possibility of sanctification.[43]

[43]Jacob Neusner, *Formative Judaism: Religious, Historical and Literary Studies,* Brown Judaic Studies 37 (Chico, Calif.: Scholars Press, 1982), p. 155.

The laws of scripture concerned with priestly food, sacrifices, and purification are now extended to the whole of the people and the land, including the family and the home. With the destruction of the temple and the dispersal of Israel, the laws are applicable everywhere. "If the people is to live, it must be as a holy people."[44] The oldest layer of the tradition incorporated in the Mishnah, which may go back to the pre-70 period, is concerned

> . . . to define and shape the ordinary lives of its adherents and to form a community expressive of its larger world-view. The foundations of an enduring community will then be laid down through rules governing what food may be eaten, under what circumstances, and with what sort of people; whom one may marry and what families may be joined in marriage; and how sexual relationships are timed. Indeed to the measure that these rules not only differ from those observed by others but in some aspect or other render the people who keep them unacceptable to those who do not, as much as, to the sect, those who do not keep them are unacceptable to those who do, the lines of difference and distinctive structure are all the more inviolable.[45]

It is as a challenge to precisely these kinds of regulations and to this boundary-drawing way of defining the convenant people that Jesus is portrayed in the first three gospels. Jesus's reinterpretation of the laws of clean and unclean, of table fellowship, and of sabbath observance put him into direct opposition with the Pharisees throughout this gospel tradition. The Pharisaic point of view (as preserved in the Mishnah, which reached its present form more than a century after Jesus's time) on one of these issues may be seen in the following excerpts:

> All utensils have outer parts and an inner part, and they further have a part by which they are held. [That is, a finger-hold sunk into the edge of the vessel, which does not become unclean if the outer part becomes unclean, and which, if unclean, does not produce uncleanness in the outer or inner part of the utensil.]
>
> R. Tarfon[46] says, "[This distinction in the outer parts applies only] to a large wooden trough."
>
> R. Aqiva[47] says, "To cups."
>
> R. Meir[48] says, "To the unclean and clean hands."
>
> Said R. Yosé,[49] "They have spoken only concerning clean hands alone." [He continues] "How so?"
>
> "[If] one's hands were clean, and the outer parts of the cup were unclean, and one took the cup with its holding part, he need not worry lest his hands be made unclean on the outer parts of the cup."

[44]Jacob Neusner, *Method and Meaning in Ancient Judaism,* Third series (Chico, Calif.: Scholars Press, 1981), pp. 20–24.

[45]Jacob Neusner, *Formative Judaism,* pp. 94–95.

[46]Pre-70 A.D.

[47]80–100 A.D.

[48]Around 150 A.D.

[49]Also around 150.

[If] one was drinking from a cup, the outer parts of which were unclean, one does not worry lest the liquid which is in his mouth be made unclean on the outer parts of the cup and go and render the [whole] cup unclean.

When one moves down to the fifth century A.D. discussions of the differences among the teachers whose opinions are recorded in the Mishnah, explanations are offered for the opinions of Hillel and Shammai (pre-70 A.D.)[50] on the issue of clean and unclean cups:

Mishnah: The House[51] of Shammai says, They wash the hands and afterwards mix the cup. And the house of Hillel says, They mix the cup first and afterwards wash the hands.

Gemara: What is the reason of the House of Shammai?

So that the liquids which are on the outer side of the cup may not be made unclean by his hands and go and make the cup unclean.

What is the reason of the House of Hillel? The outer side of the cup is always unclean [so there is no reason to protect it from the hand's uncleanness . . .]

Rabbi Biban in the name of Rabbi Yochanan said, "The opinion of the House of Shammai is in accord with Rabbi Yosé, and that of the House of Hillel with Rabbi Meir, as we have learned there. [See the previous excerpt.]

In all vessels an outer part and an inner part are distinguished, and also a part by which they are held.

Rabbi Meir says, "For the hands they are clean and unclean."

Rabbi Yosé said, "This applied to clean hands only."

Yosé and the House of Shammai agree that the outer part of the cup may be clean, as well as the holding place, even though the inner part is unclean, and the holding place may be clean even if the outer part is unclean. The Hillelites, on the other hand, assume the outside is always unclean, and are concerned rather about the cleanness of the hands and of the inside of the cup. If the inside is clean, then the cup as a whole may be regarded as clean. The condition of the outside is a neutral factor in the issue of cleanness. If the Shammaite view was dominant in the time of Jesus, with its careful distinctions between the state of cleanness of the inside and the outside of vessels, then the saying of Jesus preserved in two different forms (Mt. 23:25–26; Lk. 11:39–40) can be seen as a metaphor of moral cleanness built on a serious item of debate among Pharisees before A.D. 70.[52]

Other issues discussed in the Mishnah, which also appear in the gospel tradition, include divorce, personal purity (ritual cleanness), fasting, and

[50]That is, in the Gemara, which is part of the Palestinian Talmud.

[51]"House" was used in the Talmud to refer to the various rabbinic schools of interpretation, which competed for the claim of having the true view of the Law.

[52] The argument set forth here, and the quotations from the Mishnah, derive from a detailed assessment of the issue of cleansing the inside and the outside offered by Jacob Neusner in *New Testament Studies* 22 (1976), pp. 486–95.

For other translations and detailed analyses of the mishnaic material, see Jacob Neusner in the series, *Studies in Judaism in Late Antiquity* (Leiden: E.J. Brill), on the following: (1) On divorce, *A History of the Mishnaic Law of Women* (1980); (2) on purity, *A History of the Mishnaic Law of Purities* (1974); (3) on fasting, *A History of the Mishnaic Laws of Appointed Times,* Part Four (1982); (4) on sabbath, *A History of the Mishnaic Laws of Appointed Times,* Part One (1981).

abstinence from work on the sabbath. The relevant passages from the gospels are noted in the margins of the excerpts from the Mishnah. It must be borne in mind that this material is here presented in the form that it achieved by the end of the second century A.D. The extent to which it incorporates points of view that go back to the time of Jesus is difficult to determine, but the issues discussed in the Mishnah correlate with those debated in the gospels.

MISHNAH: ON DIVORCE (*GITTIN 1*)

This tractate details the specific circumstances under which a bill of divorce may be drawn up and is to be considered either binding or invalid.

7. Howbeit women that are not deemed trustworthy if they say, "Her
husband is dead," are deemed trustworthy when they bring her bill of divorce; namely, her mother-in-law, her mother-in-law's daughter, her co-
MK. wife, her husband's brother's wife, and her husband's daughter. Wherein
10:1–12 does [evidence of] divorce differ from [evidence of] a death? The written
document [in divorce] affords proof. The woman herself may bring her
own bill of divorce, save only that she must say, "It was written in my pres-
MT. ence and it was signed in my presence."
19:1–12 3. I. No bill of divorce is valid that is not written expressly for the
woman. Thus if a man was passing through the market and heard the scribes calling out, "Such a man is divorcing such a woman of such a place," and he said, "That is my name and that is the name of my wife," it is not a valid document wherewith to divorce his wife. Moreover, if he had drawn up a document wherewith to divorce his wife but he changed his mind, and a man of his city found him and said to him, "My name is like thy name and my wife's name like thy wife's name," it is not a valid document wherewith to divorce his wife; moreover if he had two wives and their names were alike and he had drawn up a document wherewith to divorce the elder, he may not therewith divorce the younger; moreover if he said to the scrivener, "Write it so that I may divorce therewith whom I will," it is not a valid document wherewith to divorce any one.

4. I. If a man sent a bill of divorce to his wife and then overtook the messenger or sent another messenger after him, and said to him, "The bill of divorce that I gave to thee is void," it thereby becomes void. If he reached his wife first or sent another messenger to her, and said to her, "The bill of divorce that I have sent to thee is void," it thereby becomes void. But [if he or the messenger reached her] after the bill of divorce came into her hand he can no more render it void.

2. Beforetime a man used to set up a court [of three] elsewhere and disannul it [before them]; but Rabban Gamaliel the Elder ordained that they should not do so, as a precaution for the general good. Beforetime a man used to change his name and her name, and the name of his city and the name of her city. Rabban Gamaliel the Elder ordained that [in the bill of divorce] there should be written, "Such-a-man" and all other names that he had, and "Such-a-woman" and all other names that she had, as a precaution for the general good.

ON CLEAN AND UNCLEAN (FROM *KELIM* 1)

The term *kelim*, though usually translated "vessels," means not only any kind of container but also any article used for some instrumental purpose, such as clothing, utensils, and other kinds of implements. At issue is the circumstances under which such objects are to be regarded as ritually unclean, and therefore unsuitable for use by the pious, who wished to eat their ordinary meals in a state of cultic cleanness, as if they were eating holy food in the Temple.

Kelim ("Vessels")

1. I. These Fathers of Uncleanness [namely] a [dead] creeping thing, male semen, he that has contracted uncleanness from a corpse, a leper in his days of reckoning, and Sin-offering water too little in quantity to be sprinkled, convey uncleanness to men and vessels by contact and to earthenware vessels by [presence within their] air-space; but they do not convey uncleanness by carrying.

MK. 2. They are exceeded by carrion and by Sin-offering water sufficient in
7:1–23 quantity to be sprinkled, for these convey uncleanness to him that carries them, so that he, too, conveys uncleanness to garments by contact but the garments do not become unclean by contact [alone].

3. They are exceeded by him that has connexion with a menstruant, for he conveys uncleanness to what lies beneath him in like degree as [he that has a flux conveys uncleanness] to what lies above him. They are exceeded by the issue of him that has a flux, by his spittle, his semen, and his urine, and by the blood of a menstruant, for they convey uncleanness both by contact and by carrying. They are exceeded by [the uncleanness of] what is ridden upon [by him that has a flux], for it conveys uncleanness even to what
MT. lies beneath a heavy stone. [The uncleanness of] what is ridden upon [by
9:18–26 him that has a flux] is exceeded by what he lies upon, since [the uncleanness caused by] contact with it is equal to [the uncleanness caused by] carrying it.
MK. [The uncleanness of] what he lies upon is exceeded by [the uncleanness of]
5:21–43 him that has a flux; for it is he that conveys uncleanness to what he lies upon, while what he lies upon does not convey the like uncleanness to that upon which it lies.

4. [The uncleanness of] the man that has a flux is exceeded by the uncleanness of the woman that has a flux, for she conveys uncleanness to him that has connexion with her. [The uncleanness of] the woman that has a flux is exceeded by [the uncleanness of] the leper, for he renders [a house] unclean by entering into it. [The uncleanness of] the leper is exceeded by [the uncleanness of] a barleycorn's bulk of bone [from a corpse], for it conveys seven-day uncleanness. These are all exceeded by [the uncleanness of] a corpse, for it conveys uncleanness by overshadowing, which uncleanness is conveyed by naught else.

* * *

6. There are ten degrees of holiness. The Land of Israel is holier than any other land. Wherein lies its holiness? In that from it they may bring the *Omer*, the Firstfruits, and the Two Loaves, which they may not bring from any other land.

7. The walled cities [of the Land of Israel] are still more holy, in that they must send forth the lepers from their midst; moreover they may carry around a corpse therein wheresoever they will, but once it is gone forth
MK. [from the city] they may not bring it back.
11:15– 8. Within the wall [of Jerusalem] is still more holy, for there [only] they
19 may eat the Lesser Holy Things and the Second Tithe. The Temple Mount is still more holy, for no man or woman that has a flux, no menstruant, and no woman after childbirth may enter therein. The Rampart is still more holy, for no gentiles and none that have contracted uncleanness from a corpse may enter therein.

ON FASTING (FROM *TAANITH* 2)

Here the questions under discussion are the days and the conditions under which the faithful must fast. All is coordinated with the cycle of holy days of the Jewish year. Chislev and Nisan are months in the Jewish calendar.

5. If the 1st of Chislev was come and no rain had fallen, the court enjoins on the congregation three days of fasting. They may eat and drink after nightfall, and they are permitted to work, to wash themselves, to anoint themselves, to put on sandals, and to have marital intercourse.

6. If these days passed by and their prayers were not answered, the court
MK. enjoins on the congregation three more days of fasting. They may eat and
2:18–22 drink [only] while it is yet day, and they are forbidden to work, to wash themselves, to anoint themselves, to put on sandals, or to have marital intercourse; and the bath-houses are shut up. If these days passed by and their prayers were not answered, the court enjoins on the congregation seven more [days of fasting]—thirteen days in all. These days surpass the first days, in that on these days they blow the *shofar* and close the shops. On Mondays they may partially open [the shops] when it grows dark, and on
MT. Thursdays they are permitted [to open the shops the whole day] because of
9:14–17 the honour due to the Sabbath.

7. If these days passed by and their prayers were not answered, they must give themselves but little to business, building or planting, betrothals or marriages, or greetings one to another, as becomes men that suffer God's displeasure. Single persons continue to fast until the end of Nisan. If Nisan ended and then the rain fell, it is a sign of [God's] curse, for it is written, *Is it not wheat harvest to-day? I will call unto the Lord that he send thunder and rain, and ye shall know and see that great is your wickedness which ye have wrought in the sight of God to ask for yourselves a king.*

* * *

6. On the first three days of fasting, the priests of the Course fasted but not the whole day; and they of the father's house did not fast at all. On the second three days, the priests of the Course fasted throughout the whole day, and they of the father's house fasted but not the whole day. But on the last seven days, both of them fasted throughout the whole day. So R. Joshua. But the Sages say: On the first three days of fasting neither fasted at all. On the second three days the priests of the Course fasted but not the whole day, and they of the father's house did not fast at all. On the last

seven days, the priests of the Course fasted throughout the whole day, and they of the father's house fasted but not the whole day.

7. The priests of the Course were permitted to drink wine during the night but not during the day, and they of the father's house neither during
MT. the night nor during the day. The priests of the Course and the men of the
6:16–18 *Maamad*[53] were forbidden to cut their hair or wash their clothes; but on a
Thursday it was permitted because of the honour due to the Sabbath.

8. Any day whereof it is written in the Scroll of Fasting that "None may mourn," it is [also] forbidden to mourn [the day] before; but it is permitted the following day. R. Jose says: It is forbidden both the day before and the following day. [Where it is written,] "None may fast," it is permitted [to fast] both the day before and the following day. R. Jose says: It is forbidden the day before but permitted the following day.

9. They may not decree a public fast beginning with a Thursday lest they disturb [market] prices, but they appoint the first three days of fasting for a Monday and the following Thursday and Monday; but they may appoint the second three days of fasting for a Thursday and the following Monday and Thursday. R. Jose says: Like as the first [three days of fasting] may not begin on a Thursday so the second [three] and the last [seven] may not begin on a Thursday.

ON SABBATH (FROM *SHABBATH*)

This constitutes a detailed analysis of the prohibition of work on the Sabbath, including the list of human activities which are to be considered work.

7. 1. A great general rule have they laid down concerning the Sabbath: whosoever, forgetful of the principle of the Sabbath, committed many acts of work on many Sabbaths, is liable only to one Sin-offering; but if, mindful of the principle of the Sabbath, he yet committed many acts of work on many Sabbaths, he is liable for every Sabbath [which he profaned]. If he knew that it was the Sabbath and he yet committed many acts of work on many Sabbaths, he is liable for every main class of work [which he performed]; if he committed many acts of work of one main class, he is liable only to one Sin-offering.

2. The main classes of work are forty save one: sowing, ploughing, reap-
MK. ing, binding sheaves, threshing, winnowing, cleansing crops, grinding, sift-
2:23–28 ing, kneading, baking, shearing wool, washing or beating or dyeing it, spinning, weaving, making two loops, weaving two threads, separating two threads, tying [a knot], loosening [a knot], sewing two stitches, tearing in order to sew two stitches, hunting a gazelle, slaughtering or flaying or salt-
MK. ing it or curing its skin, scraping it or cutting it up, writing two letters, eras-
3:1–6 ing in order to write two letters, building, pulling down, putting out a fire,
lighting a fire, striking with a hammer and taking out aught from one domain into another. These are the main classes of work: forty save one.

3. Another general rule have they laid down: whatsoever it is proper to keep stored and is in such quantity as it is usual to keep stored, and a man takes it out on the Sabbath, he is liable thereby to a Sin-offering. But what-

[53]The members of the priestly families were apportioned certain periods of time during which each must serve in the Temple. Their terms were referred to as "courses."

soever it is not proper to keep stored or that is not in such quantity as it is usual to keep stored, and a man takes it out on the Sabbath, he only is culpable that [usually] keeps [the like of] its stored.

4. [He is culpable] that takes out straw equal to a cow's mouthful, or pea-stalks equal to a camel's mouthful, or ears of grain equal to a lamb's mouthful, or grass equal to a kid's mouthful, or a dried fig's bulk of fresh garlic or onion-leaves, or, if dry, a kid's mouthful [thereof]; and these may not be included together [to make up the forbidden quantity] since their prescribed measures are not equal. But if a man takes out even a dried fig's bulk of foodstuff he is culpable, and they can be included together [to make up the forbidden quantity] since their prescribed measures are equal, excepting their husks, kernels, and stalks, and coarse or fine bran. R. Judah says: Excepting the husks of lentils which are cooked together with them.

The Passover Haggadah

Another kind of midrash composition is the Passover Haggadah, which moves through the biblical texts phrase by phrase, explaining how they are now to be carried out. Preparations for the first night of Passover include the placing on a table of three plates: In one are three matzoth, or loaves of unleavened bread; in the second are a lamb bone, an egg, some parsley, and a mixture of nuts, fruit, and wine; in the third is some vinegar or salt water. The ceremony is celebrated in the private home, not in the synagogue. Following are selections from the liturgy, which begins with praise to God for his holiness and his favor to Israel, his covenant people:

Praised be You, Eternal our God, Ruler of the world, Who selected us from among all people and exalted us among all nations, by making us holy through the commandments. Out of love You gave us the festivals for happiness, holidays and seasons for rejoicing, as this day, the season of our freedom, which is a holy assembly, in remembrance of the going out of Egypt.

Praised be you, Eternal our God, Ruler of the world, who makes a distinction between the holy and the profane, between the light and darkness, between Israel and other people, between the seventh day and the six days of work. You have distinguished and made holy your people Israel with your holiness. Praised be You, Eternal our God, Ruler of the world, who has given us life and sustenance and brought us to this happy season.

Then follows the ceremonial washing of the hands, the dipping of some parsley into the salt water, and the distribution of it to all participants. Then a matzo is broken; half of it is put aside until the end of the ceremony.

Behold this bread! It is like the bread which our forefathers ate in the land of Egypt. All who are hungry—let them come and eat. All who are needy—let them come and celebrate with us the Passover. Now we are here, next year may we be in the land of Israel. Now we are slaves, next year may we be free men.

Why is this night different from all other nights?

1) On all other nights we eat either leavened or unleavened bread; on this night why only unleavened bread?

2) On all other nights we eat herbs of any kind; on this night why only bitter herbs?

3) On all other nights we do not dip our herbs even once; on this night why do we dip them twice?

4) On all other nights we eat either sitting upright or leaning; on this night why do we eat in a leaning position?

Then the unleavened bread is uncovered and the answers are recited.

We were slaves in Egypt; the Eternal our God brought us out from there with a strong hand and an outstretched arm. Now, if God had not brought out our forefathers from Egypt, then even we, our children, and our children's children might still have been enslaved to Pharaoh in Egypt. Therefore, even were we all wise, all men of understanding, and even if we were all old and learned in the Torah; it would still be our duty to tell the story of the Departure from Egypt. So the more one tells of the Departure from Egypt, the more is he to be praised.

The liturgy then goes on to explain why the ceremony is performed on this date, and what were the events that shaped the destiny of Israel, beginning with God's call of Abraham out of Mesopotamia into the land of Canaan, and culminating in the migration of the sons of Jacob into Egypt, where they became enslaved. The account then shifts to an extended explanation of Deut. 26:5–8, which is a summary of Israel's history:

DEUT. A Syrian sought to destroy my father [Jacob], and he went down to
26:5 Egypt and dwelled there, a handful, few in number. There he became a
great nation, mighty and numerous.

He went down to Egypt—Why did he go down to Egypt? He was compelled by God's decree.

He dwelled there. This means that Jacob our father did not go down to
GEN. Egypt to settle there but only to stay for a short while; for it is said, "And
47:4 they said to Pharaoh, we have come to dwell in the land because there is no
pasture for the flocks of your servants, since the famine is very bad in the
land of Canaan, and now let your servants live in the land of Goshen."

Few in number—as it is said: "Your forefathers went down into Egypt with
DEUT. seventy persons." Now the Eternal your God has made you as numerous as
10:22 the stars in heaven.

And there he became a nation, teaching us that Israel became a distinct nation in Egypt.

Great and mighty—as it is said: "And the children of Israel were fruitful
EXOD. and increased and multiplied and became very strong and numerous, so
1:7 that the land was full of them."

And numerous—as it is said: "I have increased you as the growth of the
field and you have become numerous and grown big and reached to excel-
EZEK. lence in beauty. Your breasts are fashioned, your hair full grown, yet you
16:7 remain bare and naked."
And the Egyptians did evil unto us. It is said in the Bible, "Come, let us deal
EXOD. craftily with them, lest they increase yet more, and it may be that when war
1:10 occurs they will be added to our enemies, fight against us and go up out of
the land."
And he made us suffer, as the Bible relates, "So the Egyptians set taskmas-
EXOD. ters over them in order to oppress them with their burdens; and they built
1:11 Pithom and Raamses as store cities for Pharaoh."
And they set upon us hard work—as the Bible declares: "And Egypt made
EXOD. the children of Israel serve with rigor."
1:13 *So we cried unto the Eternal, the God of our fathers*—as the Bible recounts,
DEUT. "And it came to pass in the course of those many days that the King of
26:7 Egypt died, and the children of Israel moaned because of their servitude
EXOD. and cried out, and their outcry from their servitude came up to God."
2:23 *And the Eternal heard our voice*—as the Bible tells, "And God heard our
EXOD. groaning, for God remembered His covenant with Abraham, with Isaac and
2:24 with Jacob."
And he saw our affliction—this phrase suggests the enforced separation of
EXOD. husband and wife under Pharaoh's persecution. "And God saw the children
2:25 of Israel and God took knowledge of them."
EXOD. *And our burden*—this recalls the drowning of the male children, as it is
1:22 said, "And Pharaoh charged all his people saying, 'Every son that is born
you shall cast into the Nile, though every daughter you may keep alive.' "
And our oppression—this refers to crushing our life, as the Bible says,
EXOD. "And now, behold, the outcry of the children of Israel has come unto me,
3:9 and I also have seen the oppression with which the Egyptians are oppressing them."
And the Eternal brought us forth from Egypt, not by a ministering angel, not
DEUT. by a fiery angel, not by a messenger, but by Himself, in His glory, the Holy
26:8 One, blessed be He, as the Bible records: "And I will pass through the land
of Egypt on that night, and I will smite all the first-born in the land of Egypt
from man to beast, and against all the gods of Egypt I will execute judgments. It is I, the Eternal."
EXOD. *And I will pass through the land of Egypt on that night*—I and not a minister-
12:12 ing angel, and I will smite the first-born in the land of Egypt—I and not a
fiery angel; and against all the gods of Egypt I will execute judgments—I
and not a messenger; it is I the Eternal—I and no other.
EXOD. *With a strong hand*—this phrase refers to the cattle plague as it is said in
9:3 the Bible, "Behold the hand of the Eternal will be against the cattle that is
in the field, against the horses, the asses, the camels, the herds, and the
flocks, a very grievous cattle plague."
And with outstretched arm—refers to the sword, just as the Bible states,
I CHRON. "His sword unsheathed in his hand, outstretched against Jerusalem."
21:16 *And with great revelation*—this is the revelation of the Spirit of God to Israel, as it is said, "Or has God adventured to come to draw a nation for
Himself, out of another nation, with trials, with signs and with portents, and
DEUT. with battle, and with a strong hand and outstretched arm, and with great
4:34 revelations, as all that the Eternal your God did for you in Egypt before
your eyes?"
EXOD. *And signs*—this is the rod of Moses, as it is said, "And thou, Moses, shalt
4:17 take in thy hand this rod wherewith thou shalt do the signs."

JOEL 2:30–31 *And wonders*—this refers to the plague of blood, as is suggested by the verse of the prophet Joel, "I will put portents in heaven and on earth."

There follows at this point a ceremonial pouring out of ten drops of blood, symbolizing each of the ten plagues that God brought on the Egyptians in order to force the release of the Israelites. The lamb bone represents the Passover lamb offered by Israel in Egypt to protect its members from the Death Angel that passed over the land, destroying all the non-Israelite first-born sons. The unleavened bread reminds them of the hasty departure of Israel from Egypt, and the bitter herbs recall the lives of the Israelites, embittered by hard labor. Perhaps the high point of the liturgy comes in the expression of gratitude to God:

> How thankful we must be to God, the All Present, for all the good He did for us:
>
> That He brought us out from Egypt, and executed judgments.
> He did justice to their idols, and slew their first-born.
> He gave us their treasures, and divided for us the sea.
> He brought us through it dry-shod, and drowned our oppressors in it.
> He helped us for forty years in the desert, and fed us manna.
> He gave us the Sabbath, and brought us to Mount Sinai.
> He gave us the Torah, and brought us into the land of Israel.
> He built for us the Holy Temple, to forgive us our sins.
>
> Therefore it is our happy duty to thank and to praise in song and prayer, glorify, and extol Him who wrought all these wonders for our forefathers and for us. He brought us out of slavery to freedom, from anguish to joy, from sorrow to festivity, from darkness to great light. Let us therefore sing before Him a new song:
>
> Praise ye the Eternal.

The Synagogue

This word, which is a transliteration from the Greek, was used to translate the Aramaic word *keneseth,* which means "gathering" or "assembly." Originally, the term referred to the people gathered. Only much later—perhaps late in the first century A.D.—did it come to be used of the special structure where the gathering took place. The early "synagogues" took place in private homes and in public halls, with the aim of prayer and instruction in the scriptures. Another Greek word used for these gatherings was *proseuchē,* which means literally "prayer," but which also came to mean "a place where the faithful gather to pray." An example of this use of the latter term may be found in Acts 16:13, where there is a place of prayer outside the city where Jewish women gather to pray. There is no evidence in either literary or architectural remains of special buildings constructed or arranged for formal worship prior to the last quarter of the first century. Even these post-70 A.D. sites have none of the distinctive features that are to be seen in later synagogues, such as a pulpit or a shrine in which the Books of the Law were kept. Just as *ekklēsia* (church) was originally the assembled community and only later became the building dedicated for that purpose, so the synagogue became an identifiable structure only in the second and third centuries.[54] This development was apparently concurrent with the development of the rabbinic practices of prayers, reading, and exposition of scripture, and more formal patterns of instruction. The same impression is provided by the evidence of the "gatherings" of Jews reported by Philo as occurring in Alexandria. Since the Temple in Jerusalem was the divinely appointed place where Israel worshipped her God, there seems to have been no provision for worship elsewhere. Even at Qumran, where the Dead Sea community gathered, there is evidence of an assembly room where the scriptures were read and where common meals were shared, but no trace of a worship center resembling the formal synagogue structures of the third and fourth centuries.

In recent decades several buildings have been excavated in Israel and the occupied territories that may have been used for synagogal gatherings. One of these is a rectangular theater at Masada, which was apparently pressed into service by the Zealots who occupied it as a stronghold against the Romans in the period immediately following the fall of Jerusalem in A.D. 70. Similarly, an audience hall or theater at Herodium (a hilltop fortress-palace east of Jerusalem) was made to serve as a gathering place for Jewish worshippers at about the same time. An earlier structure of similar shape, dating from around the time of the birth of Jesus, has been found at Gamla, on the Syrian heights north of the Sea of Galilee. None of the distinctive features of the later Palestinian synagogues is present in the remains of any of these gathering places: There is no trace of a Torah shrine, nor are there the mosaic pavements, which regularly picture such unmistakably Jewish features as the menorah (a seven-branched lampstand) and the shrine in which the scriptures were kept. The probability is that—if these were indeed synagogues—they were merely adapted from large rectangular rooms with benches along the sides and a central platform from which a lecturer could be heard.

The negative evidence fits well with the picture that emerges when the Mishnah and Talmud are carefully analyzed: Both the formal process of interpretation of the law and the formal meeting place where the exposition and instruction took place were later developments in the period following the destruction of the Temple and the designation by the Romans of the Pharisees as the official group to organize the Jewish religion.

[54]A possible exception is the Theodotos synagogue in Jerusalem, the inscription from which has long been known (see p. 204). The date usually assigned to this inscription is A.D. 70, but it is almost certainly of a later time. Since it was not found in connection with datable archaeological evidence, it is a precarious base on which to build a theory of a developed synagogue tradition in the pre-70 period.

Mosaic Pavements from the Synagogue at Beth Alpha. Unlike the earlier synagogue gatherings, which seem to have taken place in private homes or in public meeting halls, by the third century synagogues had developed distinctive architectural and decorative features, which borrowed heavily from Greco-Roman art. Although later Jewish interpretation of the commandment against "graven images" was understood to prohibit representational art, this was obviously not the case in these early synagogues. The scene above depicts Abraham's offering of Isaac, which is recounted in Genesis 22. On the left is the central floor panel of the synagogue, in which are the signs of the zodiac, representations of the four seasons in the corners, and the God of Israel portrayed as Helios, driving the four-horse sun chariot in the center. *(Courtesy of the Oxford University Press)*

Surprisingly, the synagogues of the third and subsequent centuries were elaborately decorated with mural paintings (as at Dura Europos) and with other representational art on the mosaic pavements. The distinctive decorative features included the twelve signs of the zodiac, and Yahweh depicted as the sun god, driving the sun chariot, in the center of the floor.

In all probability, the very term *synagogue* originally meant simply a gathering of pious Jews for prayer and study of the scriptures. Later, it came to designate the meeting place as well. Since one of the major themes of the Pharisees was to apply to themselves in their own homes the provisions for worship and ritual purity linked with the temple by the biblical writers, the transfer of these procedures and obligations to informal gatherings of the faithful was simple. Only when the temple was gone and the synagogue developed as an institution central to Jewish identity did the characteristic features of those structures begin to emerge. In the first century A.D., however, synagogues (which means literally *coming together*) probably took place in private homes or in public halls, as Paul is reported to have assembled the Christians in Ephesus (Acts 19:9). Among the earliest literary evidence for preaching in synagogues are the gospel narratives of Jesus's activities in Nazareth and elsewhere (Lk. 4:16; Mk. 1:39, 6:2). The term here almost certainly means the gatherings themselves, rather than a special structure dedicated to that purpose, as came to be the practice later on.

Throne Mysticism: The Angelic Liturgy

Among the fragmentary documents from Qumran, of great importance is the Angelic Liturgy, which describes how the chief angels ("princes") carry on the worship of God ("the God of gods"). In a second section, the document describes the honoring of God offered by the Cherubim to Him as he is seated on his chariot-throne. The most detailed account of God on a wheeled throne is found in Ezek. 1:4–28. But the concept of God's presence as symbolized by the chariot (Merkavah) was to become significant in Jewish mysticism. The basic pattern of this mystical approach to God was that certain faithful persons were privileged to ascend to the highest heaven where God was seated on his chariot-throne. The result of this experience was to give reassurance to those enduring suffering and a promise of ultimate vindication. It is probably this type of mystical transport that lies behind the gospel story of Jesus's transfiguration (Mk. 9:2–8), and behind Paul's reassuring vision in II Cor. 12: 1–10.

> He shall bless all the perfect of way
>   with seven marvellous words
>   that they may stand with them that live for [ever].
> He shall bless all who wait for Him
>   with seven marvellous words
>   that they may obtain the return
>   of the [grace] of His favours.
> In the name of His holiness,
>   the seventh sovereign Prince shall bless
>   with seven words of His marvellous holiness
>   all the holy founders [of knowledge.
> He shall bless] all who exalt His Statutes
>   with seven marvellous words
>   that they may be for them stout shields.
> He shall bless all the [companions] of righteousness
>   who endlessly [praise] His glorious kingship
>   with seven [marvellous words]
>   (that they may obtain) everlasting peace.
> In the name of . . .
>   all the [sovereign] Princes [shall bless] the God of gods
>   . . .

The Divine Throne-Chariot

. . . the [ministers] of the Glorious Face in the abode of [the gods] of knowledge fall down before Him, [and the Cheru]-bim utter blessings. And as they rise up, there is a divine small voice . . . and loud praise; (there is) a divine [small] voice as they fold their wings.

The Cherubim bless the image of the Throne-Chariot above the firmament, and they praise the [majesty] of the fiery firmament beneath the seat of His glory. And between the turning wheels, Angels of Holiness come and go, as it were a fiery vision of most holy spirits; and about them (flow) seeming rivulets of fire, like gleaming bronze, a radiance of many gorgeous colours, of marvellous pigments magnificently mingled.

The spirits of the Living God move perpetually with the glory of the wonderful Chariot. The small voice of blessing accompanies the tumult as they depart, and on the path of their return they worship the Holy One. Ascending, they rise marvellously; settling, they [stay] still. The sound of joyful praise is silenced and there is a small voice of blessing in all the camp of God. And a voice of praise [resounds] from the midst of all their divisions in [worship of] . . . and each one in his place, all their numbered ones sing hymns of praise.

Scriptures for the Diaspora: Letter of Aristeas

A novelistic and apologetic account of the circumstances and process by which the Hebrew Bible was translated into Greek—with some significant supplements—is the Letter of Aristeas. It purports to have been written by an Egyptian courtier, Aristeas, during the reign of Ptolemy Philadelphus (285–247 B.C.). But the historical anachronisms, including references to the Hebrew writings as scripture—a term that did not come into use until centuries afterward—betray the letters as pseudonymous and as coming from centuries after the time of Philadelphus. Their aim is to foster social respect and political freedom for Jews living in the lands of the Dispersion, and to invite intellectual respect for the Jewish sacred books. Of great interest to the modern reader is the attempt of the author to provide rational explanations for the dietary and other laws that Jews must have had difficulty in justifying to their Gentile associates. The letters incorporate older material, but probably gained their present form in the early part of the first century A.D.

The first excerpt is an account given to Aristeas's brother, Philocrates, of the journey to Jerusalem undertaken to secure permission from the High Priest, Eleazar, for the translation project. The second demonstrates Aristeas's piety and his shrewdness in persuading the king to free the Jewish slaves while he is favorably disposed toward Judaism during the negotiations about the translation of the Law. It is the third excerpt that offers rational explanations for the dietary laws. The fourth, regarding a favorite setting of ancient writers—a royal banquet—provides the translators an opportunity to show their wisdom, and the final excerpt serves as a testimony to the divine nature of the Jewish Law and as a warning to those who might want to tamper with it.

SECTIONS 3–11

(3) It was my devotion to the pursuit of religious knowledge that led me to undertake the embassy to the man[55] I have mentioned, who was held in the highest esteem by his own citizens and by others both for his virtue and his majesty and who had in his possession *documents of* the highest value to the Jews in his own country and in foreign lands for the interpretation of the divine law, for their (4) laws are written on leather parchments in Jewish characters. This *embassy* then I undertook with enthusiasm, having first of all found an opportunity *of pleading* with the king[56] on behalf of the Jewish captives who had been transported from Judea to Egypt by the king's father, when he first obtained possession of this city and conquered (5) the land of Egypt. It is worthwhile that I should tell you this story, too, since I am convinced that you, with your disposition towards holiness and your sympathy with men who are living in accordance with the holy law, will all the more readily listen to the account which I propose to set forth, since you yourself have lately come to us from the island and are anxious to hear everything that (6) tends to build up the soul. On a former occasion, too, I sent you a record of the facts which I thought worth relating about the Jewish race—the record which I had obtained from the most learned high (7) priests of the most learned land of Egypt. As you are so eager to acquire the knowledge of those things which can benefit the mind, I feel it incumbent upon me to impart to you *all the information in my power. I should feel the same duty* towards all who possessed the same disposition but I feel it especially towards you since you have aspirations which are so noble, and since you are not only my brother in character no less than in blood but are one with me as (8) well in the pursuit of goodness. For neither the pleasure derived from gold nor any other of the possessions which are prized by shallow minds confers the same benefit as the pursuit of culture and the study which we expend in securing it. But that I may not weary you by a too lengthy introduction, I will proceed at once to the substance of my narrative. (9) Demetrius of Phalerum,[57] the president of the king's library, received vast sums of money, for the purpose of collecting together, as far as he possibly could, all the books in the world. By means of purchase and transcription, he carried out, to the best of his ability, the purpose of the king. On one occasion when I was present he was asked, "How many thousand books are there *in the library?*" (10) and he replied, "More than two hundred thousand, O king, and I shall make endeavour in the immediate future *to gather together* the remainder also, so that the total of five hundred thousand may be reached. I am told that the laws of the Jews are worth transcribing and deserve (11) a place in your library." "What is to prevent you from doing this?" replied the king. "Everything that is necessary has been placed at your disposal." "They need to be translated," answered Demetrius, "for in the country of the Jews they use a peculiar alphabet (just as

[55]Eleazar, the High Priest in Jerusalem.

[56]Ptolemy II Philadelphus.

[57]An Athenian politician and philosopher of the peripatetic school, who fled to Egypt when he and his clique were driven out of power in Athens. He is credited with having supplied the ruler of Egypt, Ptolemy Lagus, with the idea of the great library of Alexandria.

the Egyptians, too, have a special form of letters) and speak a peculiar dialect. They are supposed to use the Syriac tongue, but this is not the case; their language is quite different." And the king when he understood all the facts of the case ordered a letter to be written to the Jewish High Priest that his purpose (which has already been described) might be accomplished.

SECTIONS 14–20

(14) . . . Having, as has already been stated, obtained an opportunity for securing their emancipation, I addressed the king with the following arguments. "Let us not be so unreasonable as to allow our (15) deeds to give the lie to our words. Since the law which we wish not only to transcribe but also to translate belongs to the whole Jewish race, what justification shall we be able to find for our embassy while such vast numbers of them remain in a state of slavery in your kingdom? In the perfection and wealth of your clemency release those who are held in such miserable bondage, since as I have been at pains to discover, the God who gave them their law is the God who maintains your kingdom. They worship the same God—the Lord and Creator of the Universe, as all other men, as we ourselves, O king, though we call him by different names, such as Zeus or Dis. (16) This name was very appropriately bestowed upon him by our first ancestors, in order to signify that He through whom all things are endowed with life and come into being, is necessarily the ruler and lord of the universe. Set all mankind an example of magnanimity by releasing those who are held in bondage."

(17) After a brief interval, while I was offering up an earnest prayer to God that He would so dispose the mind of the king that all the captives might be set at liberty—(18) for the human race, being the creation of God, is swayed and influenced by Him. Therefore with many divers prayers I called upon Him who ruleth the heart that *the king* might be constrained to grant my request. For I had great hopes with regard to the salvation of the men since I was assured that God would grant a fulfillment of my prayer. For when men from pure motives plan some action in the interest of righteousness and the performance of noble deeds, Almighty God brings their efforts and purposes to a successful issue—*the king* raised his head and looking up at me with a cheerful countenance asked, "How many thousands do you think they will number?" Andreas, who was standing (19) near, replied, "A little more than a hundred thousand." "It is a small boon indeed," said the king, "that Aristeas asks of us!" Then Sosibius and some others who were present said, "Yes, but it will be a fit tribute to your magnanimity for you to offer the enfranchisement of these men as an act of devotion to the supreme God. You have been greatly honoured by Almighty God and exalted above all your forefathers in glory and it is only fitting that you should render to Him the greatest thankoffering in your power." Extremely (20) pleased *with these arguments* he gave orders that an addition should be made to the wages *of the soldiers by the amount of the redemption money,* that twenty drachmae should be paid *to the owners* for every slave, that a public order should be issued and that registers of the captives should be attached to it. He showed the greatest enthusiasm in the business, for it was God who had brought our purpose to fulfilment in its entirety and constrained him to redeem not only those who had come into Egypt with the army of his father but any who had come before that time or had been subsequently brought into the kingdom. It was pointed out to him that the ransom money would exceed four hundred talents.

SECTIONS 139–151

(139) Now our Lawgiver[58] being a wise man and specially endowed by God to understand all things, took a comprehensive view of each particular detail, and fenced us round with impregnable ramparts and walls of iron, that we might not mingle at all with any of the other nations, but remain pure in body and soul, free from all vain imaginations, worshipping the one Almighty God above the whole creation. (140) Hence the leading Egyptian priests having looked carefully into many such matters, and being cognizant with [our] affairs, call us "men of God." This is a title which does not belong to the rest of mankind but only to those who worship the true God. The rest are *not of God* but of meats and drink and clothing. For their whole (141) disposition leads them to find solace in these things. Among our people such things are reckoned of no account, but throughout their (142) whole life their main consideration is the sovereignty of God. Therefore lest we should be corrupted by any abomination, or our lives be perverted by evil communications, he hedged us round on all sides by rules of purity, affecting alike what we eat, or drink, or touch, (143) or hear, or see. For though, speaking generally, all things are alike in their natural constitution, since they are all governed by one and the same power, yet there is a deep reason in each individual case why we abstain from the use of certain things and enjoy the common use of others. For the sake of illustration I will run over (144) one or two points and explain them to you. For you must not fall into the degrading idea that it was out of regard to mice and weasels and other such things that Moses drew up his laws with such exceeding care. All these ordinances were made for the sake of righteousness (145) to aid the quest for virtue and the perfecting of character. For all the birds that we use are tame and distinguished by their cleanliness, feeding on various kinds of grain and pulse, such as for instance pigeons, turtle-doves, locusts, partridges, geese also, (146) and all other birds of this class. But the birds which are forbidden you will find to be wild and carnivorous, tyrannising over the others by the strength which they possess, and cruelly obtaining food by (147) preying on the tame birds enumerated above. And not only so, but they seize lambs and kids, and injure human beings too, whether dead or alive, and so by naming them unclean, he gave a sign by means of them that those, for whom the legislation was ordained, must practise righteousness in their hearts and not tyrannise over any one in reliance upon their own strength nor rob them of anything, but steer their course of life in accordance with justice, just as the tame birds, already mentioned, consume the different kinds of pulse that grow upon the earth and do not tyrannise to the destruction of their (148) own kindred. Our legislator taught us therefore that it is by such methods as these that indications are given to the wise, that they must be just and effect nothing by violence, and refrain from tyrannising (149) over others in reliance upon their own strength. For since it is *considered* unseemly even to touch such *unclean* animals, as have been mentioned, on account of their particular habits, ought we not to take every precaution lest our own characters should be (150) destroyed to the same extent? Wherefore all the rules which he has laid down with regard to what is permitted in the case of these *birds* and other animals, he has enacted with the object of teaching us a moral lesson. For the division of the hoof and

[58]Moses, to whom was attributed the whole of the Pentateuch (the first five books of the Jewish Bible), including even the account of his own death.

the separation of the claws are intended to teach us that we must discriminate between our individual actions with a view to the practice of (151) virtue. For the strength of our whole body and its activity depend upon our shoulders and limbs. Therefore he compels us to recognise that we must perform all our actions with discrimination according to the standard of righteousness—more especially because we have been distinctly separated from the rest of mankind.

SECTIONS 277–292

(277) The king loudly applauded the answer and asked another, "Why is it that the majority of men never become virtuous?" "Because," he replied, "all men are by nature intemperate and inclined to pleasure.
(278) Hence, injustice springs up and a flood of avarice. The habit of virtue is a hindrance to those who are devoted to a life of pleasure because it enjoins upon them the preference of temperance and righteousness. For it is God who is the master of these things."

(279) The king said that he had answered well, and asked, "What ought kings to obey?" And he said, "The laws, in order that by righteous enactments they may restore the lives of men. Even as you by such conduct in obedience to the Divine command have laid up in store for yourself a perpetual memorial."
(280) The king said that this man, too, had spoken well, and asked the next, "Whom ought we to appoint as governors?" And he replied, "All who hate wickedness, and imitating your own conduct act righteously that they may maintain a good reputation constantly. For this is what you do, O mighty King," he said, "and it is God who has bestowed upon you the crown of righteousness."
(281) The king loudly acclaimed the answer and then looking at the next man said, "Whom ought we to appoint as officers over the forces?" And he explained. "Those who excel in courage and righteousness and those who are more anxious about the safety of their men than to gain a victory by risking their lives through rashness. For as God acts well towards all men, so too you in imitation of Him are the benefactor of all your subjects."

(282) The king said that he had given a good answer and asked another, "What man is worthy of admiration?" And he replied, "The man who is furnished with reputation and wealth and power and possesses a soul equal to it all. You yourself show by your actions that you are most worthy of admiration through the help of God who makes you care for these things."

(283) The king expressed his approval and said to another "To what affairs ought kings to devote most time?" And he replied, "To reading and the study of the records of official journeys, which are written in reference to the *various* kingdoms, with a view to the reformation and preservation of the subjects. And it is by such activity that you have attained to a glory which has never been approached by others, through the help of God who fulfills all your desires."

(284) The king spoke enthusiastically to the man and asked another, "How ought a man to occupy himself during his hours of relaxation and recreation?" And he replied, "To watch those plays which can be acted with propriety and to set before one's eyes scenes taken from life and enacted with dignity and decency is profitable and
(285) appropriate. For there is some edification to be found even in these amusements, for often some desirable lesson is taught by the most insignif-

icant affairs of life. But by practising the utmost propriety in all your actions, you have shown that you are a philosopher and you are honoured by God on account of your virtue."

(286) The king, pleased with the words which had just been spoken, said to the ninth man, "How ought a man to conduct himself at banquets?" And he replied, "You should summon to your side men of learning and those who are able to give you useful hints with regard to the affairs of your kingdom and the lives of your subjects (for you could not find any theme more suitable or more educative than this)
(287) since such men are dear to God because they have trained their minds to contemplate the noblest themes—as you indeed are doing yourself, since all your actions are directed by God."

(288) Delighted with the reply, the king inquired of the next man, "What is best for the people? That a private citizen should be made king over them or a member of the royal family?" And he replied,
(289) "He who is best by nature. For kings who come of royal lineage are often harsh and severe towards their subjects. And still more is this the case with some of those who have risen from the ranks of private citizens, who after having experienced evil and borne their share of poverty, when they rule over multitudes turn out to be
(290) more cruel than the godless tyrants. But, as I have said, a good nature which has been properly trained is capable of ruling, and you are a great king, not so much because you excel in the glory of your rule and your wealth but rather because you have surpassed all men in clemency and philanthropy, thanks to God who has endowed you with these qualities."

(291) The king spent some time in praising this man and then asked the last of all, "What is the greatest achievement in ruling an empire?" And he replied, "That the subjects should continually dwell in a state of peace, and that justice should be speedily administered
(292) in cases of dispute. These results are achieved through the influence of the ruler, when he is a man who hates evil and loves the good and devotes his energies to saving the lives of men, just as you consider injustice the worst form of evil and by your just administration have fashioned for yourself an undying reputation, since God bestows upon you a mind which is pure and untainted by any evil."

SECTIONS 312–319

(312) When the matter was reported to the king, he rejoiced greatly, for he felt that the design which he had formed had been safely carried out. The whole book was read over to him and he was greatly astonished at the spirit of the lawgiver. And he said to Demetrius, "How is it that none of the historians or the poets have ever thought it worth their while to allude to such a wonderful achievement?"
(313) And he replied, "Because the law is sacred and of divine origin. And some of those who formed the intention of *dealing with it* have been smitten by God and therefore desisted from their purpose."
(314) He said that he had heard from Theopompus that he had been driven out of his mind for more than thirty days because he intended to insert in his history some of the incidents from the earlier and somewhat unreliable translations of the law. When he had recovered a little, he besought God to make it clear to him why the misfortune
(315) had befallen him. And it was revealed to him in a dream, that from

idle curiosity he was wishing to communicate sacred truths to common men, and that if he desisted he would recover his health. I have heard too from the lips of Theodektes, one of the tragic poets, that when he was about to adapt some of the incidents recorded in the book for one of his plays, he was affected with cataracts in both his eyes. And when he perceived the reason why the misfortune had befallen him, he prayed to God for many days and was afterwards restored.

(317) And after the king, as I have already said, had received the explanation of Demetrius on this point, he did homage and ordered that great care should be taken of the books, and that they should
(318) be sacredly guarded. And he urged the translators to visit him frequently after their return to Judea, for it was only right, he said, that he should now send them home. But when they came back, he ordered preparations to be made for them to return home, and
(319) treated them most munificently. He presented each one of them with three robes of the finest sort, two talents of gold, a sideboard weighing one talent, all the furniture for three couches.

B. GRECO-ROMAN RELIGIONS

Personal Religions

In both Athens and Rome at the time of the beginning of Christianity, there were probably few who believed in the gods and goddesses of the ancient myths, but it was thought by many to be important to maintain the state cult honoring the traditional gods in order to guarantee the stability of the political system. The divinities were thought of as personifications of certain powers or virtues, with Zeus regarded as the epitome of cosmic power, and therefore the one with whom the ruler figure sought to identify. The gods were in control of history, including the rise and fall of earthly leaders, and conveyed their intentions to those who had the insight to discern the divine hand at work in the form of portents or omens that accompanied the birth, the death, or the rise to power of the ruler. We shall examine some reports of these portents, as well as comments on them offered by the rationalistic moralist, Cicero.

Personal religion among Greeks and Romans in the period from about 150 B.C. to 150 A.D. centered on certain divine figures who were not part of the Olympian deities of Homer and the Greek tradition. Chief among these divinities who were sought by those with personal or even physical needs were Dionysus, Asklepios, and Isis. Dionysus, who was thought to have migrated from Phrygia in Asia Minor, was a figure of tragedy and exaltation, of sorrow and ecstasy. Associated with wine and fertility, he was also the god who dies and is reborn. Participating in his cult, therefore, enabled one to experience the mystery of life and death. As one scholar has described him, from his all-too-early birth, from his origin in his mother who persished in flames, sorrow and pain pursue him. His victories become defeats, and from radiant heights a god plunges down into the horrors of destruction. But it is just because of this that the earth also brings forth its most precious fruits through him and for him. Out of the vine, "the wild mother," there erupts for his sake the drink whose magic extends all that is confined and lets a blissful drink blossom forth out of pain.[59]

Also known as Bacchus, this god was worshipped in wild ecstatic rites by devotees over a period of centuries. Euripedes (480–406 B.C.), in his tragedy *The Bacchae,* tells how some women, seized with madness, attack a wild animal with their bare hands and dismember it, only to find that it is the son of their leader. Livy (59 B.C.–A.D.19) describes a group of women in Italy who were involved in the orgiastic rites of Bacchus, and relates how the authorities tried in vain to stamp out this religious movement. One can sense how these wild rites gave the participants a sense of directly sharing in the life and power of the god. Far from the remoteness of the traditional gods carrying on their games and schemes on Mount Olympus, Dionysus (Bacchus) was a god at work among and even within his followers.

Devotion to the healing gods, Asklepios and Isis, went through significant change in the hellenistic and Roman periods. In the hellenistic period these deities were sought out by those with specific needs: chiefly an illness or some sort of disability, such as blindness. Testimonies to the healing benefits of Asklepios have been preserved at his major shrine in Epidauros, not far from Corinth in Greece. Stories and dramas preserve the details of how he healed the ailing. The stricken person would come to the shrine and prepare to sleep in its precincts for the night. The chamber in which the seekers slept, hoping for a vision of or visit from the god, was called the *Abaton.* When all was dark, the sacred serpents would slither up from the depths of the grotto under the temple, or sacred dogs would come to lick the wounds of the afflicted, or specially favored persons might be visited by the god himself. The preserved testimonies of the cured have survived to modern times, although we have no way of guessing what percentage of the sick went away as they had come.

Similarly, shrines of Isis attest to her healing powers. Originally a lesser goddess in the Egyptian pantheon, by hellenistic times she became identified with Ma'at, the goddess of justice and divine order, and then as the wife of Osiris she became the instrument that restored him to life and could do the same for all who turned to her in faith. The inscriptions and documents celebrating her curative powers and her role in ordering the universe are called *aretalogies,* which derives from the word *aretē,*

[59]Walter F. Otto, *Dionysus: Myth and Cult,* tr. R.B. Palmer (Bloomington: Indiana University Press, 1965), p. 201.

meaning "virtue" or "power." Later both Asklepios and Isis came to be seen as the divine instruments through whom pious seekers could find meaning and renewal in their lives. Through them the faithful could commune with the gods and experience personal transformation. The fullest account of the change effected through Isis is the *Metamorphoses* of Apuleius (123–180 A.D.).[60] The life-transforming results of mystic communion with Asklepios are recounted by Aelius Aristides (117–189 A.D.) in his *Sacred Discourses.* He tells his readers that, although his ailments were alleviated by the god rather than cured, the visions and sacred communications that came from Asklepios gave meaning and purpose to his life, and greatly heightened his skill as a public orator.

The Bacchic or Dionysiac Mysteries

Livy, a Roman historian (59 B.C.–A.D.17), reports in Book 39 of his *History of Rome* how the authorities discovered a fairly widespread religious movement in the early part of the second century B.C. In addition to the orgiastic rites that were said to have been performed in connection with the Bacchic cult, it was believed by the senate that there was a political plot involved in this secret activity. Livy passes on the testimony of a woman who was found to be involved in this illicit sect.

> At first, she said, it was a ritual for women, and it was the custom that no man should be admitted to it. There had been three days appointed each year on which they held initiations into the Bacchic rites by day; it was the rule to choose the matrons in turn as priestesses. Paculla Annia, a Campanian, she said, when priestess, had changed all this; for she had been the first to initiate men, her sons, Minius and Herennius Cerrinius; she had held the rites by night and not by day, and instead of a mere three days a year she had established five days of initiation in every month.

> 186 B.C. From the time that the rites were performed in common, men mingling with women and the freedom of darkness added, no form of crime, no sort of wrong-doing, was left untried. There were more lustful practices among men with one another than among women. If any of them were disinclined to endure abuse or reluctant to commit crime, they were sacrificed as victims. To consider nothing wrong, she continued, was the highest form of religious devotion among them. Men, as if insane, with fanatical tossings of their bodies, would utter prophecies. Matrons in the dress of Bacchantes, with dishevelled hair and carrying blazing torches, would run down to the Tiber, and plunging their torches in the water (because they contained live sulphur mixed with calcium) would bring them out still burning. Men were alleged to have been carried off by the gods who had been bound to a machine and borne away out of sight to hidden caves: they were those who had refused either to conspire or to join in the crimes or to suffer abuse. Their number, she said, was very great, almost constituting a second state; among them were certain men and women of high rank. Within the last two years

[60]Excerpts from the *Metamorphoses* of Apuleius appear on pp. 197–202, under *Romances*.

Dionysus. The god of wine, here accompanied by maenads and satyrs, attracted both men and women to his cult. In the ceremonies honoring him, his followers achieved ecstasy, and believed themselves to be participating in the life of the god, which could transcend death itself. In addition to the visual evidence of vase paintings like this one from the fifth or sixth century B.C., there is testimony from both historical and literary figures over the centuries down to the Roman period of the popularity of this god among Greeks and Romans. *(Courtesy of the Metropolitan Museum of Art, New York)*

it had been ordained that no one beyond the age of twenty years should be initiated: such ages could be involved in error and also were ready to permit abuse.

Such was the decree of the senate. The consuls ordered the curule aediles to search out all the priests of this cult and to keep them under surveillance, in free custody for the investigation; the plebeian aediles were to see to it that no celebration of the rites should be held in secret. The task was entrusted to the *triumviri capitales* of placing guards through the City, of seeing that no night meetings were held, and of making provision against fire; as assistants to the *triumviri,* the *quinqueviri uls cis Tiberim* were to stand guard each over the buildings of his own district.

* * *

As to the Bacchanalia, I am assured that you have learned that they have long been celebrated all over Italy and now even within the City in many places, and that you have learned this not only from rumour but also from their din and cries at night, which echo throughout the City, but I feel sure that you do not know what this thing is: some believe that it is a form of worship of the gods, others that it is an allowable play and pastime, and, whatever it is, that it concerns only a few. As regards their number, if I shall say that there are many thousands of them, it cannot but be that you are terrified, unless I shall at once add to that who and of what sort they are. First, then, a great part of them are women, and they are the source of this mischief; then there are men very like the women, debauched and debauchers, fanatical, with senses dulled by wakefulness, wine, noise and shouts at night. The conspiracy thus far has no strength, but it has an immense source of strength in that they grow more numerous day by day. Your ancestors did not wish that even you should assemble casually and without reason, except when the standard was displayed on the citadel and the army was assembled for an election, or the tribunes had announced a meeting of

the plebeians, or some of the magistrates had called you to an informal gathering; and wherever there was a crowd collected they thought that
186 B.C. there should also be a legal leader of the crowd. Of what sort do you think are, first, gatherings held by night, second, meetings of men and women in common? If you knew at what ages males were initiated, you would feel not only pity for them but also shame. Do you think, citizens, that youths initiated by this oath should be made soldiers? That arms should be entrusted to men mustered from this foul shrine? Will men covered with the signs of their own debauchery and that of others fight to the death on behalf of the chastity of your wives and children?

XVI. "Yet it would be less serious if their wrong-doing had merely made them effeminate—that was in great measure their personal dishonour—and if they had kept their hands from crime and their thoughts from evil designs: never has there been so much evil in the state nor affecting so many people in so many ways. Whatever villainy there has been in recent years due to lust, whatever to fraud, whatever to crime, I tell you, has arisen from this one cult. Not yet have they revealed all the crimes to which they have conspired. Their impious compact still limits itself to private crimes, since as yet it does not have strength enough to crush the state. Daily the evil grows and creeps abroad. It is already too great to be purely a private matter: its objective is the control of the state."

Testimonies to the Healing Powers of Asklepios

INSCRIPTIONS FROM HIS SHRINE IN EPIDAUROS

Cleo was with child for five years. After she had been pregnant for five years she came as a suppliant to the god and slept in the Abaton. As soon as she left it and got outside the temple precincts she bore a son who, immediately after birth, washed himself at the fountain and walked about with his mother. In return for this favor she inscribed on her offering: "Admirable is not the greatness of the tablet, but the Divinity, in that Cleo carried the burden in her womb for five years, until she slept in the Temple and He made her sound."

* * *

The goblet. A porter, upon going up to the Temple, fell when he was near the ten-stadia stone. When he had gotten up he opened his bag and looked at the broken vessels. When he saw that the goblet from which his master was accustomed to drink was also broken, he was in great distress and sat down to try to fit the pieces together again. But a passer-by saw him and said: "Foolish fellow, why do you put the goblet together in vain? For this one not even Asclepius of Epidaurus could put to rights again." The boy, hearing this, put the pieces back in the bag and went on to the Temple. When he got there he opened the bag and brought the goblet out of it, and it was entirely whole; and he related to his master what had happened and had been said; when he [the master] heard that, he dedicated the goblet to the god.

* * *

Aeschines, when the suppliants were already asleep, climbed up a tree and tried to see over into the Abaton. But he fell from the tree on to some fencing and his eyes were injured. In a pitiable state of blindness, he came as a suppliant to the god and slept in the Temple and was healed.

* * *

Euhippus had had for six years the point of a spear in his jaw. As he was sleeping in the Temple the god extracted the spearhead and gave it to him into his hands. When day came Euhippus departed cured, and he held the spearhead in his hands.

* * *

A man had his toe healed by a serpent. He, suffering dreadfully from a malignant sore in his toe, during the daytime was taken outside by the servants of the Temple and set upon a seat. When sleep came upon him, then a snake issued from the Abaton and healed the toe with its tongue, and thereafter went back again to the Abaton. When the patient woke up and was healed he said that he had seen a vision: it seemed to him that a youth with a beautiful appearance had put a drug upon his toe.

Alcetas of Halieis. This blind man saw a dream. It seemed to him that the god came up to him and with his fingers opened his eyes, and that he first saw the trees in the sanctuary. At daybreak he walked out sound.

Sostrata, a woman of Pherae, was pregnant with worms. Being in a very bad way, she was carried into the Temple and slept there. But when she saw no distinct dream she let herself be carried back home. Then, however, near a place called Kornoi, a man of fine appearance seemed to come upon her and her companions. When he had learned from them about their bad luck, he asked them to set down on the ground the litter in which they were carrying Sostrata. Then he cut open her abdomen and took out a great quantity of worms—two wash-basins full. After having stitched her belly up again and made the woman well, Asclepius revealed to her his presence and enjoined her to send thank-offerings for her treatment to Epidauros.

* * *

Anticrates of Cnidos, eyes. In a battle he had been hit by a spear in both eyes and had become blind; and the spear point he carried with him, sticking in his face. While sleeping he saw a vision. It seemed to him that the god pulled out the missile and then fitted into his eyelids again the so-called pupils. When day came he walked out sound.

* * *

Diaetus of Cirrha. He happened to be paralyzed in his knees. While sleeping in the Temple he saw a dream. It seemed to him that the god ordered his servants to lift him up and to carry him outside the Adyton and to lay him down in front of the Temple. After they had carried him outside, the god yoked his horses to a chariot and drove three times around him in a circle and trampled on him with his horses and he got control over his knees instantly. When day came he walked out sound.

* * *

Cleimenes of Argus, paralyzed in body. He came to the Abaton and slept there and saw a vision. It seemed to him that the god wound a red woolen fillet around his body and led him for a bath a short distance away from the Temple to a lake of which the water was exceedingly cold. When he behaved in a cowardly way Asclepius said he would not heal those people who

Asklepios, the god of healing, was acclaimed by physicians who carried on their medical work in his name, and by ordinary people with ailments or desperate needs who turned to him for healing or help. The chief center of the Asklepios cult was in Epidauros, on the Greek Peleponnesus, although it was rivaled in the second century A.D. by his shrine in Pergamum. This relief shows the stricken person being visited by the god himself. The practice was for the needy one to spend the night in his shrine in the hopes of being visited by the sacred dogs or snakes, whose licking the patient might effect healing, or by the god himself. *(Courtesy of the Deutches Archäologisches Institut, Athens)*

were too cowardly for that, but those who came to him into his Temple, full of hope that he would do no harm to such a man, he would send him away well. When he woke up he took a bath and walked out unhurt.

Aelius Aristides, Sacred Discourses

IV:15–20

Autumn 145 A.D.

While I now rested in Pergamum because of a divine summons and my supplication, I received from the God a command and exhortation not to abandon rhetoric. It is impossible to say through the multitude of years whatever dreams came first, or the nature of each on the whole. Here is one of those exhortatory dreams, which occurred at the very beginning. *It befits you to converse with Socrates, Demosthenes, and Thucydides. And someone who was distinguished before our time was pointed out, so that I was especially moved to speak. And he commanded me to go to the Temple Stoa, which is at the Theater, and to offer to him the very first fruits of these improvised and competitive orations.* And so it happened. There was a very magnificent spectacle in the city, either a bull hunt, I think, or some such thing. Therefore all those from the Temple had rushed down, and the city was engaged in these things. We had been left alone in the Temple, two of the more distinguished worshippers, I and a Nicean, a man of praetorian rank, called Sedatius, but originally Theophilus. Therefore we were sitting in the Temple of Hygieia,[61] where the statue of Telesphorus is, and we were asking one another, as we were accustomed, whether the God had prescribed anything new. For some of our diseases were also the same. Therefore I said that I did not know what I should do, the prescription was like an order to fly, the practice of rhetoric, for one who could not breathe, and this here—I meant the Stoa—and I recounted the dream to him. And when he heard it, he said, "What will you do, and how do you feel about it?" "What else," I said, "than I shall do whatever I can? Put on my cloak, stand so, make a note of the problem to myself, begin some little thing, and then I shall stop. And so my religious obligation has been fulfilled." "Not at all," he said, "not so. But you have me here as a listener. Then contend with all zeal. Strength will be the God's concern. How do you know whether your dream portends even more?" And at the same time, he told me a marvellous deed of the God, how he commanded some sick man to contend in this way, and by causing him to perspire through the exercize, brought an end to the whole disease. It seemed necessary to do this. And while we were talking and taking counsel, Maximus the Libyan entered in the third place, a worshipper of the ancients, and in a fashion zealous about rhetoric. It was he who proposed the problem. And the problem was as follows, for I remember it, since it was the first, which I received: "While Alexander," he said, "is in India, Demosthenes advises that it is time to act." Therefore I immediately accepted the omen of Demosthenes speaking again and of the subject, which was about empire. And pausing a little, I contended, and my other strength was such as is the God's devising, and the year seemed not to belong to silence, but to training.

Then this was the beginning of the practice of rhetoric for us, and so we returned to it. But there were also many other dreams which pertained to the same, and the following was particularly encouraging. Rosander was a philosopher and especially diligent in the service of the God. *This man seemed to me to come from a gentleman who was a distinguished philosopher and who had just now lectured, and to stand before my bed, as it were, inspired and very serious. Next he spoke about the great improvement of my speeches. He remembered Plato and Demosthenes, for whatever he remembered each. Finally he added, "For us you have surpassed Demosthenes in dignity, so that not even the philosophers can scorn you."* This remark kindled all my later ambition. This made me feel that everything, which I might do in rhetoric, was less than I should do. Moreover, the God himself set his seal to this in a waking state. For after that night which brought the dream at dawn, I immediately began practicing, still at the beginning, as I said. And those present, having learned nothing of the dream before, but hearing my words then for the first time, especially approved of their dignity, and this caused them much excitement.

* * *

II:15–23

January 27
149 A.D.

After this, he kept me in Phocaea and sent me marvellous symbolic dreams, which pertained not only to my body, but also to many, many other things. And we heard in advance about the winds which would probably occur, so that whenever

[61]The goddess of health.

our host, Rufus, heard our dreams—in other respects he was the first of the Phocaeans, and himself also not ignorant of Asclepius—, he was greatly amazed to hear these things from us indoors, which he had left without, when he entered. Once at the God's command, there was need of milk. And there was none, for it was near a fourth in the month of Dystrus, according to our usage in Asia. But it seemed necessary to search for it. And Rufus went out to the end of his estate and found a sheep, who had given birth that very night. And he brought and provided the milk.

Finally the God remitted our sailing to Chius, both with signs and other prophecies, and after all these *I thought that the ship had been smashed to pieces and was no more.* There is a region called Genais, not far from Phocaea. He diverted us here for some days, at the warm springs, and then brought us back to Smyrna.

Then when we were in Smyrna, he appeared to me in some such form. *He was at the same time Asclepius, and Apollo, both the Clarian, and he who is called the Callitecnus in Pergamum and whose is the first of the three temples. Standing before my bed in this form, when he had extended his fingers and calculated the time, he said, "You have ten years from me and three from Sarapis," and at the same time the three and the ten appeared by the position of the fingers as seventeen. And he said that "this was not a dream, but a waking state* (Odyssey 19:547)," *and that I would also know it. And at the same time he commanded that I go down to the river, which flows before the city, and bathe, and that a young boy lead the way. And he pointed out the boy.* This is a summary of the divine manifestation, and I would place a high premium on being able to recount exactly each particular of it. It was the middle of winter and the north wind was strong and it was icy cold, and the pebbles were fixed to one another by the frost so that they seemed like a continuous piece of ice, and the water was such as is likely in such weather. When the divine manifestation was announced, friends escorted us, and various doctors, some of them acquaintances, and others who came either out of concern or even for the purposes of investigation. And there was also another great crowd, for some distribution happened to be taking place beyond the gates. And everything was visible from the bridge. There was a certain doctor, Heracleon, a companion of ours, who confessed to me on the day after, that he had gone having persuaded himself that if I should fare as well as possible, I should be afflicted with recurvation of the spine or some other such thing. When we were at the river, there was no need for anyone to encourage us. But being still full of warmth from the vision of the God, I cast off my clothes, and not wanting to be massaged, flung myself where the river was deepest. Next, as in a pool of very gentle and tempered water, I passed my time swimming all about and splashing myself all over. When I came out, all my skin had a rosy hue and my body was comfortable everywhere. And there was a great shout from those present and those coming up, shouting that celebrated phrase, "Great is Asclepius!" Who could indicate what came next. During all the rest of the day and night till bed time, I preserved the condition which I had after the bath, nor did I feel any part of my body to be drier or moister, nor did any of the warmth abate, nor was any added, nor again was the warmth such as one would have from a human contrivance, but it was a certain continuous body heat, bringing an even power throughout the whole of my body and during the whole time. My mental state was nearly the same. For there was neither, as it were, conspicuous pleasure, nor would you say it was like a human joy. But there were inexplicable high spirits, which counted all things second to the present moment, so that when I was other things, I seemed not to see them. Thus I was wholly with the God.

* * *

I:78

January 148 A.D.

Then he saved countless times beyond expectation, my old nurse, named Philumene, than whom nothing was dearer to me. Once when she was in bed, he restored her by sending me from Pergamum *and foretelling that I would make my nurse easier. And at the same time, I found a letter lying before my feet in the Temple of Zeus Asclepius, and made it an omen. Then I discovered every particular written in it, all but explicitly.* So I departed in great joy, and I found my nurse with strength enough only to recognize me approaching. But when she recognized me, she cried out and got up very soon thereafter.

* * *

II:26–28

end of March 146 A.D.

This one thing, I remember, was also done by him once. *He said that it was fated that I die in two days, and that this was inevitable. And at the same time, he gave me tokens about certain events on the following day, and the state of the weather, and where the constellation of the Charioteer would appear, and he gave me other tokens of his truthfulness. But he said that it was necessary to do the following. First having mounted a wagon, to go to the river which flows through the city, and when I was at the place where it is outside the city, to make sacrifices "at the trench"—for so he called them. Therefore it was necessary to dig a trench and to make sacrifices in it to whomever of the Gods it was necessary. Next upon turning back to take some small coins, to cross the river and cast them away. And he ordered some things, I think, in addition to this. After this to go to the Temple and make a full sacrifice to Asclepius, and to have sacred bowls set up, and to distribute the sacred portions of the sacrifice to all my fellow pilgrims. Also it was necessary to cut off some part of my body for the sake of the well being of the whole. But since this was difficult, he remitted it for me. Instead of this, he ordered me to remove the ring which I wore and dedicate it to Telesphorus—for this had the same effect, as if I should give up my finger—and to inscribe on the band of the ring, "O son of Cronus." And if I did this, I would be saved.* After this it is impossible to imagine our condition, and into what kind of harmony the God again brought us. For we engaged in all this, almost as if in an initiation, since there was great hope together with fear.

Isis Aretalogy

Discovered in the Macedonian section of Greece, the following inscription from the end of the second century B.C. was prepared in behalf of someone who had been healed of blindness. It is of significance, not only as testimony to Isis's healing powers, but also as a witness to the role assigned to this goddess in the hellenistic period as the agent of order in the world. Just as in Judaism, wisdom was the personification of divine activity in creating and ordering the universe in both its cosmic and human dimensions, so Isis is here represented as fulfilling those divine functions. The sense of personal devotion and gratitude on the part of this person who has benefitted from Isis's kindness shows through in this inscription, and expresses a widespread view of the gods that is to be found in documents of the hellenistic period.

> Just as you, O Isis, heeded the prayers that I addressed to you on the subject of my eyes, come to receive the praises that I extend to you in another prayer. . . . Your praise is, indeed, more important than my eyes. With these eyes I have seen the sun, and now I see the world which is yours. I am convinced that you will assist me in this way. If you came when I invoked you concerning my health, how will you not come when it is a matter honoring you? It is, therefore, with confidence that I approach you, knowing that eulogy is the spirit of the divine and that it is recorded by human hands.
>
> I come first to the matter of your family origin as I begin my praises for the beginnings of your race.
>
> Earth, it is said, became the Mother of All.
> She, who is the first, had you as her daughter.
> You took Sarapis as your spouse, and after you had
> instituted marriage, the world was resplendent before you,
> under the care of Helios and Selene.
>
> Thus you are gods, although you are invoked among humans by many names. You know life only as gods. Why then will the subject of my eulogy not be difficult, when it must begin with the evoking of many deities?
>
> With Hermes, she discovered the writings, among which are those sacred to the mystery initiates and other writings which are public in character.
>
> She has instituted justice in order that all of us, made equal with respect to death, might live in conditions of equality.
>
> She instituted language among human beings, for some a barbarous tongue, for others the Greek language, in order that the races might live in harmony, not only men and women, but all with all.
>
> She has given laws, which are originally *thesmoi.*
>
> This is why the cities have been solidly established, for she founded them, not by violence established through law, but by law without violence. You have arranged that children should honor their parents, not only as parents, but as divine ones. Therefore it is more widely recognized that you have made from natural necessity a law.
>
> Egypt has pleased you as a place of residence. As for Greece, you have especially honored Athens. It is there that you first revealed the fruits of the earth. Triptolemus, after having subdued the sacred serpents, distributed the seed among the Greeks, carrying it in his chariot. This is why we have the courage to come to see you in Greece, in Athens; and in Athens, in Eleusis, since we consider the city to be the soul of Europe, and the sanctuary [at Eleusis] to be the soul of the city. . . .

* * *

Other aretalogies have been preserved by historians, such as Didodorus Siculus Siculus (first century B.C.):

> I am Isis, the Queen of every land;
> She who was instructed by Hermes,
> And whatsoever laws I have established,
> These no one is able to destroy.
> I am the eldest daughter of the youngest god, Chronos.
> I am the wife and sister of Osiris, the king;
> I am she who first discovered fruits for mankind;
> I am the mother of Horus the king;
> I am she that riseth in the star that is in the Dog constellation;
> By me was Bubastis built.
> Farewell, farewell, O Egypt that nurtured me. (I. 27:3–4)

Describing her healing role, Didorus wrote:

> For standing above the sick in their sleep she gives aid for their diseases and works remarkable cures upon such as submit themselves to her; and many who have been despaired of by their physicians because of the difficult nature of their malady are restored to health by her, while numbers who have altogether lost the use of their eyes or some other part of the body, whenever they turn for help to this goddess are restored to their previous condition. (I. 25:5)

ORACLES, PORTENTS, AND DIVINATION

For seeking individuals in the Greco-Roman world, a different method of communication with the gods was consultation with oracles. The most famous of these was the shrine of Apollo at Delphi in central Greece, where a priestess under a spell gave answers to direct questions about problems of the present or the future. Although the Delphic oracle was viewed by many in the first century A.D. as no longer significant or reliable, it was still sought for advice, even by emperors down into the late third century.

Philosophers, including such different types as the skeptical, moralistic Cicero and the mystical Plutarch, expressed doubts about the oracles, and were critical of the established priestly system that operated the venerable oracular shrine at Delphi. The leading historians, on the other hand—including Suetonius (69–140 A.D.) and Tacitus (55–120)—describe in detail the extraordinary events that show the hand of the gods at work in preparing for major changes in the course of history, including the birth, coming to power, and death of the emperors.

Given wide credence in the popular mind were the Sibylline Oracles. The sibyls were prophetesses who provided answers on important issues to those who consulted them. The most famous of these was lo-

Temple of Apollo. Although Apollo was known chiefly in the older mythology of Greece as the god of the sun, one of his most important roles was as the instrument of prophecy. The oracle of his shrine at Delphi was visited by innumerable people from all stations in life with the aim of learning through the priestess (who was the mouthpiece of Apollo's oracle) what the future held in store for them, or how they might resolve a complex problem. The temple here pictured was a major feature of Corinth, a crossroads of culture and commerce, which was visited by Paul and became an important base of operations for his evangelism of the eastern Mediterranean. *(Courtesy of the American School of Classical Studies, Athens)*

cated south of Rome at Cumae. The oracles uttered—or allegedly uttered—by the sibyls were collected in books, which continued to be used by wandering prophets down into the Roman period. For a fee, they would provide answers, or even furnish copies of the Sibylline pronouncements. Jews, and later Christians, as well as important Roman authors, utilized the tradition of the Sibylline Oracles for their own purposes. Virgil's *Aeneid,* for example, describes how the sibyl instructed Aeneas to enter the underworld. In his *Fourth Eclogue,* Virgil's prophecy of the age of peace and prosperity that is to come on the earth through a divinely chosen agent is attributed to the Cumean Sibyl.

Portions of Jewish Sibylline books, written in Egypt, have been preserved as well. These adapt and expand the style of the oracles to present an analysis of the present state of the human race and a vision of its future. Instead of seeking to live in conformity to the divine image and the sacred laws that God bestowed upon humans, all nations—including many Jews—live in idolatry and disobedience. God will punish the nations and chastise his faithless people, but will ultimately send his agent to rule over his people and over the whole of a transformed creation.

These Sibylline Oracles were probably written in the second century B.C. and were widely used by the Christians in later centuries. The sibyls appear, along with the saints, as decorative features of medieval cathedrals. Central to their significance was the belief that they were indeed messengers of God foretelling the future of his people and of the human race.

Cicero

In his treatise "On Divination," Cicero carries on a debate with his brother as to whether the gods do indeed reveal to humankind their plans and purposes. Quintus, the brother of Cicero, argues as follows:

> I, at any rate, find sufficient proof to satisfy me of the existence of gods and of their concern in human affairs in my conviction that there are some kinds of divination which are clear and manifest. . . . There is nothing new or original in my views; for those which I adopt are not only very old, but they are endorsed by the consent of all peoples and nations. There are two kinds of divination: the first is dependent on art, the other on nature. Now—to mention those almost entirely dependent on art—what nation or what state disregards the prophecies of soothsayers, or interpreters of prodigies and lightnings, or of augurs, or of astrologers, or of oracles, or—to mention the two kinds which are classified as natural means of divination—the forewarnings of dreams, or of frenzy. Of these methods of divining it behooves us, I think, to examine the results rather than the causes. For there is a certain natural power, which now, through long-continued observation of signs and now, through some divine excitement and inspiration, makes prophetic announcement of the future (I. 6).
>
> Those diviners employ art, who, having learned the known by observation, seek the unknown by deduction. On the other hand those do without art who, unaided by reason or deduction or by signs which have been observed and recorded, forecast the future while under the influence of mental excitement, or of some free and unrestrained emotion. This condition often occurs to persons while dreaming and sometimes to those who prophesy while in a frenzy. In this latter class must be placed oracles . . . uttered under the impulse of divine inspiration; although divination by lot is not in itself to be despised . . . for in spite of everything, I am inclined to think that they may, under the power of God, be so drawn as to give an appropriate response. Those capable of correctly interpreting all these signs of the future seem to approach very near to the divine sport of the gods whose wills they interpret, just as scholars do when they interpret the poets (I. 18).

In his response to Quintus, Cicero is thoroughly skeptical of any factors or theories that cannot be accounted for on a strictly natural basis, although he does want to affirm the existence of the gods and the importance of honoring them:

> What do the gods mean by sending us in our dreams visions which we cannot understand ourselves and which we cannot find anybody to interpret

for us? If the gods send us these unintelligible and inexplicable dream-messages they are acting as Carthaginians and Spaniards would if they were to address our Senate in their own vernacular without the aid of an interpreter. Besides, what purpose is served by dark and enigmatic dreams? Surely the gods ought to want us to understand the advice they give us for our good (II. 64).

Astronomers have recorded the movements of the planets and thereby have discovered an orderly course of the stars, not thought of before. But tell me, if you can, what is the orderly course of dreams and what is the harmonious relation between them and subsequent events . . . If one dream turns out to be true, your Stoics do not withdraw their belief in the prophetic value of that one though it is only one out of many; rather, from the character of one true dream, they establish the character of countless others that are false. Therefore, if God is not the creator of dreams; if there is no connection between them and the laws of nature; and finally, if, by means of observation no art of divining can be found in them, it follows that absolutely no reliance can be placed in dreams (II. 71).

Cicero goes on to class dreams, along with all other forms of divination, as superstition. He declares that he wants to uphold religion even while exposing superstition:

I consider it the part of wisdom to preserve the institutions of our forefathers by retaining their sacred rites and ceremonies. Furthermore, the celestial order and the beauty of the universe compel me to confess that there is some excellent and eternal Being, who deserves the respect and homage of human beings. Wherefore, just as it is a duty to extend the influence of true religion, which is so closely associated with the knowledge of nature, so it is a duty to weed out every root of superstition (II. 72).

Plutarch

Plutarch (46–120 A.D.) in his *Moralia* (407) observes that the earlier age has passed in which communication among human beings and with the gods was carried out in poetic, mythical, and musical forms. Even Apollo conveyed his messages to the seekers at his Delphic shrine in verse form. Now, however, attention to artful form has given way to directness and intelligibility. That shift in style is apparent at Delphi as well, since the priestess who utters the oracles now speaks in simple, direct prose. Plutarch goes on to call into question the durability, not only of the oracular system, but of the gods who are thought to speak through it. He does, however, continue to believe that divine inspiration is possible.

So, as language also underwent a change and put off its finery, history descended from its vehicle of versification, and went on foot in prose, whereby the truth was mostly sifted from the fabulous. Philosophy welcomed clearness and teachability in preference to creating amazement, and pursued its investigations through the medium of everyday language. The god put an end to having his prophetic priestess call her own citizens "fire-blazers," the Spartans "snake-devourers," men "mountain-roamers," and rivers "mountain-engorgers." When he had taken away from the oracles epic versification, strange words, circumlocutions, and vagueness, he had thus made them ready to talk to his consultants as the laws talk to States, or as kings meet with common people, or as pupils listen to teachers, since he adapted the language to what was intelligible and convincing.

(25) Men ought to understand thoroughly, as Sophocles says, that the god is

> For wise men author of dark edicts aye,
> For dull men a poor teacher, if concise.

The introduction of clearness was attended also by a revolution in belief, which underwent a change along with everything else. And this was the result: in days of old what was not familiar or common, but was expressed altogether indirectly and through circumlocution, the mass of people imputed to an assumed manifestation of divine power, and held it in awe and reverence; but in later times, being well satisfied to apprehend all these various things clearly and easily without the attendant grandiloquence and articificiality, they blamed the poetic language with which the oracles were clothed, not only for obstructing the understanding of these in their true meaning and for combining vagueness and obscurity with the communication, but already they were coming to look with suspicion upon metaphors, riddles, and ambiguous statements, feeling that these were secluded nooks of refuge devised for furtive withdrawal and retreat for him that should err in his prophecy. Moreover, there was the oft-repeated tale that certain men with a gift for poetry were wont to sit about close by the shrine waiting to catch the words spoken, and then weaving about them a fabric of extempore hexameters or other verses or rhythms as "containers," so to speak, for the oracles. I forbear to mention how much blame men like Onomacritus, Prodicus, and Cinaethon have brought upon themselves from the oracles by foisting upon them a tragic diction and a grandiloquence of which they had no need, nor have I any kindly feeling toward their changes.

However, the thing that most filled the poetic art with disrepute was the tribe of wandering soothsayers and rogues that practised their charlatanry about the shrines of the Great Mother and of Serapis, making up oracles, some using their own ingenuity, others taking by lot from certain treatises oracles for the benefit of servants and womenfolk, who are most enticed by verse and a poetic vocabulary. This, then, is not the least among the reasons why poetry, by apparently lending herself to the service of tricksters, mountebanks, and false prophets, lost all standing with truth and the tripod.

(26) I should not, therefore, be surprised if there were times when there was need of *double entendre,* indirect statement, and vagueness for the people of ancient days. As a matter of fact, this or that man assuredly did not go down to consult the oracle about the purchase of a slave or about business. No, powerful States and kings and despots, who cherished no moderate designs, used to appeal to the god regarding their course of action; and it was not to the advantage of those concerned with the oracle to vex and provoke these men by unfriendliness through their hearing many of the things that

they did not wish to hear. For the god does not follow Euripides when he asserts as if he were laying down a law:

> None but Phoebus ought
> For men to prophesy.

But inasmuch as the god employs mortal men to assist him and declare his will, whom it is his duty to care for and protect, so that they shall not lose their lives at the hands of wicked men while ministering to a god, he is not willing to keep the truth unrevealed, but he caused the manifestation of it to be deflected, like a ray of light, in the medium of poetry, where it submits to many reflections and undergoes subdivisions, and thus he did away with its repellent harshness. There were naturally some things which it was well that despots should fail to understand and enemies should not learn beforehand. About these, therefore, he put a cloak of intimations and ambiguities which concealed the communication so far as others were concerned, but did not escape the persons involved nor mislead those that had need to know and who gave their minds to the matter. Therefore anyone is very foolish who, now that conditions have become different, complains and makes unwarranted indictment if the god feels that he must no longer help us in the same way, but in a different way.

Suetonius

In his *Lives of the Twelve Caesars,* Suetonius reports details of occurrences that he regards as signs of the hand of the gods at work in the birth and coming to power of the various emperors, as well as in connection with their deaths.

JULIUS CAESAR (LXXXI)

Now Caesar's approaching murder was foretold to him by unmistakable signs. A few months before, when the settlers assigned to the colony at Capua by the Julian Law were demolishing some tombs of great antiquity, to build country houses, and plied their work with the greater vigour because as they rummaged about they found a quantity of vases of ancient workmanship, there was discovered in a tomb, which was said to be that of Capys, the founder of Capua, a bronze tablet, inscribed with Greek words and characters to this purport: "Whenever the bones of Capys shall be moved, it will come to pass that a son of Ilium shall be slain at the hands of his kindred, and presently avenged at heavy cost to Italy." And let no one think this tale a myth or a lie, for it is vouched for by Cornelius Balbus, an intimate friend of Caesar. Shortly before his death, as he was told, the herds of horses which he had dedicated to the river Rubicon when he crossed it, and had let loose without a keeper, stubbornly refused to graze and wept copiously. Again, when he was offering sacrifice, the soothsayer Spurinna warned him to beware of danger, which would come not later than the Ides of March; and on the day before the Ides of that month a little bird called the king-bird flew into the Hall of Pompey with a sprig of laurel, pursued by others of various kinds from the grove hard by, which tore it to pieces in the hall. In fact the very night before his murder he dreamt now that he was flying above the clouds, and now that he was clasping the hand of Jupiter; and his wife Calpurnia thought that the pediment of their house fell, and that her husband was stabbed in her arms; and on a sudden the door of the room flew open of its own accord.

CAESAR AUGUSTUS (FROM BK. II)

As Marcus Cicero was attending Gaius Caesar to the Capitol, he happened to tell his friends a dream of the night before; that a boy of noble countenance was let down from heaven on a golden chain and, standing at the door of the temple, was given a whip by Jupiter. Just then suddenly catching sight of Augustus, who was still unknown to the greater number of those present and had been brought to the ceremony by his uncle Caesar, he declared that he was the very one whose form had appeared to him in his dream.

When Augustus was assuming the gown of manhood, his senatorial tunic was ripped apart on both sides and fell at his feet, which some interpreted as a sure sign that the order of which the tunic was the badge would one day be brought to his feet.

As the Deified Julius was cutting down a wood at Munda and preparing a place for his camp, coming across a palm tree, he caused it to be spared as an omen of victory. From this a shoot at once sprang forth and in a few days grew so great that it not only equalled the parent tree, but even overshadowed it; moreover many doves built their nests there, although that kind of bird especially avoids hard and rough foliage. Indeed, it was that omen in particular, they say, that led Caesar to wish that none other than his sister's grandson should be his successor.

VESPASIAN

In addition to reports of portents linked with the coming to power of Vespasian (A.D. 69–79) are miracles performed through him.

Once when he was taking breakfast, a stray dog brought in a human hand from the cross-roads and dropped it under the table. Again, when he was dining, an ox that was ploughing shook off its yoke, burst into the dining-room, and after scattering the servants, fell at the very feet of Vespasian as he reclined at table, and bowed its neck as if suddenly tired out. A cypress tree, also, on his grandfather's farm was torn up by the roots, without the agency of any violent storm, and thrown down, and on the following day rose again greener and stronger than before.

He dreamed in Greece that the beginning of good fortune for himself and his family would come as soon as Nero had a tooth extracted; and on the next day it came to pass that a physician walked into the hall and showed him a tooth which he had just then taken out.

When he consulted the oracle of the god of Carmel in Judaea, the lots were highly encouraging, promising that whatever he planned or wished, however great it might be, would come to pass; and one of his high-born prisoners, Josephus by name, as he was being put in chains, declared most confidently that he would soon be released by the same man, who would then, however, be emperor. Omens were also reported from Rome: Nero in his latter days was admonished in a dream to take the sacred chariot of Ju-

Vespasian. After the death of Nero (in A.D. 68), there were four rival claimants to the position of emperor. In 69, the Roman senate declared in favor of Vespasian, who was at the time engaged successfully in putting down the Jewish Revolt. Rumors of acclaim of him by oracles and gods in the east conveniently reached Rome while the senate was seeking an appropriate leader. With the choice of Vespasian, the Flavian line of emperors was established, and continued until near the end of that century. *(Courtesy of the Alinari Art Reference Bureau)*

piter Optimus Maximus from its shrine to the house of Vespasian and from there to the Circus. Not long after this, too, when Galba was on his way to the elections which gave him his second consulship, a statue of the Deified Julius of its own accord turned towards the East; and on the field of Betriacum, before the battle began, two eagles fought in the sight of all, and when one was vanquished, a third came from the direction of the rising sun and drove off the victor.

Tacitus

In his *Histories,* Tacitus describes many portents, including those that purportedly occurred at the time of the coming of the Roman troops to suppress the Jewish nationalists in their effort to establish an autonomous Jewish state (A.D. 65–70).

BOOK V:13

Prodigies had indeed occurred, but to avert them either by victims or by vows is held unlawful by a people which, though prone to superstition, is opposed to all propitiatory rites. Contending hosts were seen meeting in the skies, arms flashed, and suddenly the temple was illumined with fire from the clouds. Of a sudden the doors of the shrine opened and a superhuman voice cried: "The gods are departing"; at the same moment the mighty stir of their going was heard. Few interpreted these omens as fearful; the majority firmly believed that their ancient priestly writings contained the prophecy that this was the very time when the East should grow strong and that men starting from Judea should possess the world. This mysterious prophecy had in reality pointed to Vespasian and Titus, but the common people, as is the way of human ambition, interpreted these great destinies in their own favour, and could not be turned to the truth even by adversity. We have heard that the total number of the besieged of every age and both sexes was six hundred thousand: there were arms for all who could use them, and the number ready to fight was larger than could have been anticipated from the total population. Both men and women showed the same determination; and if they were to be forced to change their home, they feared life more than death.

Such was the city and people against which Titus Caesar now proceeded; since the nature of the ground did not allow him to assault or employ any sudden operations, he decided to use earthworks and mantlets: the legions were assigned to their several tasks, and there was a respite of fighting until they made ready every device for storming a town that the ancients had ever employed or modern ingenuity invented.

Jewish Sibylline Oracles

The excerpts included here offer a mixture of warning and promise. The warning concerns the human race, which has ignored and corrupted its having been created in the divine image. The consequences of this alienation from the Creator are detailed. But at the same time, assurance is given that the power of Rome will give way to God's rule over the world through his chosen agent. After a prediction of the end of the power of Greece and Rome, there is an exhortation to humankind to bring the appropriate sacrifices to God. (From Bk. III.)

(8) Ye men that bear the form that God did mould in his image, (9) why do ye wander at random and walk not in the straight path, (10) being ever mindful of the eternal Creator? (11) There is one sovereign God, ineffable, whose dwelling is in heaven, (12) self sprung, unseen yet seeing all himself alone. (13) No mason's hand did make him, nor does some model formed from gold (14) or ivory by the varied skill of man represent him. (15) But he, himself Eternal, hath revealed himself (16) as One who is and was before, yea and shall be hereafter. (17) For who, being mortal, can gaze on God with his eyes? (18) Or who could bear even to hear the mere name (19) of the mighty, heavenly God, the World-Ruler? (20) Who by his word created all, both heaven and sea (21) and tireless sun and moon at full (22) and twinkling stars, mighty mother Ocean, (23) springs and rivers, fire immortal, days and nights. (24) Yea it is God Himself who fashioned four-lettered Adam, (25) the first man fashioned, who completes in his name (26) morn and dusk, antarctic and arctic. (27) He too both established the fashion of the form of mortal men (28) and made the beasts and things that creep and fly. (29) Ye do not worship nor fear God, but wander at haphazard, (30)

bowing down to serpents and doing sacrifice to cats, (31) and to dumb idols and stone statues of mortal wights, (32) and sitting down before the doors of godless temples (33) ye weary the God who ever is, who guards all (34), taking your delight in miserable stones, forgetting the judgement (35) of the Eternal Saviour Who created heaven and earth. (36) O race that delights in blood, crafty, wicked race of godless men, (37) liars and double-tongued, immoral, (38) adulterous, idolatrous, of wily devices, (39) within whose heart is evil, a frenzied spur, (40) snatching for yourselves, having a shameless mind! (41) For no man of wealth endowed with goods will give any part to another, (42) but miserable meanness shall be among all mortals, (43) and faith they shall never keep at all, (44) but many widowed women shall have other secret lovers for lucre's sake, (45) and gaining husbands shall not keep hold of the rope of life.

(46) But when Rome shall rule over Egypt as well, (47) as she still hesitates to do, then the mightiest kingdom (48) of the immortal king over men shall appear. (49) And a holy prince shall come to wield the sceptre over all the world (50) unto all ages of hurrying time. (51) And then there shall be inexorable wrath on Latin men. (52) Three with piteous fate shall bring ruin on Rome, (53) and all its people shall perish in their own dwellings, (54) whensoever a cataract of fire shall flow from heaven. (55) O wretched me! when shall that day arrive, (56) even the judgement of the eternal God, the mighty King? (57) Yet for the present be ye founded, O ye cities, and adorned all of you (58) with temples and race-courses, with markets and statues (59) of gold and silver and stone, that ye may come to the day of bitterness. (60) For come it will, whenever the odour of brimstone pervades (61) all mankind. But I will tell out in particular (62) all those cities in which men are to suffer woe.

* * *

III:545–630

(45) Hellas, why dost thou put thy trust in governors, (46) mortal men who are powerless to escape the consummation of death? (47) With what view dost thou proffer vain gifts to the dead (48) and sacrifice to idols? Who has put error in thine heart, (49) that thou shouldst perform these rites and forsake the face of Mighty God? (50) Reverence the name of the Father of all and forget him not. (51) There are a thousand years and five hundred more, (52) since the reign of the haughty kings (53) of the Greeks who were the pioneers of evils to mankind, (54) holding fast to many idols of defunct gods, (55) whereby ye have been taught to think vain things. (56) But when the wrath of the great God shall be upon you, (57) then shall ye know the face of the great God. (58) And every soul of men with deep groans, (59) upraising their hands straight to the broad heaven, (60) shall begin to call to his succour the Mighty king, (61) and to seek who shall come as a deliverer from the mighty wrath.

(62) But come and learn this and store it in thy mind, (63) how many shall be the woes of the circling years. [For not even if thou shouldst offer up hecatombs of sacrifices], (64) as many as Hellas offered of old, of kine and bellowing bulls, (65) bringing whole burnt sacrifices to the temple of the Mighty God, (66) not even so wilt thou escape from jarring war and panic (67) and pestilence, and the yoke of bondage again. (68) But so long

the race of godless men shall exist, (69) until the day of fate reaches its appointed end. (70) Ye shall not sacrifice to God until all these things come to pass. (71) Whatsoever the one God purposes fails not of its accomplishment. (72) For that all things be accomplished the stress of necessity will insist.

(73) There shall be thereafter a holy race of God-fearing men, (74) adhering to the counsels and the mind of the Most High: (75) who pay full honour to the temple of the mighty God, (76) with drink offerings and fat offerings and sacred hecatombs, (77) with sacrifices of lusty bulls and unblemished rams, (78) and piously offer as whole burnt sacrifices rich flocks of firstling sheep and lambs upon the great altar. (80) And in righteousness possessing the law of the Most High, (81) they shall dwell happily in their cities and rich fields, (82) themselves as prophets exalted by the Immortal One, (83) and bringing great joy to all mortals. (84) For to them alone the Mighty God has given discreet counsel, (85) and faith and an excellent understanding in their hearts: (86) in that they give not themselves to vain deceits, nor honour the works of men's hands, (87) of gold and brass, silver or ivory, (88) idols of dead gods of wood and stone, (89) idols of clay vermilion painted, pictured likenesses of beasts, (90) such things as men with minds void of counsel do honour. (91) But they instead raise heavenwards holy arms, (92) rising early from their bed and ever cleansing their flesh (93) with water, and they honour Him alone who reigns for ever, (94) the Eternal, and after him their parents: and more than any (95) men they are mindful of the purity of marriage. (96) Nor do they hold unholy intercourse with boys, (97) as do the Phoenicians, Egyptians, and Latins, (98) and *spacious* Hellas, and many nations of other men, (99) Persians and Galatians and all Asia, transgressing (600) the holy law of the immortal God which he ordained. (601) For which cause the Eternal shall impose on all men (602) retribution and famine and woes and groans, (603) war, too, and pestilence and fearful calamities; (604) because they would not honour in holiness the eternal Father of all men, (605) but reverenced and honoured idols (606) made by men's hands, which men themselves shall cast (607) into the crannies of rocks and hide in shame, (608) whensoever a youthful king of Egypt, seventh in line, (609) of his own land reckoned from the Greeks shall reign over (10) an empire, over which the doughty Macedonians shall reign; (11) and there comes from Asia a mighty king, a fiery eagle, (12) who shall darken every land with foot and horse, (13) and shall break up everything and fill everything with miseries: (14) he shall cast down the kingdom of Egypt, and taking all (15) its wealth, shall ride upon the broad surface of the sea. (16) And then at length to God the great King, the Eternal, (17) they shall bend the white knee upon the fruitful earth, (18) and the works of men's hand shall all fall into the flame of fire. (19) And then God shall give great joy to men. (20) For the earth and the trees and the innumerable flocks of sheep, (21) shall give their true fruit to mankind, (22) of wine and sweet honey and white milk (23) and corn which is to men the most excellent gift of all.

(24) But thou, O man of wiles, tarry not with hesitation, (25) but turning round again make intercession to God. (26) Sacrifice to God hundreds of bulls and firstling lambs (27) and of goats in the circling seasons. (28) Yea, make intercession to Him, the Immortal God, if perchance He may have mercy upon thee. (29) For He alone is God, and there is none beside. (30) Honour righteousness and oppress no man: (31) for these are the commands of the Eternal to wretched mortals.

Virgil: Fourth Eclogue

The Fourth Eclogue of Virgil is an enigma; it is impossible to determine what the poet's precise aim was or what lies behind the veiled allusions and imagery. He probably wrote in praise of Caesar Augustus and in the hope that the new era that began with him would culminate in the renewal of the creation. Lily Ross Taylor's[62] plausible proposal is that the "new child" of this eclogue combines elements of Aion (meaning "age"; an abstract divinity compounded of Egyptian and Iranian elements), Horus from Egypt, and Mithra from Iran. The poem's perspective on history has been shaped by the Jewish Sibylline Oracles, which had been growing by accretion since the second century B.C. The Greek and Roman sibyls, whose oracles were highly regarded and often consulted in Rome, were prophetesses, the counterparts of the Hebrew prophets. Alexandrine Jews began to produce their own Sibylline Oracles which, though retaining many aspects of pagan mythology and hellenistic history, set forth eschatological views like those of the later Hebrew prophets and predicted the coming of the Messiah. The fact that Virgil would espouse such hopes and express them in terms drawing from such a wide range of cultural traditions is itself testimony both to the syncretism that characterized the period and to the widespread longing for a new beginning.

> Sicilian Muses, let us sing a somewhat loftier strain. Not all do the orchards please and the lowly tamarisks. If our song is of the woodland, let the woodland be worthy of a consul.
>
> Now is come the last age of the song of Cumae; the great line of the centuries begins anew. Now the Virgin returns, the reign of Saturn returns; now a new generation descends from heaven on high. Only do thou, pure Lucina, smile on the birth of the child, under whom the iron brood shall first cease, and a golden race spring up throughout the world! Thine own Apollo now is king!
>
> And in thy consulship, Pollio, yea in thine, shall this glorious age begin, and the mighty months commence their march; under thy sway, and lingering traces of our guilt shall become void, and release the earth from its continual dread. He shall have the gift of divine life, shall see heroes mingled with gods, and shall himself be seen of them, and shall sway a world to which his father's virtues have brought peace.
>
> But for thee, child, shall the earth untilled pour forth, as her first pretty gifts, straggling ivy with foxglove everywhere, and the Egyptian bean blended with the smiling acanthus. Uncalled, the goats shall bring home their udders swollen with milk, and the herds shall fear not huge lions; unmasked, thy cradle shall pour forth flowers for thy delight. The serpent, too, shall perish, and the false poison-plant shall perish; Assyrian spice shall spring up on every soil.

[62] *The Divinity of the Roman Emperor* (Middletown, Conn.: American Philological Association, 1931), pp. 113–14.

(26) But soon as thou canst read of the glories of heroes and thy father's deeds, and canst know what valour is, slowly shall the plain yellow with the waving corn, on wild brambles shall hang the purple grape, and the stubborn oak shall distil dewy honey. Yet shall some few traces of olden sin lurk behind, to call men to essay the sea in ships, to gird towns with walls, and to cleave the earth with furrows. A second Tiphys shall then arise, and a second Argo to carry chosen heroes; a second warfare, too, shall there be, and again shall a great Achilles be sent to Troy.

(37) Next, when now the strength of years has made thee man, even the trader shall quit the sea, nor shall the ship of pine exchange wares; every land shall bear all fruits. The earth shall not feel the harrow, nor the vine the pruning-hook; the sturdy ploughman, too, shall now loose his oxen from the yoke. Wool shall no more learn to counterfeit varied hues, but of himself the ram in the meadows shall change his fleece, now to sweetly blushing purple, now to a saffron yellow; of its own will shall scarlet clothe the grazing lambs.

(46) "Ages such as these, glide on!" cried to their spindles the Fates, voicing in unison the fixed will of Destiny!

(48) Enter on thy high honours—the hour will soon be here—O thou dear offspring of the gods, mighty seed of a Jupiter to be! Behold the world bowing with its massive dome—earth and expanse of sea and heaven's depth! Behold, how all things exult in the age that is at hand! O that then the last days of a long life may still linger for me, with inspiration enough to tell of thy deeds! Not Thracian Orpheus, not Linus shall vanquish me in song, though his mother be helpful to the one, and his father to the other, Calliope to Orpheus, and fair Apollo to Linus. Even Pan, were he to contend with me and Arcady be judge, even Pan, with Arcady for judge, would own himself defeated.

(60) Begin, baby boy, to know thy mother with a smile—to thy mother ten months have brought the weariness of travail. Begin, baby boy!

GNOSTICISM

By the second century A.D. there had developed in the eastern Mediterranean world an assortment of teachers of religious philosophy who, in spite of important differences among them, agreed that the salvation of human beings depended on their gaining knowledge of the origin of the world. One of the Greek words for knowledge, *gnosis,* was used in the literature for this special kind of divine information, and gave its name to the movement: *gnosticism.* The basic issue for the gnostics was the problem of evil: How did a world beset by evil come into existence? The assumption was that there must be some superior power in the universe that was above and beyond evil to which enlightened human beings could escape from their miserable involvement in the material world.

The source of this elaborate and complicated kind of speculation seems to have been Jewish wisdom theories, which flourished in the hellenistic period. In its earlier forms, wisdom speculation sought to show how the remote, transcendent God of the universe had created the world through his chosen agent, Wisdom.[63] Later, as Judaism came increasingly under the influence of Greek philosophy, the effort was made to show that the truth revealed by God to the fathers of Israel and the prophets was compatible with truth arrived at by human reasoning.[64] Gnosticism went far beyond these proposals to make the claim that the world of matter was fundamentally evil, not the work of God (as in Genesis 1 and 2), but of an arrogant evil power, intent on its own wicked schemes. Human beings were caught in this material world, but they had within them a seed or spark of the divine that could be released through true knowledge and thus return to its heavenly source.

The teachings of the gnostics were formerly known almost solely through attacks on them made by the fathers of the church in the second and third centuries. But in 1945 a collection of gnostic writings was found in upper Egypt, where a gnostic monastic settlement had collected and preserved them. Known as the Nag Hammadi library, from the modern name of the find site, their publication has shown the diversity of the gnostic teachings. But it has also provided overwhelming evidence that these gnostic writings are based on either the Old or the New Testament, or both, and that they represent a way of radically reinterpreting the biblical tradition. Central to these documents is the figure of Wisdom (Sophia): Sometimes she is beneficent, but at other times she is pictured as the agent of evil. There is a strong influence of the basic Platonic philosophical distinction between the eternal heavenly world and the material world, subject to decay and corruption. Conversely, the Stoic teaching of nature as divinely ordered and of human responsibility to live in accord with the law of nature is dismissed as profound error. The redemptive figure is not described in many of the writings, and where he or she is, the role is by no means uniform. The writings that show the strongest Christian influence are composed in vigorous opposition to the biblical teachings of the goodness of the creation or to the truly human nature of Christ.

The following excerpts represent three different themes in the gnostic tradition: a description of the role of Wisdom in creation; a depiction of how knowledge or truth is the agent of human redemption; a radical modification of the Jesus tradition, which pictures him seeking to free his people from such earthy aspects of human existence as sexual differentiation, which was regarded by the gnostics as the product of the evil creator god. The second and third of these writings, though called gospels, lack any details of the career of Jesus, his miracles, his death or resurrection.

[63]As evident in Proverbs 8 and Sirach 24 (see pp. 77–82).

[64]As seen in Wisdom of Solomon 8 (see pp. 82–84).

Wisdom: On the Origin of the World

II:97, 24–108, 14

Since everyone—the gods of the world and men—says that nothing has existed prior to Chaos, I shall demonstrate that [they] all erred, since they do not know the [structure] of Chaos and its root. Here [is the] demonstration:

> If it is [agreed by] **98** all men concerning [Chaos] that it is a darkness, then it is something derived from a shadow. It was called darkness.
>
> But the shadow is something derived from a work existing from the beginning.
>
> So it is obvious that it (the first work) existed before Chaos came into being, which followed after the first work.

Now let us enter into the truth, but also into the first work, from whence Chaos came; and in this way the demonstration of truth will appear.

After the nature of the immortals was completed out of the boundless one, then a likeness called "Sophia" flowed out of Pistis. ⟨She⟩ wished ⟨that⟩ a work ⟨should⟩ come into being which is like the light which first existed, and immediately her wish appeared as a heavenly likeness, which possessed an incomprehensible greatness, which is in the middle between the immortals and those who came into being after them, like what is above, which is a veil which separates men and those belonging to the (sphere) above.

Now the aeon of truth has no shadow ⟨within⟩ it because the immeasurable light is everywhere within it. Its outside, however, is a shadow. It was called "darkness." From within it (darkness) a power appeared (as ruler) over the darkness. And (as for) the shadow, the powers which came into being after them called ⟨it⟩ "the limitless Chaos." And out of it [every] race of gods was brought forth, both [one and] the other and the whole place. Consequently, [the shadow] too is posterior to the first **99** work [which] appeared. The abyss is derived from the aforementioned Pistis.

Then the shadow perceived that there was one stronger than it. It was jealous, and when it became self-impregnated, it immediately bore envy. Since that day the origin of envy has appeared in all of the aeons and their worlds. But that envy was found to be a miscarriage without any spirit in it. It became like the shadows in a great watery substance.

Then the bitter wrath which came into being from the shadow was cast into a region of Chaos. Since that day ⟨a⟩ watery substance has appeared, i.e. what was ⟨enclosed⟩ in it (the shadow) flowed forth, appearing in Chaos. Just as all the useless afterbirth of one who bears a little child falls, likewise the matter which came into being from the shadow was cast aside. And it did not come out of Chaos, but matter was in Chaos, (existing) in a part of it.

Now after these things happened, then Pistis came and appeared over the matter of Chaos, which was cast off like a miscarriage since there was no spirit in ⟨her⟩. For all of that is a boundless darkness and water of unfathomable depth. And when Pistis saw what came into being from her deficiency, she was disturbed. And the disturbance appeared as a fearful work. And it fled [in order to dwell] in the Chaos. Then she turned to it and [breathed] into its face in the abyss, [which is] beneath **100** all of the heavens.

Now when Pistis Sophia desired [to cause] the one who had no spirit to receive the pattern of a likeness and rule over the matter and over all its powers, a ruler first appeared out of the waters, lion-like in appearance, androgynous, and having a great authority within himself, but not knowing whence he came into being.

Then when Pistis Sophia saw him moving in the depth of the waters, she said to him, "O youth, pass over here," which is interpreted "Yaldabaoth." Since that day, the first principle of the word which referred to the gods and angels and men has appeared. And the gods and angels and men constitute that which came into being by means of the word. Moreover, the ruler Yaldabaoth is ignorant of the power of Pistis. He did not see her face, but the likeness which spoke with him he saw in the water. And from that voice he called himself "Yaldabaoth." But the perfect ones call him "Ariael" because he was a lion-likeness. And after this one came to possess the authority of matter, Pistis Sophia withdrew up to her light.

When the ruler saw his greatness—and he saw only himself; he did not see another one except water and darkness—then he thought that [he] alone existed. His [thought was] made complete by means of the word, **101** and it appeared as a spirit moving to and fro over the waters. And when that spirit appeared, the ruler separated the watery substance to one region, and the dry (substance) he separated to another region. And from the (one) matter he created a dwelling place for himself. He called it "heaven." And from the (other) matter the ruler created a footstool. He called it "earth."

Afterward the ruler thought within his nature, and he created an androgynous being by means of the word. He opened his mouth (and) boasted to himself. When his eyes were opened, he saw his father and he said to him "y." His father called him "Yao." Again he created the second son (and) boasted to himself. He opened his eyes (and) he said to his father "e." His father called him "Eloai." Again he created the third son (and) boasted to himself. He opened his eyes, (and) he said to his father "as." His father called him "Astophaios." These are the three sons of their father.

Seven appeared in Chaos as androgynous beings. They have their masculine name and their feminine name. The feminine name (of Yaldabaoth) is Pronoia Sambathas, i.e. the Hebdomad. (As for) his son called "Yao," his feminine name is "lordship." Sabaoth's feminine name is "divinity." Adonaios' feminine name is "kingship." Eloaios' feminine name is "envy." Oraios' feminine name is "[riches]." Astaphaios' [feminine] name **102** is "Sophia." These [are the seven] powers of the seven heavens of Chaos. And they came into being as androgynous beings according to the deathless pattern which existed before them and in accord with the will of Pistis, so that the likeness of the one who existed from the first might rule until the end.

You will find the function of these names and the masculine power in "the Archangelikē of Moses the Prophet." But the feminine names are in "the First Book of Noraia."

Now since the First Father, Yaldabaoth, had great authority, he created for each of his sons by means of the word beautiful heavens as dwelling places, and for each heaven great glories, seven times more exquisite (than any earthly glory), thrones and dwelling places and temples and chariots and spiritual virgins and their glories, ⟨looking⟩ up to an invisible (realm), each one having these within his heaven; (and also) armies of divine, lordly, angelic, and archangelic powers, myriads without number, in order to serve.

The report concerning these you will find accurately in "the First Logos of Noraia."

Now they were completed in this ⟨way⟩ up to the sixth heaven, the one belonging to Sophia. And the heaven and his earth were overturned by the troubler who was beneath all of them. And the six heavens trembled. For the powers of Chaos knew ⟨not⟩ who it was who destroyed the heaven beneath them. And when Pistis knew the scorn of the troubler, she sent her breath, and she [bound him and] cast him down to Tartaros.

[Since] that [day], the heaven has been consolidated along with **103** its earth by means of the Sophia of Yaldabaoth, the one which is beneath them all. But after the heavens and their powers and all of their government set themselves aright, the First Father exalted himself, and was glorified by ⟨the⟩ whole army of angels. And all the ⟨gods⟩ and their angels gave him praise and glory. And he rejoiced in his heart, and he boasted continually, saying to them, "I do not need anything." He said, "I am god and no other one exists except me." But when he said these things, he sinned against all of the immortal ⟨imperishable⟩ ones, and they protected him. Moreover, when Pistis saw the impiety of the chief ruler, she was angry. Without being seen, she said, "You err, Samael," i.e. "the blind god." "An enlightened, immortal man exists before you. This will appear within your molded bodies. He will trample upon you like potter's clay, ⟨which⟩ is trampled. And you will go with those who are yours down to your mother, the abyss. For in the consummation of your works all of the deficiency which appeared in the truth will be dissolved. And it will cease, and it will be like that which did not come into being." After Pistis said these things, she revealed the likeness of her greatness in the waters. And thus she withdrew up to her light.

But when Sabaoth, the son of Yaldabaoth, heard the voice of Pistis, he worshipped [her. He] condemned the father **104** [on] account of the word of Pistis. [He] glorified her because she informed them of the deathless man and his light. Then Pistis Sophia stretched forth her finger, and she poured upon him a light from her light for a condemnation of his father. Moreover when Sabaoth received light, he received a great authority against all of the powers of Chaos. Since that day, he has been called "the lord of the powers." He hated his father, the darkness, and his mother, the abyss. He loathed his sister, the thought of the First Father, the one who moves to and fro over the water.

And on account of his light, all of the authorities of Chaos were jealous of him. And when they were disturbed, they made a great war in the seven heavens. Then when Pistis Sophia saw the war, she sent seven archangels from her light to Sabaoth. They snatched him away up to the seventh heaven. They took their stand before him as servants. Furthermore, she sent him three other archangels. She established the kingdom for him above every one so that he might come to be above the twelve gods of Chaos.

But when Sabaoth received the place of repose because of his repentance, Pistis moreover gave him her daughter Zoe with a great authority so that she might inform him about everything that exists in the eighth (heaven). And since he had an authority, he first created a dwelling place for himself. It is a large place which is very excellent, sevenfold (greater) than all those which exist [in the] seven heavens.

Then in front of **105** his dwelling place he created a great throne on a four-faced chariot called "Cherubin." And the Cherubin has eight forms for each of the four corners—lion forms, and bull forms, and human forms, and eagle forms—so that all of the forms total sixty-four forms. And seven archangels stand before him. He is the eighth, having authority. All of the forms total seventy-two. For from this chariot the seventy-two gods receive a pattern; and they receive a pattern so that they might rule over the seventy-two languages of the nations. And on that throne he created some other dragon-shaped angels called "Seraphin," who glorify him continually.

Afterward he created an angelic church—thousands and myriads, without number, (belong to her)—being like the church which is in the eighth. And a first-born called "Israel," i.e. "the man who sees god," and (also) having another name, "Jesus the Christ," who is like the Savior who is above the eighth, sits at his right upon an excellent throne. But on his left the virgin of the holy spirit sits upon a throne praising him. And the seven virgins stand before her while thirty (other virgins) ⟨with⟩ lyres and harps [and] **106** trumpets in their hands glorify him. And all of the armies of angels glorify him and praise him. But he sits on a throne concealed by a great light-cloud. And there was no one with him in the cloud except Sophia Pistis, teaching him about all those which exist in the eighth so that the likeness of those might be created, in order that the kingdom might continue for him until the consummation of the heavens of Chaos and their powers.

Now Pistis Sophia separated him from the darkness. She summoned him to her right. But she left the First Father on her left. Since that day right has been called "justice," but left has been called "injustice." Moreover, because of this they all received an order of the assembly of justice; and the injustice stands above all ⟨their⟩ creations.

Moreover, when the First Father of Chaos saw his son, Sabaoth, and that the glory in which he (dwells) is more exquisite than all the authorities of Chaos, he was jealous of him. And when he was angry, he begot Death from his (own) death. It was set up over the sixth heaven. Sabaoth was snatched away from that place. And thus the number of the six authorities of Chaos was completed.

Then since Death was androgynous, he mixed with his nature and begot seven androgynous sons. These are the names of the males: Jealousy, Wrath, Weeping, Sighing, Mourning, Lamenting, Tearful groaning. And these are the names of the females: Wrath, Grief, Lust, Sighing, Cursing, Bitterness, Quarrelsomeness. They had intercourse with one another, and each one begot seven so that they total **107** forty-nine androgynous demons.

Their names and their functions you will find in "the Book of Solomon."

And vis-à-vis these, Zoe, who exists with Sabaoth, created seven androgynous good powers. These are the names of the males: One-who-is-not-jealous, the Blessed, Joy, the True One, One-who-is-not-envious, the Beloved, the Trustworthy One. (As for) the females, however, these are their names: Peace, Gladness, Rejoicing, Blessedness, Truth, Love, Faith. And many good and guileless spirits are derived from these.

Their accomplishments and their functions you will find in "the Schemata of the Heimarmene of the Heaven Which is Beneath the Twelve."

But when the First Father saw the likeness of Pistis in the waters, he grieved. Especially when he heard her voice, it was like the first voice which called to him out of the water, and when he knew that this was the one who named him, he groaned and was ashamed on account of his transgression. And when he actually knew that an enlightened, immortal man existed before him, he was very much disturbed, because he had first said to all the gods and their angels, "I am god. No other one exists except me." For he had been afraid lest perhaps they know that another one existed before him and condemn him. But he, like a fool, despised the condemnation and acted recklessly, and said, "If **108** someone exists before me, let him appear so that we might see his light." And immediately, behold, ⟨a⟩ light came out of the eighth, which is above, and passed through all of the heavens of the earth.

When the First Father saw that the light was beautiful as it shone forth, he was amazed and was very much ashamed. When the light appeared, a human likeness, which was very wonderful, was revealed within it; and no one saw it except the First Father alone and Pronoia who was with him. But its light appeared to all the powers of the heavens. Therefore they were all disturbed by it. Then when Pronoia saw the angel, she became enamored of him. But he hated her because she was in darkness. Moreover she desired to embrace him, and she was not able. When she was unable to cease her love, she poured out her light upon earth. From that day, the angel was called "Light Adam," which is interpreted "the enlightened bloody (one)."

Gospel: The Gospel of Truth

1:16–21

The gospel of truth is a joy for those who have received from the Father of Truth the gift of knowing him, through the power of the Word that came forth from the pleroma—the one who is in the thought and the mind of the Father, that is, the one who is addressed as the Savior, (that) being the name of the work he is to perform for the redemption of those who were **17** ignorant of the Father, while the name (of) the gospel is the proclamation of hope, being discovery for those who search for him.

Indeed the all went about searching for the one from whom it (pl.) had come forth, and the all was inside of him, the incomprehensible, inconceivable one who is superior to every thought. Ignorance of the Father brought about anguish and terror. And the anguish grew solid like a fog so that no one was able to see. For this reason error became powerful; it fashioned its own matter foolishly, not having known the truth. It set about making a creature, with (all its) might preparing, in beauty, the substitute for the truth.

This was not, then, a humiliation for him, the incomprehensible, inconceivable one, for they were nothing—the anguish and the oblivion and the creature of lying—while the established truth is immutable, imperturbable, perfect in beauty. For this reason, despise error.

Being thus without any root, it fell into a fog regarding the Father, while it was involved in preparing works and oblivions and terrors in order that by means of these it might entice those of the middle and capture them. The oblivion of error was not revealed. It is not a **18** [. . .] under the Father. Oblivion did not come into existence under the Father, although it did indeed come into existence because of him. But what comes into existence in him is knowledge, which appeared in order that oblivion might vanish and the Father might be known. Since oblivion came into existence because the Father was not known, then if the Father comes to be known, oblivion will not exist from that moment on.

This ⟨is⟩ the gospel of the one who is searched for, which ⟨was⟩ revealed to those who are perfect through the mercies of the Father—the hidden mystery, Jesus, the Christ. Through it he enlightened those who were in darkness. Out of oblivion he enlightened them, he showed (them) a way. And the way is the truth which he taught them.

For this reason error grew angry at him, persecuted him, was distressed at him, (and) was brought to naught. He was nailed to a tree; he became a fruit of the knowledge of the Father, which did not, however, become destructive because it ⟨was⟩ eaten, but to those who ate it it gave (cause) to become glad in the discovery. For he discovered them in himself, and they discovered him in themselves, the incomprehensible, inconceivable one, the Father, the perfect one, the one who made the all, while the all is within him and the all has need of him, since he retained its (pl.) perfection within himself which he did not give to the all. The Father was not jealous. What jealousy indeed (could there be) between himself and his members? **19** For if the aeon had thus [received] their [perfection], they could not have come [. . .] the Father, since he retained their perfection within himself, granting it to them as a return to him and a knowledge unique in perfection. It is he who fashioned the all, and the all is within him and the all had need of him.

As in the case of one of whom some are ignorant, who wishes to have them know him and love him, so—for what did the all have need of if not knowledge regarding the Father?—he became a guide, restful and leisurely. He went into the midst of the schools (and) he spoke the word as a teacher. There came the wise men—in their own estimation—putting him to the test. But he confounded them because they were foolish. They hated him because they were not really wise.

After all these, there came the little children also, those to whom the knowledge of the Father belongs. Having been strengthened, they learned about the impressions of the Father. They knew, they were known; they were glorified, they glorified. There was revealed in their heart the living book of the living—the one written in the thought and the mind **20** [of the] Father, and which from before the foundation of the all was within the incomprehensible (parts) of him—that (book) which no one was able to take since it is reserved for the one who will take it and will be slain. No one could have appeared among those who believed in salvation unless that book had intervened. For this reason the merciful one, the faithful one, Jesus, was patient in accepting sufferings until he took that book, since he knows that his death is life for many.

Just as there lies hidden in a will, before it ⟨is⟩ opened, the fortune of the deceased master of the house, so (it is) with the all, which lay hidden while the Father of the all was invisible, the one who is from himself, from whom all spaces come forth. For this reason Jesus appeared; he put on that book; he was nailed to a tree; he published the edict of the Father on the cross. O such great teaching! He draws himself down to death though life eternal clothes him. Having stripped himself of the perishable rags, he put on imperishability, which no one can possibly take away from him. Having entered the empty spaces of terrors, he passed through those who were stripped naked by oblivion, being knowledge and perfection, proclaiming the things that are in the heart **21** of the [Father] in order to [. . .] teach those who will receive teaching.

The Gospel of Thomas

II:32, 10–39, 5

These are the secret sayings which the living Jesus spoke and which Didymos Judas Thomas wrote down.

(1) And he said, "Whoever finds the interpretation of these sayings will not experience death."

(2) Jesus said, "Let him who seeks continue seeking until he finds. When he finds, he will become troubled. When he becomes troubled, he will be astonished, and he will rule over the All."

(3) Jesus said, "If those who lead you say to you, 'See, the Kingdom is in the sky,' then the birds of the sky will precede you. If they say to you, 'It is in the sea,' then the fish will precede you. Rather, the Kingdom is inside of you, and it is outside of you. When you come to know yourselves, then you will become known, **33** and you will realize that it is you who are the sons of the living Father. But if you will not know yourselves, you dwell in poverty and it is you who are that poverty."

(4) Jesus said, "The man old in days will not hesitate to ask a small child seven days old about the place of life, and he will live. For many who are first will become last, and they will become one and the same."

(5) Jesus said, "Recognize what is in your sight, and that which is hidden from you will become plain to you. For there is nothing hidden which will not become manifest."

(6) His disciples questioned Him and said to Him, "Do You want us to fast? How shall we pray? Shall we give alms? What diet shall we observe?"

Jesus said, "Do not tell lies, and do not do what you hate, for all things are plain in the sight of Heaven. For nothing hidden will not become manifest, and nothing covered will remain without being uncovered."

(7) Jesus said, "Blessed is the lion which becomes man when consumed by man; and cursed is the man whom the lion consumes, and the lion becomes man."

(8) And He said, "The man is like a wise fisherman who cast his net into the sea and drew it up from the sea full of small fish. Among them the wise fisherman found a fine large fish. He threw all the small fish **34** back into the sea and chose the large fish without difficulty. Whoever has ears to hear, let him hear."

(9) Jesus said, "Now the sower went out, took a handful (of seeds), and scattered them. Some fell on the road; the birds came and gathered them up. Others fell on rock, did not take root in the soil, and did not produce ears. And others fell on thorns; they choked the seed(s) and worms ate them. And others fell on the good soil and produced good fruit: it bore sixty per measure and a hundred and twenty per measure."

(10) Jesus said, "I have cast fire upon the world, and see, I am guarding it until it blazes."

(11) Jesus said, "This heaven will pass away, and the one above it will pass away. The dead are not alive, and the living will not die. In the days when you consumed what is dead, you made it what is alive. When you come to dwell in the light, what will you do? On the day when you were one you became two. But when you become two, what will you do?"

(12) The disciples said to Jesus, "We know that You will depart from us. Who is to be our leader?"

Jesus said to them, "Wherever you are, you are to go to James the righteous, for whose sake heaven and earth came into being."

(13) Jesus said to His disciples, "Compare me to someone and tell Me whom I am like."

Simon Peter said to Him, "You are like a righteous angel."

Matthew said to Him, **35** "You are like a wise philosopher."

Thomas said to Him, "Master, my mouth is wholly incapable of saying whom You are like."

Jesus said, "I am not your master. Because you have drunk, you have become intoxicated from the bubbling spring which I have measured out."

And He took him and withdrew and told him three things. When Thomas returned to his companions, they asked him, "What did Jesus say to you?"

Thomas said to them, "If I tell you one of the things which he told me, you will pick up stones and throw them at me; a fire will come out of the stones and burn you up."

(14) Jesus said to them, "If you fast, you will give rise to sin for yourselves; and if you pray, you will be condemned; and if you give alms, you will do harm to your spirits. When you go into any land and walk about in the districts, if they receive you, eat what they will set before you, and heal the sick among them. For what goes into your mouth will not defile you, but that which issues from your mouth—it is that which will defile you."

(15) Jesus said, "When you see one who was not born of woman, prostrate yourselves on your faces and worship him. That one is your Father."

(16) Jesus said, "Men think, perhaps, that it is peace which I have come to cast upon the world. They do not know that it is dissension which I have come to cast upon the earth: fire, sword, and war. For there will be five **36** in a house: three will be against two, and two against three, the father against the son, and the son against the father. And they will stand solitary."

(17) Jesus said, "I shall give you what no eye has seen and what no ear has heard and what no hand has touched and what has never occurred to the human mind."

(18) The disciples said to Jesus, "Tell us how our end will be."

Jesus said, "Have you discovered, then, the beginning, that you look for the end? For where the beginning is, there will the end be. Blessed is he who will take his place in the beginning; he will know the end and will not experience death."

(19) Jesus said, "Blessed is he who came into being before he came into being. If you become My disciples and listen to My words, these stones will minister to you. For there are five trees for you in Paradise which remain undisturbed summer and winter and whose leaves do not fall. Whoever becomes acquainted with them will not experience death."

(20) The disciples said to Jesus, "Tell us what the Kingdom of Heaven is like."

He said to them, "It is like a mustard seed, the smallest of all seeds. But when it falls on tilled soil, it produces a great plant and becomes a shelter for birds of the sky."

(21) Mary said to Jesus, "Whom are Your disciples like?"

He said, "They are like **37** children who have settled in a field which is not theirs. When the owners of the field come, they will say, 'Let us have back our field.' They (will) undress in their presence in order to let them have back their field and to give it back to them. Therefore I say to you, if the owner of a house knows that the thief is coming, he will begin his vigil before he comes and will not let him dig through into his house of his domain to carry away his goods. You, then, be on your guard against the world. Arm yourselves with great strength lest the robbers find a way to come to you, for the difficulty which you expect will (surely) materialize. Let there be among you a man of understanding. When the grain ripened, he came quickly with his sickle in his hand and reaped it. Whoever has ears to hear, let him hear."

(22) Jesus saw infants being suckled. He said to His disciples, "These infants being suckled are like those who enter the Kingdom."

They said to Him, "Shall we then, as children, enter the Kingdom?"

Jesus said to them, "When you make the two one, and when you make the inside like the outside and the outside like the inside, and the above like the below, and when you make the male and the female one and the same, so that the male not be male nor the female female; and when you fashion eyes in place of an eye, and a hand in place of a hand, and a foot in place of a foot, and a likeness in place of a likeness; then you will enter [the Kingdom]." **38**

(23) Jesus said, "I shall choose you, one out of a thousand, and two out of ten thousand, and they shall stand as a single one."

(24) His disciples said to Him, "Show us the place where You are, since it is necessary for us to seek it."

He said to them, "Whoever has ears, let him hear. There is light within a man of light, and he (or: it) lights up the whole world. If he (or: it) does not shine, he (or: it) is darkness."

(25) Jesus said, "Love your brother like your soul, guard him like the pupil of your eye."

(26) Jesus said, "You see the mote in your brother's eye, but you do not see the beam in your own eye. When you cast the beam out of your own eye, then you will see clearly to cast the mote from your brother's eye."

(27) ⟨Jesus said,⟩ "If you do not fast as regards the world, you will not find the Kingdom. If you do not observe the Sabbath as a Sabbath, you will not see the Father."

(28) Jesus said, "I took My place in the midst of the world, and I appeared to them in flesh. I found all of them intoxicated; I found none of them thirsty. And My soul became afflicted for the sons of men, because they are blind in their hearts and do not have sight; for empty they came into the world, and empty too they seek to leave the world. But for the moment they are intoxicated. When they shake off their wine, then they will repent."

(29) Jesus said, "If the flesh came into being because of spirit, it is a wonder. But if spirit came into being because of the body, it is a wonder of wonders. Indeed, I am amazed **39** at how this great wealth has made its home in this poverty."

(30) Jesus said, "Where there are three gods, they are gods. Where there are two or one, I am with him."

CHURCH TRADITION OF THE SECOND CENTURY

For information concerning the history of the church after the period of the New Testament and for the fate of the apostles and others mentioned in the New Testament we are largely dependent on the writings of Eusebius of Caesarea (264–349) in his *Ecclesiastical History*. For much of his material he draws on legends or traditions written by or attributed to leaders of the church in the second century. Because nearly all the works he mentions are otherwise lost, we are indebted to him for the material he has preserved, but we are often in no position to evaluate it.

What is excerpted here are passages in which he tells where the apostles went, how they met death, and what writings they left behind, if any. In discussing the origins of the gospels, he makes an attempt to account for the differences among them, thus setting an early example for critical historical study of the New Testament, even though modern critics are often unconvinced by his arguments.

Eusebius: Ecclesiastical History

XV . . . At that same time also JAMES,[65] who was called the brother of the Lord, inasmuch as the latter too was styled the child of Joseph, and Joseph was called the father of Christ, for the Virgin was betrothed to him when, before they came together, she was discovered to have conceived by the Holy Spirit, as the sacred writing of the Gospels teaches—this same James, to whom the men of old had also given the surname of Just for his excellence of virtue, is narrated to have been the first elected to the throne of the bishopric of the Church in Jerusalem. Clement in the sixth book of the *Hypotyposes* adduces the following: "For," he says, "PETER and JAMES and JOHN after the Ascension of the Saviour did not struggle for glory, because they had previously been given honour by the Saviour, but chose James the Just as bishop of Jerusalem." The same writer in the seventh book of the same work says in addition this about him, "After the Resurrection the Lord gave the tradition of knowledge to James the Just and John and Peter, these gave it to the other Apostles and the other Apostles to the seventy, of whom Barnabas also was one. Now there were two Jameses, one James the Just, who was thrown down from the pinnacle of the temple and beaten to death with a fuller's club, and the other he who was beheaded." Paul also mentions the same James the Just when he writes, "And I saw none other of the Apostles save James the brother of the Lord."

At this time too the terms of our Saviour's promise to the king of the Osrhoenes were receiving fulfilment. THOMAS was divinely moved to send THADDAEUS to Edessa[66] as herald and evangelist of the teaching concerning Christ, as we have shown just previously from the writing preserved there. When he reached the place Thaddaeus healed Abgar by the word of Christ, and amazed all the inhabitants by his strange miracles. By the mighty influence of his deeds he brought them to reverence the power of Christ, and made them disciples of the saving teaching. From that day to this the whole city of Edessenes has been dedicated to the name of Christ, thus displaying no common proof of the beneficence of our Saviour to them. Of such evil was SIMON[67] the father and fabricator, and the Evil Power, which hates that which is good and plots against the salvation of men, raised him up at that time as a great antagonist for the great and inspired Apostles of our Saviour. Nevertheless the grace of God which is from heaven helped its ministers and quickly extinguished the flames of the Evil One by their advent and presence, and through them humbled and cast down "every high thing that exalteth itself against the knowledge of God." Wherefore no conspiracy, either of Simon, or of any other of those who

[65]James, the brother of Jesus; not to be confused with James the son of Zebedee and brother of John.

[66]A city in northern Syria.

[67]Simon Magus (the Magician), mentioned in Acts 8:9 ff., and considered by early Christian writers to have been the father of heresies, especially of gnosticism.

arose at that time, succeeded in those Apostolic days; for the light of the truth and the divine Logos himself, which had shone from God upon men by growing up on the earth and dwelling among his own Apostles, was overcoming all things in the might of victory. The aforesaid sorcerer, as though the eyes of his mind had been smitten by the marvellous effulgence of God when he had formerly been detected in his crimes in Judaea by the Apostle PETER, at once undertook a great journey across the sea, and went off in flight from east to west, thinking that only in this way could he live as he wished. He came to the city of the Romans, where the power which obsessed him wrought with him greatly, so that in a short time he achieved such success that he was honoured as a god by the erection of a statue by those who were there. But he did not prosper long. Close after him in the same reign of Claudius the Providence of the universe in its great goodness and love towards men guided to Rome, as against a gigantic pest on life, the great and mighty Peter, who for his virtues was the leader of all the other Apostles. Like a noble captain of God, clad in divine armour, he brought the costly merchandise of the spiritual light from the east to the dwellers in the west, preaching the Gospel of the light itself and the word which saves souls, the proclamation of the Kingdom of Heaven. XV. Thus when the divine word made its home among them the power of Simon was extinguished and perished immediately, together with the fellow himself.

But a great light of religion shone on the minds of the hearers of PETER, so that they were not satisfied with a single hearing or with the unwritten teaching of the divine proclamation, but with every kind of exhortation besought Mark whose Gospel is extant, seeing that he was Peter's follower, to leave them a written statement of the teaching given them verbally, nor did they cease until they had persuaded him, and so became the cause of the Scripture called the Gospel according to Mark. And they say that the Apostle, knowing by the revelation of the spirit to him what had been done, was pleased at their zeal, and ratified the scripture for study in the churches. Clement quotes the story in the sixth book of the *Hypotyposes,* and the bishop of Hierapolis, named Papias, confirms him. He also says that Peter mentions MARK in his first Epistle, and that he composed this in Rome itself, which they say that he himself indicates, referring to the city metaphorically as Babylon, in the words, "the elect one in Babylon greets you, and Marcus my son."

XVI. They say that this MARK was the first to be sent to preach in Egypt the Gospel which he had also put into writing, and was the first to establish churches in Alexandria itself. The number of men and women who were there converted at the first attempt was so great, and their asceticism was so extraordinarily philosophic, that Philo thought it right to describe their conduct and assemblies and meals and all the rest of their manner of life.

When PAUL appealed to Caesar and was sent over to Rome by Festus the Jews were disappointed of the hope in which they had laid their plot against him and turned against JAMES, the brother of the Lord, to whom the throne of the bishopric in Jerusalem had been allotted by the Apostles. The crime which they committed was as follows. They brought him into the midst and demanded a denial of the faith in Christ before all the people, but when he, contrary to the expectation of all of them, with a loud voice and with more courage than they had expected, confessed before all the people that our Lord and Saviour Jesus Christ is the son of God, they could no longer endure his testimony, since he was by all men believed to be most righteous because of the height which he had reached in a life of philosophy and religion, and killed him, using anarchy as an opportunity for power since at that moment Festus had died in Judaea, leaving the district without government or procurator. The manner of James's death has been shown by the words of Clement already quoted, narrating that he was thrown from the battlement and beaten to death with a club, but Hegesippus, who belongs to the generation after the Apostles, gives the most accurate account of him speaking as follows in his fifth book: "The charge of the Church passed to James the brother of the Lord, together with the Apostles. He was called the 'Just' by all men from the Lord's time to ours, since many are called James, but he was holy from his mother's womb. He drank no wine or strong drink, nor did he eat flesh; no razor went upon his head; he did not anoint himself with oil, and he did not go to the baths. He alone was allowed to enter into the sanctuary, for he did not wear wool but linen, and he used to enter alone into the temple and be found kneeling and praying for forgiveness for the people, so that his knees grew hard like a camel's because of his constant worship of God, kneeling and asking forgiveness for the people. So from his excessive righteousness he was called the Just and Oblias, that is in Greek, 'Rampart of the people and righteousness,' as the prophets declare concerning him.

"And many were convinced and confessed at the testimony of James and said, 'Hosanna to the Son of David.' Then again the same Scribes and Pharisees said to one another, 'We did wrong to provide Jesus with such testimony, but let us go up and throw him down that they may be afraid and not believe him.' And they cried out saying, 'Oh, oh, even the just one erred.' And they fulfilled the Scripture written in Isaiah, 'Let us take the just man for he is unprofitable to us. Yet they shall eat the fruit of their works.' So they went up and threw down the Just, and they said to one another, 'Let us stone James the Just,' and they began to stone him since the fall had not killed him, but he turned and knelt saying, "I beseech thee, O Lord, God and Father, forgive them, for they know not what they do." And while they were thus stoning him one of the priests of the sons of Rechab, the son of Rechabim, to whom Jeremiah the prophet bore witness, cried out saying, 'Stop! what are you doing? The Just is praying for you.' And a certain man among them, one of the laundrymen, took the club with which he used to beat out the clothes, and hit the Just on the head, and so he suffered martyrdom. And they buried him on the spot by the temple, and his gravestone still remains by the temple. He became a true witness both to Jews and to Greeks that Jesus is the Christ, and at once Vespasian began to besiege them."

XXV. When the rule of Nero was now gathering strength for unholy objects he began to take up arms against the worship of the God of the universe. It is not part of the present work to describe his depravity: many indeed have related his story in accurate narrative, and from them he who wishes can study the perversity of his degenerate madness, which made him compass the unreasonable destruction of so many thousands, until he reached that final guilt of sparing neither his nearest nor dearest, so that in various ways he did to death alike his mother, brothers, and wife, with thousands of others attached to his family, as though they were enemies and foes. But with all this there was still lacking to him this—that it should be attributed to him that he was the first of the emperors to be pointed out as a foe of divine religion. This again the Latin writer Tertullian mentions in one place as follows: "Look at your records: there you will find that Nero was the first to persecute this belief when, having overcome the whole East, he was specially cruel in Rome against all. We boast that such a man was the author of our chastisement; for he who knows him can understand that nothing would have been condemned by Nero had it not been great and good."

In this way then was he the first to be heralded as above all a fighter against God, and raised up to slaughter against the Apostles. It is related that in his time PAUL was beheaded in Rome itself, and that PETER likewise was crucified, and the title of "Peter and Paul," which is still given to the cemeteries there, confirms the story, no less than does a writer of the Church named Caius, who lived when Zefyrinus was bishop of Rome. Caius in a written discussion with Proclus, the leader of the Montanists, speaks as follows of the places where the sacred relics of the Apostles in question are deposited: "But I can point out the trophies of the Apostles, for if you will go to the Vatican or to the Ostian Way you will find the trophies of those who founded this Church." And that they both were martyred at the same time DIONYSIUS, bishop of Corinth, affirms in this passage of his correspondence with the Romans: "By so great an admonition you bound together the foundations of the Romans and Corinthians by Peter and Paul, for both of them taught together in our Corinth and were our founders, and together also taught in Italy in the same place and were martyred at the same time."

Such was the condition of things among the Jews, but the holy Apostles and disciples of our Saviour were scattered throughout the whole world, THOMAS, as tradition relates, obtained by lot Parthia, ANDREW Scythia, JOHN Asia[68] (and he stayed there and died in Ephesus), but PETER seems to have preached to the Jews of the Dispersion in Pontus and Galatia and Bithynia, Cappadocia, and Asia, and at the end he came to Rome and was crucified head downwards, for so he had demanded to suffer. What need be said of PAUL, who fulfilled the gospel of Christ from Jerusalem to Illyria and afterward was martyred in Rome under Nero?

ROM. Now it would be clear from Paul's own words and from the narrative of
15:19 Luke in the Acts that Paul, in his preaching to the Gentiles, laid the foundations of the churches from Jerusalem round about unto Illyricum. And from the Epistle which we have spoken of as indisputably PETER's, in which he writes to those of the Hebrews in the Dispersion of Pontus and Galatia, Cappadocia, Asia, and Bithynia, it would be clear from his own words in how many provinces he delivered the word of the New Testament by preaching the Gospel of Christ to those of the circumcision. But it is not easy to say how many of these and which of them were genuinely zealous and proved their ability to be the pastors of the churches founded by the Apostles, except by making a list of those mentioned by Paul. For there were many thousands of his fellow-workers and, as he called them himself, fellow-soldiers, of whom the most were granted by him memorial past forgetting, for he recounts his testimony to them unceasingly in his own letters, and, moreover, Luke also in the Acts gives a list of those known to him and mentions them by name. Thus TIMOTHY is related to have been the first ap-
COL. pointed bishop of the diocese of Ephesus, as was TITUS of the churches in
4:14 Crete. Luke, who was by race an Antiochian and a physician by profession, was long a companion of Paul, and had careful conversation with the other Apostles, and in two books left us examples of the medicine for souls which he had gained from them—the Gospel, which he testifies that he had
LK. 1:1–4 planned according to the tradition received by him by those who were from

[68]The Roman province of Asia; what is now the western edge of Turkey.

A Harbor in Campania. On a mural preserved from Pompeii, a flourishing city near the site of present-day Naples that was destroyed by the eruption of Mt. Vesuvius in A.D. 79, is this picture of one of the harbor cities in the district of southern Italy known as Campania. It was at one of these harbors that Paul would have landed on his final journey to Rome, as reported in Acts 28. *(Courtesy of Il Soprintendente alle Antichita della Campania, Naples)*

the beginning, and Acts of the Apostles which he composed no longer on the evidence of hearing but of his own eyes. And they say that Paul was actually accustomed to quote from LUKE's Gospel since when writing of some Gospel as his own he used to say, "According to my Gospel." Of the other followers of Paul there is evidence that Crescens was sent by him to Gaul, and Linus, who is mentioned in the second Epistle to Timothy as present with him in Rome has already been declared to have been the first after Peter to be appointed to the bishopric of the Church in Rome. Of CLEMENT too, who was himself made the third bishop of the church of Rome, it is
PHIL. testified by Paul that he worked and strove in company with him. In addi-
4:3 tion to these Dionysius, one of the ancients, the pastor of the diocese of the Corinthians, relates that the first bishop of the Church at Athens was that member of the Areopagus, the other DIONYSIUS, whose original conversion after Paul's speech to the Athenians in the Areopagus Luke described in the Acts.[69]

MK. . . . the people of the church in Jerusalem were commanded by an oracle
13:14 given by revelation before the war to those in the city who were worthy of
(?) it to depart and dwell in one of the cities of Perea which they called Pella.[70]
To it those who believed in Christ migrated from Jerusalem, that when holy men had altogether deserted the royal capital of the Jews and the whole land of Judaea, the judgement of God might at last overtake them for all their crimes against the Christ and his Apostles, and all that generation of the wicked be utterly blotted out from among men. Those who wish can retrace accurately from the history written by Josephus how many evils at that time overwhelmed the whole nation in every place and especially how the inhabitants of Judaea were driven to the last point of suffering, how

[69]Acts 17:34.

[70]A hellenistic city on the eastern side of the upper Jordan Valley, and a part of the loose federation of cities known as *Decapolis*. Recently excavated, it contains extensive Roman remains and evidence of having continued as a center of Christianity down to the sixth century, when the Muslim invasion of Palestine occurred.

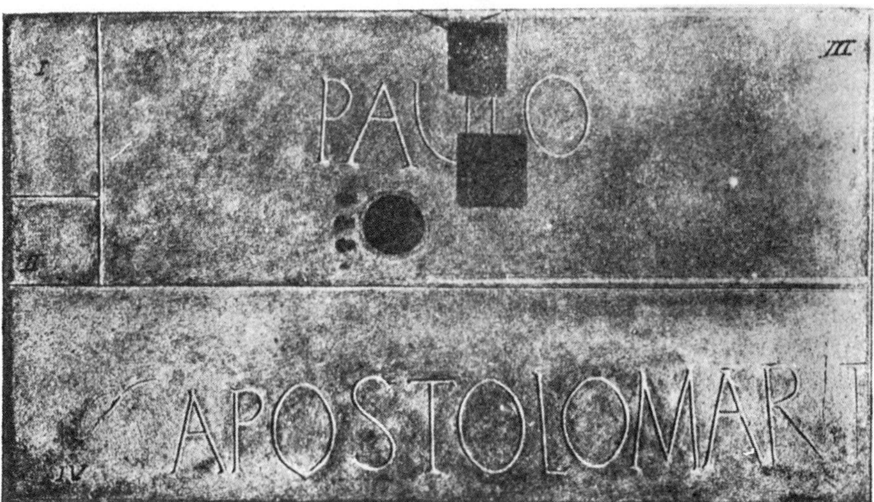

Memorial of Paul. This stone slab set in the floor of the old Church of St. Paul in Rome is the traditional site of his burial, following his martyrdom under the Emperor Nero in the late sixties. The inscription identifies him simply as Apostle, Martyr. *(From Guilio Belvedere, "L'Origine della Basilica Ostiense,"* Rivista di Archeologia Cristiana *22 (1946))*

many thousands of youths, women, and children perished by the sword, by famine, and by countless other forms of death; they can read how many and what famous Jewish cities were besieged, and finally how terrors and worse than terrors were seen by those who fled to Jerusalem as if to a mighty capital; they can study the nature of the whole war, all the details of what happened in it, and how at the end the abomination of desolation spoken of by the prophets was set up in the very temple of God, for all its ancient fame, and it perished utterly and passed away in flames.

After the martyrdom of JAMES and the capture of Jerusalem which immediately followed, the story goes that those of the Apostles and of the disciples of the Lord who were still alive came together from every place with those who were, humanly speaking, of the family of the Lord, for many of them were then still alive, and they all took counsel together as to whom they ought to adjudge worthy to succeed James, and all unanimously decided that SIMEON the son of CLOPAS,[71] whom the scripture of the Gospel also mentions, was worthy of the throne of the diocese there. He was, so it is said, a cousin of the Saviour, for Hegesippus relates that Clopas was the brother of Joseph, (XII.) and in addition that Vespasian, after the capture of Jerusalem, ordered a search to be made for all who were of the family of David, that there might be left among the Jews no one of the royal family and, for this reason, a very great persecution was again inflicted on the Jews.

XVIII. At this time, the story goes, the Apostle and Evangelist JOHN was still alive, and was condemned to live in the island of Patmos for his witness

[71]In Luke 24:18.

to the divine word. At any rate Irenaeus, writing about the number of the name ascribed to the anti-Christ in the so-called Apocalypse of John, states this about John in so many words in the fifth book against Heresies. "But if it had been necessary to announce his name plainly at the present time, it would have been spoken by him who saw the apocalypse. For it was not seen long ago but almost in our own time, at the end of the reign of Domitian."[72]

The same Domitian gave orders for the execution of those of the family of David and an ancient story goes that some heretics accused the grandsons
JUDE 1 of JUDAS (who is said to have been the brother, according to the flesh, of the Saviour) saying that they were of the family of David and related to the Christ himself. Hegesippus relates this exactly as follows. XX. "Now there still survived of the family of the Lord grandsons of Judas, who was said to have been his brother according to the flesh, and they were related as being of the family of David. These the officer brought to Domitian Caesar, for, like Herod, he was afraid of the coming of the Christ. He asked them if they were of the house of David and they admitted it. Then he asked them how much property they had, or how much money they controlled, and they said that all they possessed was nine thousand denarii between them, the half belonging to each, and they stated that they did not possess this in money but it was the valuation of only thirty-nine plethra of ground on which they paid taxes and lived on it by their own work." They then showed him their hands, adducing as testimony of their labour the hardness of their bodies, and the tough skin which had been embossed on their hands from their incessant work. They were asked concerning the Christ and his kingdom, its nature, origin, and time of appearance, and explained that it was neither of the world nor earthly, but heavenly and angelic, and it would be at the end of the world, when he would come in glory to judge the living and the dead and to reward every man according to his deeds. At this Domitian did not condemn them at all, but despised them as simple folk, released them, and decreed an end to the persecution against the church. But when they were released they were the leaders of the churches, both for their testimony and for their relation to the Lord, and remained alive in the peace which ensued until Trajan. Hegesippus tells this; moreover, Tertullian also has made similar mention of Domitian. "Domitian also once tried to do the same as he, for he was a Nero in cruelty, but I believe, inasmuch as he had some sense, he stopped at once and recalled those whom he had banished."

At this time that very disciple whom Jesus loved, JOHN, at once Apostle and Evangelist, still remained alive in Asia and administered the churches there, for after the death of Domitian, he had returned from his banishment on the island. And that he remained alive until this time may fully be confirmed by two witnesses, and these ought to be trustworthy for they represent the orthodoxy of the church, no less persons than Irenaeus and Clement of Alexandria. The former of these writes in one place in the second of his books *Against the Heresies,* as follows: "And all the presbyters who had been associated in Asia with JOHN, the disciple of the Lord, bear witness to his tradition, for he remained with them until the times of Trajan." And in the third book of the same work he makes the same statement as follows: "Now the church at Ephesus was founded by Paul, but John stayed there until the times of Trajan, and it is a true witness of the tradition of the Apostles."

[72]That is, prior to A.D. 96.

Clement indicates the same time, and in the treatise to which he gave the title *Who is the rich man that is saved,* adds a narrative most acceptable to those who enjoy hearing what is fine and edifying. Take and read here what he wrote. "Listen to a story which is not a story but a true tradition of JOHN the Apostle preserved in memory. For after the death of the tyrant he passed from the island of Patmos to Ephesus, and used also to go, when he was asked, to the neighbouring districts of the heathen, in some places to appoint bishops, in others to reconcile whole churches, and in others to ordain some one of those pointed out by the Spirit."

But come, let us indicate the undoubted writings of this Apostle. Let the Gospel according to him be first recognized, for it is read in all the churches under heaven. Moreover, that it was reasonable for the ancients to reckon it in the fourth place after the other three may be explained thus. Those inspired and venerable ancients, I mean Christ's Apostles, had completely purified their life and adorned their souls with every virtue, yet were but simple men in speech. Though they were indeed bold in the divine and wonder-working power given them by the Saviour, they had neither the knowledge nor the desire to represent the teachings of the Master in persuasive or artistic language, but they used only the proof of the Spirit of God which worked with them, and the wonder-working power of Christ which was consummated through them. Thus they announced the knowledge of the Kingdom of Heaven to all the world and cared but little for attention to their style. And this they did inasmuch as they were serving a
II COR. 12:2–4 greater, superhuman ministry. Thus PAUL, the most powerful of all in the preparation of argument and the strongest thinker, committed to writing no more than short epistles, though he had ten thousand ineffable things to say, seeing that he had touched the vision of the third heaven, had been caught up to the divine paradise itself, and was there granted the hearing of ineffable words. Nor were the other pupils of our Saviour without experience of the same things—the twelve Apostles and the seventy disciples and ten thousand others in addition to them. Yet nevertheless of all those who had been with the Lord only MATTHEW and JOHN have left us their recollections, and tradition says that they took to writing perforce. MATTHEW had first preached to Hebrews, and when he was on the point of going to others he transmitted in writing in his native language the Gospel according to himself, and thus supplied by writing the lack of his own presence to those from whom he was sent, and MARK and LUKE had already published the Gospels according to them, but JOHN, it is said, used all the time a message which was not written down, and at last took to writing for the following cause. The three gospels which had been written down before were distributed to all including himself; it is said that he welcomed them and testified to their truth but said that there was only lacking to the narrative the account of what was done by Christ at first and at the beginning of the preaching. The story is surely true. It is at least possible to see that the three evangelists related only what the Saviour did during one year after John the Baptist had been put in prison and that they stated this at the beginning of their narrative. At any rate, after the forty days' fast and the temptation which followed, Matthew fixes the time described in his own writing by saying that "hearing that John had been betrayed, he retreated" from Judaea
MT. 4:12 "into Galilee." Similarly MARK says, "and after John was betrayed Jesus came into Galilee." And Luke, too, makes a similar observation before beginning
LK. 3:19–20 the acts of Jesus saying that Herod added to the evil deeds which he had done by "shutting up John in prison." They say accordingly that for this

reason the apostle John was asked to relate in his own gospel the period
passed over in silence by the former evangelists and the things done during
JN. it by the Saviour (that is to say, the events before the imprisonment of the
3:22–24 Baptist), and that he indicated this at one time by saying, "this beginning of
miracles did Jesus," at another by mentioning the Baptist in the midst of the
acts of Jesus as at that time still baptizing at Aenon near Salem, and that he
makes this plain by saying, "for John was not yet cast into prison." Thus JOHN in the course of his gospel relates what Christ did before the Baptist had been thrown into prison, but the other three evangelists narrate the events after the imprisonment of the Baptist. If this be understood the gospels no longer appear to disagree, because that according to John contains the first of the acts of Christ and the others the narrative of what he did at the end of the period, and it will seem probable that John passed over the genealogy of our Saviour according to the flesh, because it had been already written out by Matthew and Luke, and began with the description of his divinity since this had been reserved for him by the Divine Spirit as for one greater than they.

The above must suffice us concerning the writing of the Gospel according to JOHN, and the cause for that according to Mark has been explained above. LUKE himself at the beginning of his treatise prefixed an account of the cause for which he had made his compilation, explaining that while many others had somewhat rashly attempted to make a narrative of the things of which he had himself full knowledge, he felt obliged to release us from the doubtful propositions of the others and related in his own gospel the accurate account of the things of which he had himself firmly learnt the truth from his profitable intercourse and life with Paul and his conversation with the other apostles.

3

The Literary Context

In order for the early Christians to communicate with their contemporaries it was essential that they use not only the languages of that era, but also the literary forms and common patterns of oral expression that were then in use. Inevitably they did not merely take over these forms unchanged, but adapted them and modified them to serve the particular purposes of the young movement. Since Christianity quickly took root among people of diverse backgrounds, the literary and oral modes of expression were different from place to place in the early Christian world.

In both Judaism and Greco-Roman culture of this period, a popular form of communication was the short story about a remarkable public figure. It might concentrate on some significant action of that person or report a saying or verbal exchange with an antagonist, a pupil, or an inquirer. These biographical anecdotes, which comprise much of the gospels and Acts, are to be found in the early rabbinic material as well as in accounts of wandering teachers and philosophers of the period. The stories were originally told randomly, in situations in which the content was appropriate. Pagan authors later joined them into a sequential account. Similarly, the gospel tradition eventually linked the stories together in a narrative sequence as we have it in the gospels—both those included in the New Testament and those written later and excluded from the canon.

A work often pointed out as an analogy to the gospels is the *Life of Apollonius of Tyana* by Philostratus. It does include a biographical account of that itinerant philosopher, and reports miracles performed by him as well as examples of his teachings. But it was not written until the third century, and was commissioned by a royal opponent of Christianity, probably to serve as a counter to the gospel. Philostratus alleges that he is using sources from the time of Apollonius (first century A.D.), but classical scholarship regards that claim as a deception.[1]

Paralleling this anecdotal material was the use by the early Christians, including Paul and possibly Jesus as well, of popular forms of public address. Both Jesus and Paul are portrayed in the New Testament as addressing randomly assembled crowds, just as the itinerant philosophers and orators of that time were accustomed to doing. Rather than formal lectures in formal settings, these teachers sought to persuade listeners in public marketplaces or in porticos or open-air theaters where the crowds would gather in Mediterranean cities. A common style of address in these circumstances was the diatribe, in which the speaker posed questions for his listeners and then provided the answers as well.

As the church recruited more of its members from the educated classes, and as it came to look forward to an extended existence (rather than a sudden end of the age), it began to employ the literary forms in use at that time. Among these were history and romance. The Roman historians were concerned that they show that the gods were at work in what the thoughtless might regard as the chance movement of history. These writers felt free to compose speeches for the leading characters in their narratives on the assumption that this is what ought to have been said, even though no contemporary record survives.

The romance, or novel, was written in an entertaining style with vivid accounts of journeys and ventures in distant or bizarre lands. But its major goal was propaganda on behalf of a cult, a god, or even for a philosophical point of view. This hellenistic form, which goes back to the second century B.C., became extremely popular in the second and third centuries. Among the best examples of this literary mode are romances concerning the devotees of Isis, who travel over the Mediterranean world in the determined effort to experience her mystically and to fulfill her purposes for their lives.

Although they are not to be classified as literature in the ordinary sense, there are four other forms of expression which are part of the significant cultural background of the New Testament: letters, hymns, magical formulas, and inscriptions. Actually, in the case of letters the distinction between literary and nonliterary is difficult to draw, since in the wider culture of that period as well as in early Christianity, there were genuine letters, written to specific persons for immediate occasions, as well as letter-like formal modes of address. The latter have often been

[1]For a detailed analysis of Philostratus's romantic account of Apollonius see H. C. Kee, *Miracle in the Early Christian World* (New Haven: Yale University Press, 1983), pp. 256–265.

called epistles, rather than merely letters. The hymns are distinguished by the lofty diction and regulated patterns of speech, as well as by the direct address to the deity and the ascriptions of praise or offering of petitions. The magical formulas were collected in later centuries, but some go back into the pre-Christian period. Characteristic of them are the use of multiple or secret names of the gods, the effort to coerce the gods to respond to the demands of the petitioner, and the instructions for the technique to be followed in order to gain from the god the desired objective.

The inscriptions that have been preserved from this period serve a variety of ends: providing dates, names, and details of events that correlate with events mentioned in the New Testament.

BIOGRAPHICAL ANECDOTES: PAGAN AND JEWISH

Known as a *chria,* the mode of biographical accounting is characteristic of nearly all the "lives" that have been preserved from the early centuries of the Roman empire and of the gospels as well. Diogenes Laertius, writing in the early third century A.D., was one who stitched together *chriae* concerning a number of philosophers, from which we have chosen typical examples depicting the life and teachings of Socrates (469–399 B.C.), and Diogenes of Sinope (412–323 B.C.), the outstanding representative of the Cynic School of philosophy.

In the rabbinic sources, there is almost no biographical interest, and most of the anecdotes that are included are edifying or amusing—sometimes both at once—concerning some activity or quality of one of the rabbis. Included here are some typical stories about the personalities of one of the most famous pairs of rabbis: Hillel and Shammai, of the first century A.D.

Lucian of Samosata offers in "Alexander the False Prophet" a delightful, cynically told story of an opportunist and trickster who makes his fortune by capitalizing on foolish, gullible people who are ready to believe anything. Reading these ancient "lives" should shed light on the distinctive features of the gospel accounts of Jesus, as well as show the influences of contemporary literary styles on the writers of the gospels.

DIOGENES LAERTIUS: SOCRATES

Demetrius of Byzantium relates that Crito removed him from his workshop and educated him, being struck by his beauty of soul; that he discussed moral questions in the workshops and the market-place, being convinced that the study of nature is no concern of ours; and that he claimed that his inquiries embraced "Whatso'er is good or evil in an house"; that frequently, owing to his vehemence in argument, men set upon him with their fists or tore his hair out; and that for the most part he was despised and laughed at, yet bore all this ill-usage patiently. So much so that, when he had been kicked, and someone expressed surprise at his taking it so quietly, Socrates rejoined, "Should I have taken legal action against a donkey, supposing that he had kicked me?" Thus far Demetrius.

Unlike most philosophers, he had no need to travel, except when required to go on an expedition. The rest of his life he stayed at home and engaged all the more keenly in argument with anyone who would converse with him, his aim being not to alter his opinion but to get at the truth. They relate that Euripides gave him the treatise of Heraclitus and asked his opinion upon it, and that his reply was, "The part I understand is excellent, and so too is, I dare say, the part I do not understand; but it needs a Delian diver to get to the bottom of it."

He took care to exercise his body and kept it in good condition. At all events he served on the expedition to Amphipolis; and when in the battle of Delium Xenophon had fallen from his horse, he stepped in and saved his life. For in the general flight of the Athenians he personally retired at his ease, quietly turning round from time to time and ready to defend himself in case he were attacked. Again, he served at Potidaea, whither he had gone by sea, as land communications were interrupted by the war; and while there he is said to have remained a whole night without changing his position, and to have won the prize of valour.

He was a man of great independence and dignity of character. Pamphila in the seventh book of her Commentaries tells how Alcibiades once offered him a large site on which to build a house; but he replied, "Suppose, then, I wanted shoes and you offered me a whole hide to make a pair with, would it not be ridiculous in me to take it?" Often when he looked at the multitude of wares exposed for sale, he would say to himself, "How many things I can do without!" And he would continually recite the lines:

> The purple robe and silver's shine
> More fits an actor's need than mine.

Moreover, in his old age he learnt to play the lyre, declaring that he saw no absurdity in learning a new accomplishment. As Xenophon relates in the Symposium, it was his regular habit to dance, thinking that such exercise helped to keep the body in good condition. He used to say that his supernatural sign warned him beforehand of the future; that to make a good start was no trifling advantage, but a trifle turned the scale; and that he knew nothing except just the fact of ignorance. . . . When Xanthippe first scolded him and then drenched him with water, his rejoinder was, "Did I not say that Xanthippe's thunder would end in rain?" When Alcibiades declared that the scolding of Xanthippe was intolerable, "Nay, I have got used to it," said he, "as to the continued rattle of a windlass. And you do not mind the cackle of geese." "No," replied Alcibiades, "but they furnish me with eggs and goslings." "And Xanthippe," said Socrates, "is the mother of my children." When she tore his coat off his back in the market-place and his acquaintances advised him to hit back, "Yes, by Zeus," said he, "in order that while we are sparring each of you may join in with 'Go it, Socrates!' 'Well done, Xanthippe!' " He said he lived with a shrew, as horsemen are fond of spirited horses, "but just as, when they have mastered these, they can easily cope with the rest, so I in the society of Xanthippe shall learn to adapt myself to the rest of the world."

* * *

The affidavit in the case, which is still preserved, says Favorinus, in the *Metroön,* ran as follows: "This indictment and affidavit is sworn by Meletus, the son of Meletus of Pitthos, against Socrates, the son of Sophroniscus of Alopece: Socrates is guilty of refusing to recognize the gods recognized by the state, and of introducing other new divinities. He is also guilty of corrupting the youth. The penalty demanded is death." The philosopher then, after Lysias had written a defence for him, read it through and said: "A fine speech, Lysias; it is not, however, suitable to me." For it was plainly more forensic than philosophical. Lysias said, "If it is a fine speech, how can it fail to suit you?" "Well," he replied, "would not fine raiment and fine shoes be just as unsuitable to me?"

Justus of Tiberias in his book entitled *The Wreath* says that in the course of the trial Plato mounted the platform and began: "Though I am the youngest, men of Athens, of all who ever rose to address you"—whereupon the judges shouted out, "Get down! Get down!" When therefore he was condemned by 281 votes more than those given for acquittal, and when the judges were assessing what he should suffer or what fine he should pay, he proposed to pay 25 drachmae. Eubulides indeed says he offered 100. When this caused an uproar among the judges, he said, "Considering my services, I assess the penalty at maintenance in the Prytaneum at the public expense."

Sentence of death was passed, with an accession of eighty fresh votes. He was put in prison, and a few days afterwards drank the hemlock, after much noble discourse which Plato records in the *Phaedo*. . . .

So he was taken from among men; and not long afterwards the Athenians felt such remorse that they shut up the training grounds and gymnasia. They banished the other accusers but put Meletus to death; they honoured Socrates with a bronze statue, the work of Lysippus, which they placed in the hall of processions.

DIOGENES LAERTIUS: DIOGENES OF SINOPE

On reaching Athens he fell in with Antisthenes. Being repulsed by him, because he never welcomed pupils, by sheer persistence Diogenes wore him out. Once when he stretched out his staff against him, the pupil offered his head with the words, "Strike, for you will find no wood hard enough to keep me away from you, so long as I think you've something to say." From that time forward he was his pupil, and, exile as he was, set out upon a simple life.

Through watching a mouse running about, says Theophrastus in the Megarian dialogue, not looking for a place to lie down in, not afraid of the dark, not seeking any of the things which are considered to be dainties, he discovered the means of adapting himself to circumstances. He was the first, say some, to fold his cloak because he was obliged to sleep in it as well, and he carried a wallet to hold his victuals, and he used any place for any purpose, for breakfasting, sleeping, or conversing. And then he would say, pointing to the portico of Zeus and the Hall of Processions, that the Athenians had provided him with places to live in. He did not lean upon a staff until he grew infirm; but afterwards he would carry it everywhere, not indeed in the city, but when walking along the road with it and with his wallet; so say Olympiodorus, once a magistrate at Athens, Polyeuctus the orator, and Lysanias the son of Aeschrio. He had written to someone to try and procure a cottage for him. When this man was a long time about it, he took for his abode the tub in the Metroön, as he himself explains in his letters. And in summer he used to roll in it over hot sand, while in winter he used to embrace statues covered with snow, using every means of inuring himself to hardship.

He was great at pouring scorn on his contemporaries. The school of Euclides he called bilious, and Plato's lectures waste of time, the performances at the Dionysia great peep-shows for fools, and the demagogues the mob's lackeys. He used also to say that when he saw physicians, philosophers and pilots at their work, he deemed man the most intelligent of all animals; but when again he saw interpreters of dreams and diviners and those who attended to them, or those who were puffed up with conceit of wealth, he thought no animal more silly. He would continually say that for the conduct of life we need right reason or a halter.

One day, observing a child drinking out of his hands, he cast away the cup from his wallet with the words, "A child has beaten me in plainness of living." He also threw away his bowl when in like manner he saw a child who had broken his plate taking up his lentils with the hollow part of a morsel of bread. He used also to reason thus: "All things belong to the gods. The wise are friends of the gods, and friends hold things in common. Therefore all things belong to the wise.". . .

All the curses of tragedy, he used to say, had lighted upon him. At all events he was

> A homeless exile, to his country dead.
> A wanderer who begs his daily bread.

But he claimed that to fortune he could oppose courage, to convention nature, to passion reason. When he was sunning himself in the Craneum, Alexander came and stood over him and said, "Ask of me any boon you like." To which he replied, "Stand out of my light." Someone had been reading aloud for a very long time, and when he was near the end of the roll pointed to a space with no writing on it. "Cheer up, my men," cried Diogenes; "there's land in sight." To one who by argument had proved conclusively that he had horns, he said, touching his forehead, "Well, I for my part don't see any." In like manner, when somebody declared that there is no such thing as motion, he got up and walked about. When someone was discoursing with celestial phenomena, "How many days," asked Diogenes, "were you in coming from the sky?" A eunuch of bad character had inscribed on his door the words, "Let nothing evil enter." "How then," he asked, "is the master of the house to get in?" When he had anointed his feet with unguent, he declared that from his head the unguent passed into the air, but from his feet into his nostrils.

The musician who was always deserted by his audience he greeted with a "Hail chanticleer," and when asked why he so addressed him, replied, "Because your song makes everyone get up."

When someone reproached him with his exile, his reply was, "Nay, it was through that, you miserable fellow, that I came to be a philosopher." Again, when someone reminded him that the people of Sinope had sentenced him to exile, "And I them," said he, "to home-staying."

. . . Being asked whether he had any maid or boy to wait on him, he said "No." "If you should die, then, who will carry you out to burial?" "Whoever wants the house," he replied.

Being asked if the wise eat cakes, "Yes," he said, "cakes of all kinds, just like other men." Being asked why people give to beggars but not to philosophers, he said, "Because they think they may one day be lame or blind, but never expect that they will turn to philosophy." He was begging of a miserly man who was slow to respond; so he said, "My friend, it's for food that I'm asking, not for funeral expenses." Being reproached one day for having falsified the currency, he said, "That was the time when I was such as you are now; but such as I am now, you will never be."

Being asked whether death was an evil thing, he replied, "How can it be evil, when in its presence we are not aware of it?" When Alexander stood opposite him and asked, "Are you not afraid of me?" "Why, what are you?" said he, "a good thing or a bad?" Upon Alexander replying "A good thing," "Who then," said Diogenes, "is afraid of the good?" Education, according to him, is a controlling grace to the young, consolation to the old, wealth to the poor, and ornament to the rich. When Didymon, who was a rake, was once treating a girl's eye, "Beware," says Diogenes, "lest the oculist instead of curing the eye should ruin the pupil." On somebody declaring that his own friends were plotting against him, Diogenes exclaimed, "What is to be done then, if you have to treat friends and enemies alike?"

Being asked what was the most beautiful thing in the world, he replied, "Freedom of speech." On entering a boys' school, he found there many statues of the Muses, but few pupils. "By the help of the gods," said he, "schoolmaster, you have plenty of pupils."

RABBINIC ANECDOTES

FROM *THE FATHERS ACCORDING TO RABBI NATHAN*

MT. 7:12 RABBI ELIEZER SAYS: LET THE HONOR OF THY FELLOW BE AS DEAR TO THEE AS THINE OWN. BE NOT EASILY ANGERED. REPENT ONE DAY BEFORE THY DEATH.

LET THE HONOR OF THY FELLOW BE AS DEAR TO THEE AS THINE OWN: how so? This teaches that even as one looks out for his own honor, so should he look out for his fellow's honor. And even as no man wishes that his own honor be held in ill repute, so should he wish that the honor of his fellow shall not be held in ill repute.

Another interpretation. LET THE HONOR OF THY FELLOW BE AS DEAR TO THEE AS THINE OWN: For example, [even] when a man has had a million and then all his wealth is taken away, let him not discredit himself over so much as a perutah's worth.

MT. 5:21 BE NOT EASILY ANGERED: what is that? This teaches that one should be patient like Hillel the Elder and not short tempered like Shammai the Elder.

What was this patience of Hillel the Elder? The story is told:

Once two men decided to make a wager of four hundred zuz with each other. They said: "Whoever can put Hillel into a rage gets the four hundred zuz."

One of them went [to attempt it]. Now that day was a Sabbath eve, toward dusk, and Hillel was washing his head. The man came and knocked on his door. "Where's Hillel? Where's Hillel?" he cried.

Hillel got into a cloak and came out to meet him. "My son," he said, "what is it?"

The man replied: "I need to ask about a certain matter."

"Ask," Hillel said.

The man asked: "Why are the eyes of the Tadmorites bleary?"

"Because," said Hillel, "they make their homes on the desert sands which the winds come and blow into their eyes. That is why their eyes are bleary."

The man went off, waited a while, and returned and knocked on his door. "Where's Hillel?" he cried, "where's Hillel?"

Hillel got into a cloak and came out. "My son," he said, "what is it?"

The man replied: "I need to ask about a certain matter."

"Ask," Hillel said.

The man asked: "Why are the Africans' feet flat?"

"Because they dwell by watery marshes," said Hillel, "and all the time they walk in water. That is why their feet are flat."

The man went off, waited a while, and returned and knocked on the door. "Where's Hillel?" he cried, "where's Hillel?"

Hillel got into a cloak and came out. "What is it thou wishest to ask?" he inquired.

"I need to ask about some matter," the man said.

"Ask," Hillel said to him. In his cloak he sat down before him and said: "What is it?"

Said the man: "Is this how princes reply! May there be no more like thee in Israel!"

"God forbid!" Hillel said, "tame thy spirit! What dost thou wish?"

The man asked: "Why are the heads of Babylonians long?"

"My son," Hillel answered, "thou hast raised an important question. Since there are no skillful midwives there, when the infant is born, slaves and maidservants tend it on their laps. That is why the heads of Babylonians are long. Here, however, there are skillful midwives, and when the infant is born it is taken care of in a cradle and its head is rubbed. That is why the heads of Palestinians are round."

"Thou hast put me out of four hundred zuz!" the man exclaimed.

Said Hillel to him: "Better that thou lose four hundred zuz because of Hillel than that Hillel lose his temper."

What was this impatience of Shammai the Elder? The story is told:

A certain man once stood before Shammai and said to him: "Master, how many Torahs have you?"

"Two," Shammai replied, "one written and one oral."

Said the man: "The written one I am prepared to accept, the oral one I am not prepared to accept."

Shammai rebuked him and dismissed him in a huff.

He came before Hillel and said to him: "Master, how many Torahs were given?"

"Two," Hillel replied, "one written and one oral."

Said the man: "The written one I am prepared to accept, the oral one I am not prepared to accept."

"My son," Hillel said to him, "sit down."

He wrote out the alphabet for him [and pointing to one of the letters] asked him: "What is this?"

"It is *'aleph,*" the man replied.

Said Hillel: "This is not *'aleph* but *bet.* What is that?" he continued.

The man answered: "It is *bet.*"

"This is not *bet,*" said Hillel, "but *gimmel.*"

[In the end] Hillel said to him: "How dost thou know that this is *'aleph* and this *bet* and this *gimmel?* Only because so our ancestors of old handed it down to us that this is *'aleph* and this *bet* and this *gimmel.* Even as thou hast taken this in good faith, so take the other in good faith."

A certain heathen once passed behind a synagogue and heard a child reciting: *And these are the garments which they shall make: a breastplate, and an ephod, and a robe* [Exod. 28:4]. He came before Shammai and asked him: "Master, all this honor, whom is it for?"

Shammai said to him: "For the High Priest, who stands and serves at the altar."

Said the heathen: "Convert me on condition that thou appoint me High Priest, so I might serve at the altar."

"Is there no priest in Israel," Shammai exclaimed, "and have we no High Priests to stand and serve in high priesthood at the altar, that a paltry proselyte who has come with naught but his staff and bag should go and serve in high priesthood!" He rebuked him and dismissed him in a huff.

The heathen then came to Hillel and said to him: "Master, convert me on condition that thou appoint me High Priest, so that I might stand and serve at the altar."

"Sit down," Hillel said to him, "and I will tell thee something. If one wishes to greet a king of flesh and blood, is it not right that he learn how to make his entrances and exits?"

"Indeed," the heathen replied.

"Thou wishest to greet the King of kings of kings, the Holy One, blessed be He: is it not all the more right that thou learn how to enter into the Holy of Holies, how to fix the lights, how to approach the altar, how to set the table, how to prepare the row of wood?"

Said the heathen: "Do what seems best in thine eyes."

First Hillel wrote out the alphabet for him and taught it to him. Then he taught him the book of Leviticus. And the heathen went on studying until he got to the verse, *And the common man that draweth nigh shall be put to death* [Num. 1:51]. Forthwith, of his own accord, he reasoned by inference as follows: "If Israel, who were called children of God and of whom the Shekinah said, *And ye shall be unto Me a kingdom of priests, and a holy nation* [Exod. 19:6], were nevertheless warned by Scripture, *And the common man that draweth nigh shall be put to death,* all the more I, a paltry proselyte, come with naught but my bag!" Thereupon that proselyte was reconciled of his own accord.

He came to Hillel the Elder and said to him: "May all the blessings of the Torah rest upon thy head! For hadst thou been like Shammai the Elder I might never have entered the community of Israel. The impatience of

Shammai the Elder well nigh caused me to perish in this world and the world to come. Thy patience has brought me to the life of this world and the one to come."

It is said: To that proselyte were born two sons; one named Hillel and the other he named Gamaliel; and they used to be called "proselytes of Hillel."

REPENT ONE DAY BEFORE THY DEATH. Rabbi Eliezer was asked by his disciples: "Does, then, a man know on what day he will die, that he should know when to repent?"

"All the more," he replied; "let him repent today lest he die on the morrow; let him repent on the morrow lest he die the day after: and thus all his days will be spent in repentance."

Rabbi Yose bar Judah says in the name of Rabbi Judah son of Rabbi Il'ai who said it in the name of Rabbi Eliezer the Great: REPENT ONE DAY BEFORE THY DEATH. KEEP WARM AT THE FIRE OF THE SAGES. BEWARE OF THEIR GLOWING COAL LEST THOU BE SCORCHED: FOR THEIR BITE IS THE BITE OF A JACKAL AND THEIR STING THE STING OF A SCORPION—MOREOVER ALL THEIR WORDS ARE LIKE COALS OF FIRE.

LUCIAN OF SAMOSATA: ALEXANDER THE FALSE PROPHET

There was no slight difference of opinion between them on that score, but in the end Alexander won, and going to Chalcedon, since after all that city seemed to them to have some usefulness, in the temple of Apollo, which is the most ancient in Chalcedon, they buried bronze tablets which said that very soon Asclepius, with his father Apollo, would move to Pontus and take up his residence at Abonoteichus. The opportune discovery of these tablets caused this story to spread quickly to all Bithynia and Pontus, and to Abonoteichus sooner than anywhere else. Indeed, the people of that city immediately voted to build a temple and began at once to dig for the foundations. Then Cocconas was left behind in Chalcedon, composing equivocal, ambiguous, obscure oracles, and died before long, bitten, I think, by a viper. It was Alexander who was sent in first; he now wore his hair long, had falling ringlets, dressed in a parti-coloured tunic of white and purple, with a white cloak over it, and carried a falchion like that of Perseus, from whom he claimed descent on his mother's side. And although those miserable Paphlagonians knew that both his parents were obscure, humble folk, they believed the oracle when it said:

Here in your sight is a scion of Perseus, dear
  unto Phoebus;
This is divine Alexander, who shareth the blood of
  the Healer!

Podaleirius, the Healer, it would appear, was so passionate and amorous that his ardour carried him all the way from Tricca to Paphlagonia in quest of Alexander's mother!

An oracle by now had turned up which purported to be a prior prediction by the Sibyl:

On the shores of the Euxine sea, in the neighborhood of
Sinope,
There shall be born, by a Tower, in the days of the Romans,
a prophet;
After the foremost unit and three times ten, he will shew
forth
Five more units besides, and a score told three times over,
Matching, with places four, the name of a valiant defender!

Well, upon invading his native land with all this pomp and circumstance after a long absence, Alexander was a man of mark and note, affecting as he did to have occasional fits of madness and causing his mouth to fill with foam. This he easily managed by chewing the root of soapwort, the plant that dyers use; but to his fellow-countrymen even the foam seemed supernatural and awe-inspiring. Then, too, they had long ago prepared and fitted up a serpent's head of linen, which had something of a human look, was all painted up, and appeared very lifelike. It would open and close its mouth by means of horsehairs, and a forked black tongue like a snake's, also controlled by horsehairs, would dart out. Besides, the serpent from Pella was ready in advance and was being cared for at home, destined in due time to manifest himself to them and to take a part in their show—in fact, to be cast for the leading role.

When at length it was time to begin, he contrived an ingenious ruse. Going at night to the foundations of the temple which were just being excavated, where a pool of water had gathered which either issued from springs somewhere in the foundations themselves or had fallen from the sky, he secreted there a goose-egg, previously blown, which contained a snake just born; and after burying it deep in the mud, he went back again. In the morning he ran out into the market-place naked, wearing a loin-cloth (this too was gilded), carrying his falchion, and tossing his unconfined mane like a devotee of the Great Mother in the frenzy. Addressing the people from a high altar upon which he had climbed, he congratulated the city because it was at once to receive the god in visible presence. The assembly—for almost the whole city, including women, old men, and boys, had come running—marvelled, prayed and made obeisance. Uttering a few meaningless words like Hebrew or Phoenician, he dazed the creatures, who did not know what he was saying save only that he everywhere brought in Apollo and Asclepius. Then he ran at full speed to the future temple, went to the excavation and the previously improvised fountain-head of the oracle, entered the water, sang hymns in honour of Asclepius and Apollo at the top of his voice, and besought the god, under the blessing of Heaven, to come to the city. Then he asked for a libation-saucer, and when somebody handed him one, deftly slipped it underneath and brought up, along with water and mud, that egg in which he had immured the god; the joint about the plug had been closed with wax and white lead. Taking it in his hands, he asserted that at that moment he held Asclepius! They gazed unwaveringly to see what in the world was going to happen; indeed, they had already marvelled at the discovery of the egg in the water. But when he broke it and received the tiny snake into his hollowed hand, and the crowd saw it moving and twisting about his fingers, they at once raised a shout, welcomed the god, congratulated their city, and began each of them to sate himself greedily with prayers, craving treasures, riches, health, and every other blessing from him. But Alexander went home again at full speed, taking with him the new-born Asclepius, "born twice, when other men are born but once," whose mother was not Coronis, by Aeus, nor yet a crow, but a goose! And the whole population followed, all full of religious fervour and crazed with expectations.

For some days he remained at home, expecting what actually happened—that as the news spread, crowds of Paphlagonians would come running in. When the city had become over-full of people, all of them already bereft of their brains and sense, and not in the least like bread-eating humans, but different from beasts of the field only in their looks, he seated himself on a couch in a certain chamber, clothed in apparel well suited to a god, and took into his bosom his Ascelpius from Pella, who, as I have said, was of uncommon size and beauty. Coiling him about his neck, and letting the tail, which was long, stream over his lap and drag part of its length on the floor, he concealed only the head at one side of his own beard, as if it certainly belonged to the creature that was in view.

Now then, please imagine a little room, not very bright and not admitting any too much daylight; also, a crowd of heterogeneous humanity, excited, wonder-struck in advance, agog with hopes. When they went in, the thing, of course, seemed to them a miracle, that the formerly tiny snake within a few days had turned into so great a serpent, with a human face, moreover, and tame! They were immediately crowded towards the exit, and before they could look closely were forced out by those who kept coming in, for another door had been opened on the opposite side as an exit. That was the way the Macedonians did, they say, in Babylon during Alexander's illness, when he was in a bad way and they surrounded the palace, craving to see him and say good-bye. This exhibition the scoundrel gave not merely once, they say, but again and again, above all if any rich men were newly arrived.

Again and again, as I said before, he exhibited the serpent to all who requested it, not in its entirety, but exposing chiefly the tail and the rest of the body and keeping the head out of sight under his arm. But as he wished to astonish the crowd still more, he promised to produce the god talking—delivering oracles in person without a prophet. It was no difficult matter for him to fasten cranes' windpipes together and pass them through the head, which he had so fashioned as to be lifelike. Then he answered the questions through someone else, who spoke into the tube from the outside, so that the voice issued from his canvas Asclepius.

These oracles were called autophones, and were not given to everybody promiscuously, but only to those who were noble, rich, and free-handed.

POPULAR RHETORIC

Self-styled philosophers wandered about from city to city, addressing whoever stopped to listen in the public squares and marketplaces. The style of rhetoric used by these teacher-preachers was a question and answer method by which the speaker posed problems or difficulties, and then provided the response that he thought the hearer needed. The following examples of these appear in Arrian's reports of the teachings of Epictetus, a Stoic philosopher of the first century A.D. An excerpt from a summary of his philosophy is also included.

OF FREEDOM

He is free who lives as he wills, who is subject neither to compulsion, nor hindrance, nor force, whose choices are unhampered, whose desires attain their end, whose aversions do not fall into what they would avoid. Who, then, wishes to live in error?—No one.—Who wishes to live deceived, impetuous, unjust, unrestrained, peevish, abject?—No one.—Therefore, there is no bad man who lives as he wills, and accordingly no bad man is free. And who wishes to live in grief, fear, envy, pity, desiring things and failing to get them, avoiding things and falling into them?—No one at all.—Do we find, then, any bad man free from grief or fear, not falling into what he would avoid, nor failing to achieve what he desires?—No one.—Then we find no bad man free, either. (IV:1)

ON THE NATURE OF THE GOOD

Do you not know that you are nourishing God, exercising God? You are bearing God about with you, you poor wretch, and know it not! Do you suppose I am speaking of some external God, made of silver or gold? It is within yourself that you bear Him, and do not perceive that you are defiling Him with impure thoughts and filthy actions. Yet in the presence of even an image of God you would not dare to do anything of the things you are now doing. But when God Himself is present within you, seeing and hearing everything, are you not ashamed to be thinking and doing such things as these, O insensible of your own nature, and object of God's wrath! (II:8)

THE ENCHEIRIDION OF EPICTETUS

1. Some things are under our control, while others are not under our control. Under our control are conception, choice, desire, aversion, and, in a word, everything that is our own doing; not under our control are our body, our property, reputation, office, and, in a word, everything that is not our own doing. Furthermore, the things under our control are by nature free, unhindered, and unimpeded; while the things not under our control are weak, servile, subject to hindrance, and not our own. Remember, therefore, that if what is naturally slavish you think to be free, and what is not your own to be your own, you will be hampered, will grieve, will be in turmoil, and will blame both gods and men; while if you think only what is your own to be your own, and what is not your own to be, as it really is, not your own, then no one will ever be able to exert compulsion upon you, no one will hinder you, you will blame no one, will find fault with no one, will do absolutely nothing against your will, you will have no personal enemy, no one will harm you, for neither is there any harm that can touch you.

With such high aims, therefore, remember that you must bestir yourself with no slight effort to lay hold of them, but you will have to give up some things entirely, and defer others for the time being. But if you wish for these things also, and at the same time for both office and wealth, it may be that you will not get even these latter, because you aim also at the former, and certainly you will fail to get the former, which alone bring freedom and happiness.

Make it, therefore, your study at the very outset to say to every harsh external impression, "You are an external impression and not at all what you appear to be." After that examine it and test it by these rules which you have, the first and most important of which is this: Whether the impression has to do with the things which are under our control, or with those which are not under our control; and, if it has to do with some one of the things not under our control, have ready to hand the answer, "It is nothing to me."

Historiography

LUCIAN OF SAMOSATA: HOW TO WRITE HISTORY (EXCERPTS)

After warning the would-be writer of history to avoid being carried away by imagination or unbridled enthusiasm, Lucian (125–180 A.D.) makes a plea for moderation and personal discipline.

As to the facts themselves, he should not assemble them at random, but only after much laborious and painstaking investigation. He should for preference be an eyewitness, but, if not, listen to those who tell the more impartial story, those whom one would suppose least likely to subtract from the facts or add to them out of malice or favor. When this happens let him show shrewdness and skill in putting together the more credible story. When he has collected all or most of the facts let him first make them into a series of notes, a body of material as yet with no beauty or continuity. Then, after arranging them into order, let him give it beauty and enhance it with the charms of expression, figure and rhythm.

* * *

Above all let him bring a mind like a mirror, clear, gleaming-bright, accurately centred, displaying the shape of things just as he receives them, free from distortion, false coloring, and misrepresentation. His concern is different from that of the orators—what historians have to relate is fact and will speak for itself, for it has already happened: what is required is arrangement and exposition. So they must look not for what to say but how to say it. In brief, we must consider that the writer of history should be like Phidias or Praxiteles or Alcamenes or one of the other sculptors—they certainly never manufactured their own gold or silver or ivory or their other material; no, their material was before them, put into their hands by Eleans or Athenians or Argives, and they confined themselves to fashioning it, sawing the ivory, polishing, glueing, aligning it, setting it off with the gold, and their art lay in handling their material properly.

The task of the historian is similar: to give a fine arrangement to events and illuminate them as vividly as possible. And when a man who has heard him thinks thereafter that he is actually seeing what is being described and then praises him—then it is that the work of our Phidias of history is perfect and has received its proper praise.

After all his preparations are made he will sometimes begin without a preface, when the subject matter requires no preliminary exposition. But even then he will use a virtual preface to clarify what he is going to say.

Whenever he does use a preface, he will make two points only, not three like the orators. He will omit the appeal for a favourable hearing and give his audience what will interest and instruct them. For they will give him their attention if he shows that what he is going to say will be important, essential, personal, or useful.

* * *

After the preface, long or short in proportion to its subject matter, let the transition to the narrative be gentle and easy. For all the body of the history is simply a long narrative. So let it be adorned with the virtues proper to narrative, progressing smoothly, evenly and consistently, free from humps and hollows. Then let its clarity be limpid, achieved, as I have said, both by diction and the interweaving of the matter. For he will make everything distinct and complete, and when he has finished the first topic he will introduce the second, fastened to it and linked with it like a chain, to avoid the breaks and a multiplicity of disjointed narratives; no, always the first and second topics must not merely be neighbors but have common material and overlap.

POPULAR ROMANCES

Apuleius (Lucius Apuleius Africans): Metamorphoses

Born in North Africa about 123 A.D., educated in Carthage and in Athens, Apuleius perfected his Latin in Rome. On his mother's side, he was related to Plutarch (A.D. 46–120) and considered himself a Platonist, although his extant writings are not philosophical but religious and mystical. Under the guise of telling a string of popular tales, Apuleius reveals the story of his own personal and religious pilgrimage. He depicts the experiences of a man who was bewitched and changed into an ass, and was then restored to pure human form through the grace of the goddess Isis. Only through her intervention and the transformation she effected in him was he able to achieve his true humanity. The *Metamorphoses* is the best ancient witness we possess to the religious appeal of initiation into the mysteries and to the inner sense of fulfillment that the experience provided.

About the first watch of the night, when as I had slept my first sleep, I awaked with sudden fear, and saw the moon shining bright as when she is at the full, and seeming as though she leaped out of the sea. Then I thought with myself that this was the most secret time, when that goddess had most puissance and force, considering that all human things be governed by her providence; and that not only all beasts private and tame, wild and savage, be made strong by the governance of her light and godhead, but also things inanimate and without life; and I considered that all bodies in the heavens, the earth, and the seas be by her increasing motions increased, and by her diminishing motions diminished: then as weary of all my cruel fortune and calamity, I found good hope and sovereign remedy, though it were very late, to be delivered of all my misery, by invocation and prayer to the excellent beauty of this powerful goddess. Wherefore shaking off my drowsy sleep I rose with a joyful face, and moved by a great affection to purify myself, I plunged my head seven times into the water of the sea; which number of seven is convenable and agreeable to holy and divine things, as the worthy and sage philosopher Pythagoras hath declared. Then very lively and joyfully, though with a weeping countenance, I made this oration to the puissant goddess:

"O blessed queen of heaven, whether Thou be the Dame Ceres which art the original and motherly nurse of all fruitful things in the earth, who, after the finding of Thy daughter Proserpine, through the great joy which Thou didst presently conceive, didst utterly take away and abolish the food of them of old time, the acorn, and madest the barren and unfruitful ground of Eleusis to be ploughed and sown, and now givest men a more better and milder food; or whether Thou be the celestial Venus, who, in the beginning of the world, didst couple together male and female with an engendered love, and didst so make an eternal propagation of human kind, being now worshipped within the temples of the Isle Paphos; or whether Thou be the sister of the god Phoebus, who hast saved so many people by lightening and lessening with thy medicines and pangs of travail and art now adored at the sacred places of Ephesus; or whether Thou be called terrible Proserpine, by reason of the deadly howlings which Thou yieldest, that hast power with triple face to stop and put away the invasion of hags and ghosts which appear unto men, and to keep them down in the closures of the Earth, which dost wander in sundry groves and art worshipped in divers manners; Thou, which dost luminate all the cities of the earth by Thy feminine light; Thou, which nourishest all the seeds of the world by Thy damp heat, giving Thy changing light according to the wanderings, near or far, of the sun: by whatsoever name or fashion or shape it is lawful to call upon Thee, I pray Thee to end my great travail and misery and raise up my fallen hopes, and deliver me from the wretched fortune which so long time pursued me. Grant peace and rest, if it please Thee, to my adversities, for I have endured enough labour and peril. Remove from me the hateful shape of mine ass, and render me to my kindred and to mine own self Lucius: and I have offended in any point Thy divine majesty, let me rather die if I may not live."

When I had ended this oration, discovering my plaints to the goddess, I fortuned to fall again asleep upon the same bed; and by and by (for mine eyes were but newly closed) appeared to me from the midst of the sea a divine and venerable face, worshipped even of the gods themselves. Then, by little and little, I seemed to see the whole figure of her body, bright and mounting out of the sea and standing before me: wherefore I propose to describe her divine semblance, if the poverty of my human speech will suffer me, or her divine power give me a power of eloquence rich enough to express it. First she had a great abundance of hair, flowing and curling, dispersed and scattered about her divine neck; on the crown of her head she bare many garlands interlaced with flowers, and in the middle of her forehead was a plain circlet in fashion of a mirror, or rather resembling the moon by the light it gave forth; and this was borne up on either side by serpents that seemed to rise from the furrows of the earth, and above it were blades of corn set out. Her vestment was of finest linen yielding divers colours, somewhere white and shining, somewhere yellow like the crocus flower, somewhere rosy red, somewhere flaming; and (which troubled my sight and spirit sore) her cloak was utterly dark and obscure covered with shining black, and being wrapped round her from under her left arm to her right shoulder in manner of a shield, part of it fell down, pleated in most subtle fashion, to the skirts of her garment so that the welts appeared comely. Here and there upon the edge thereof and throughout its surface the stars glimpsed, and in the middle of them was placed the moon in mid-month, which shone like a flame of fire; and round about the whole length of the border of that goodly robe was a crown or garland wreathing unbroken, made with all flowers and all fruits. Things quite diverse did she bear:

for in her right hand she had a timbrel of brass, a flat piece of metal curved in manner of a girdle, wherein passed not many rods through the periphery of it; and when with her arm she moved these triple chords, they gave forth a shrill and clear sound. In her left hand she bare a cup of gold like unto a boat, upon the handle whereof, in the upper part which is best seen, an asp lifted up his head with a wide-swelling throat. Her odoriferous feet were covered with shoes interlaced and wrought with victorious palm. Thus the divine shape, breathing out the pleasant spice of fertile Arabia, disdained not with her holy voice to utter these words unto me:

"Behold, Lucius, I am come; thy weeping and prayer hath moved me to succour thee. I am she that is the natural mother of all things, mistress and governess of all the elements, the initial progeny of worlds, chief of the powers divine, queen of all that are in hell, the principal of them that dwell in heaven, manifested alone and under one form of all the gods and goddesses. At my will the planets of the sky, the wholesome winds of the seas, and the lamentable silences of hell be disposed; my name, my divinity is adored throughout all the world, in divers manners, in variable customs, and by many names. For the Phrygians that are the first of all men call me the Mother of the gods at Pessinus; the Athenians, which are sprung from their own soil, Cecropian Minerva; the Cyprians, which are girt about the sea, Paphian Venus; the Cretans which bear arrows, Dictynnian Diana; the Sicilians, which speak three tongues, infernal Proserpine; the Eleusians their ancient goddess Ceres; some Juno, other Bellona, other Hecate, other Rhamnusia, and principally both sort of the Ethiopians which dwell in the Orient and are enlightened by the morning rays of the sun, and the Egyptians, which are excellent in all kind of ancient doctrine, and by their proper ceremonies accustom to worship me, do call me by my true name, Queen Isis. Behold I am come to take pity on thy fortune and tribulation; behold I am present to favour and aid thee; leave off thy weeping and lamentation, put away all thy sorrow, for behold the healthful day which is ordained by my providence. Therefore be ready and attentive to my commandment; the day which shall come after this night is dedicated to my service by an eternal religion; my priests and ministers do accustom, after the wintry and stormy tempests of the sea be ceased and the billows of his waves are still, to offer in my name a new ship, as a first-fruit of their navigation; and for this must thou wait, and not profane or despise the sacrifice in any wise. For the great priest shall carry this day following in procession, by my exhortation, a garland of roses next to the timbrel of his right hand; delay not, but, trusting to my will, follow that my procession passing amongst the crowd of the people, and when thou comest to the priest, make as though thou wouldst kiss his hand, but snatch at the roses and thereby put away the skin and shape of an ass, which kind of beast I have long time abhorred and despised. But above all things beware thou doubt not nor fear of any of those things as hard and difficult to be brought to pass; for in this same hour that I am come to thee, I am present there also, and I command the priest by a vision what he shall do, as here followeth: and all the people by my commandment shall be compelled to give thee place and say nothing. Moreover, think not that amongst so fair and joyful ceremonies, and in so good company, that any person shall abhor thy ill-favoured and deformed figure, or that any man shall be so hard as to blame and reprove thy sudden restoration to human shape, whereby they should gather or conceive any sinister opinion of thee; and know thou this of certainty, that the residue of thy life until the hour of death shall be bound and subject to me; and think it not an injury to be always serviceable towards me whilst thou shalt live, since as by my mean and benefit thou shalt return again to be a man. Thou shalt live blessed in this world, thou shalt live glorious by my guide and protection, and when after thine allotted space of life thou descendest to hell, there thou shalt see me in that subterranean firmament shining (as thou seest me now) in the darkness of Acheron, and reigning in the deep profundity of Styx, and thou shalt worship me as one that hath been favourable to thee. And if I perceive that thou art obedient to my commandment and addict to my religion, meriting by thy constant chastity my divine grace, know thou that I alone may prolong thy days above the time that the fates have appointed and ordained."

. . . Then the priest, being admonished the night before, as I might well perceive, and marvelling that now the event came opportunely to fulfil that warning, suddenly stood still, and holding out his hands thrust out the garland of roses to my mouth: which garland I (trembling and my heart beating greatly) devoured with a great affection. As soon as I had eaten them, I was not deceived of the promise made unto me: for my deform and assy face abated, and first the rugged hair of my body fell off, my thick skin waxed soft and tender, my fat belly became thin, the hoofs of my feet changed into toes, my hands were no more feet but returned again to the work of a man that walks upright, my neck grew short, my head and mouth became round, my long ears were made little, my great and stony teeth waxed less, like the teeth of men, and my tail, which before cumbered me most, appeared nowhere. Then the people began to marvel, and the religious honoured the goddess for so evident a miracle, which was foreshadowed by the visions which they saw in the night, and the facility of my reformation, whereby they lifted their hands to heaven and with one voice rendered testimony of so great a benefit which I received of the goddess.

When I saw myself in such estate, I was utterly astonished and stood still a good space and said nothing; for my mind could not contain so sudden and so great joy, and I could not tell what to say, nor what word I should first speak with my voice newly found, nor what thanks I should render to the goddess. But the great priest, understanding all my fortune and misery by divine advertisement, although he also was amazed at this notable marvel, by gestures commanded that one should give me a linen garment to cover me; for as soon as I was transformed from the vile skin of an ass to my human shape, I hid the privities of my body with my hands as far as a naked man might do. Then one of the company put off his upper robe, and put it on my back; which done, the priest, looking upon me with a sweet and benign countenance, began to say in this sort: "O my friend Lucius, after the endurance of so many labours and the escape of so many tempests of fortune, thou art now at length come to the port and haven of rest and mercy. Neither did thy noble lineage, thy dignity, neither thy excellent doctrine anything avail thee; but because thou didst turn to servile pleasures, by a little folly of thy youthfulness, thou hast had a sinister reward of thy unprosperous curiosity. But howsoever the blindness of fortune tormented thee in divers dangers, so it is that now by her unthoughtful malice thou art come to this present felicity of religion. Let fortune go and fume with fury in another place; let her find some other matter to execute her cruelty; for fortune hath no puissance against them which have devoted their lives to serve and honour the majesty of our goddess. For what availed the thieves? The beasts savage? Thy great servitude? The ill, toilsome, and dangerous ways? The fear of death every day? What availed all those, I say, to cruel fortune? Know thou that now thou art safe, and under the protection of that fortune that is not blind but can see, who by her clear light doth lighten the other gods: wherefore rejoice, and take a convenable countenance to thy white habit, and follow with joyful steps the pomp of this devout and honourable procession; let such, which be not devout to the goddess, see and acknowledge their error: 'Behold, here is Lucius that is delivered from his former so great miseries by the providence of the goddess Isis, and rejoiceth therefore and triumpheth of victory over his fortune.' And to the end thou mayest live more safe and sure, make thyself one of this holy order, to which thou wast but a short time since pledged by oath, dedicate thy mind to the obeying of our religion, and take upon thee a voluntary yoke of ministry: for when thou beginnest to serve and honour the goddess, then shalt thou feel the more the fruit of thy liberty."

When morning came and that the solemnities were finished, I came forth sanctified with twelve stoles and in a religious habit, whereof I am not forbidden to speak, considering that many persons saw me at that time. There I was commanded to stand upon a pulpit of wood which stood in the middle of the temple, before the figure and remembrance of the goddess; my vestment was of fine linen, covered and embroidered with flowers; I had a precious cope upon my shoulders, hanging down behind me to the ground, whereon were beasts wrought of divers colours, as Indian dragons, and Hyperborean griffins, whom in form of birds the other part of the world doth engender: the priests commonly call such a habit an Olympian stole. In my right hand I carried a lighted torch, and a garland of flowers was upon my head, with white palm-leaves sprouting out on every side like rays; thus I was adorned like unto the sun, and made in fashion of an image, when the curtains were drawn aside and all the people compassed about to behold me. Then they began to solemnise the feast, the nativity of my holy order, with sumptuous banquets and pleasant meats: the third day was likewise celebrated with like ceremonies, with a religious dinner, and with all the consummation of the adept order. Now when I had continued there some days, conceiving a marvellous pleasure and consolation in beholding ordinarily the image of the goddess, because of the benefits, beyond all esteem or reward, which she had brought me, at length she admonished me to depart homeward, not without rendering of thanks, which although they were not sufficient, yet they were according to my power. Howbeit I could hardly be persuaded to break the chains of my most earnest devotion and to depart, before I had fallen prostrate before the face of the goddess and wiped her feet with my face, whereby I began so greatly to weep and sigh that my words were interrupted, and as devouring my prayer I began to say in this sort: "O holy and blessed dame, the perpetual comfort of human kind, who by Thy bounty and grace nourishest all the world, and bearest a great affection to the adversities of the miserable as a loving mother, Thou takest no rest night or day, neither art Thou idle at any time in giving benefits and succouring all men as well on land as sea; Thou art she that puttest away all storms and dangers from men's life by stretching forth Thy right hand, whereby likewise Thou dost unweave even the inextricable and entangled web of fate, and appeasest the great tempests of fortune, and keepest back the harmful course of the stars. The gods supernal do honour Thee; the gods infernal have Thee in reverence; Thou dost make all the earth to turn, Thou givest light to the sun, Thou governest the world, Thou treadest down the power of hell. By Thy mean the stars give answer, the seasons return, the gods rejoice, the elements serve: at Thy commandment the winds do blow, the clouds nourish the earth, the seeds prosper, and the fruits do grow. The birds of the air, the beasts of the hill, the serpents of the den, and the fishes of the sea do tremble at Thy majesty: but my spirit is not able to give Thee sufficient praise, my patrimony is unable to satisfy Thy sacrifices; my voice hath no power to utter that which I think of Thy majesty, no, not if I had a thousand mouths and so many tongues and were able to continue forever. Howbeit as a good religious person, and according to my poor estate, I will do what I may: I will always keep Thy divine appearance in remembrance, and close the imagination of Thy most holy godhead within my breast."

INSCRIPTIONS FROM THE EASTERN MEDITERRANEAN

Of the vast numbers of inscriptions in Greek and Latin that have been found in the eastern part of the Roman Empire (W. Dittenberger's *Sylloge Inscriptionarum Graecarum Orientalis* is the most convenient and complete collection for the east), three have been chosen for inclusion here, since they shed light on the New Testament from three different perspectives: The first furnishes the date for the term of service of a public official mentioned in Acts 16 as governor of Corinth at the time Paul was there; the second was originally placed on the balustrade that separated the Court of the Gentiles from the Court of Israel in the Temple at Jerusalem; the third illustrates the claims that were being made in behalf of the Roman emperors from the reign of the first to receive the title.

(1)

Tiberius Claudius Caesar Augustus[2] Germanicus Pontifex Maximus,[3] in the twelfth year of his tribunician power, acclaimed emperor for the twenty-sixth time,[4] father of his country,[5] consul for the fifth time, censor, sends

[2]Claudius's reign began in A.D. 41, so that the "twelfth year" would be between January 25, A.D. 52 and January 24, A.D. 53.

[3]The emperor was also the chief priest of the state cult, the faithful and precisely accurate observation of which was believed by all Romans—even those inclined on philosophical grounds to be skeptical in matters religious—to be essential for the preservation of the state and for warding off baleful influences in the form of retribution wreaked on the state by offended divinities.

[4]The acclamation of the emperor could occur at any time the senate chose to do so, although it seems not to have been done more than three times in any single year. Acclamation usually followed on some military or political victory, or on the occasion of some act of divine favor in behalf of the state or its ruler.

[5]From the outset, the imperial system of Rome sought to foster a deep and reverent personal attitude on the part of citizens and subjects of Rome toward the emperor. This had its highest expression in relation to Octavian (or Augustus) in Virgil's *Eclogue,* according to which the stability of the world and the universal peace that (for the moment) prevailed was directly traceable to the emperor, who guarded the welfare of the state like a father.

greetings to the city of Delphi.[6] I have long been zealous for the city of Delphi and favorable to it from the beginning, and I have always observed the cult of the Pythian Apollo,[7] but with regard to the present stories, and those quarrels of the citizens of which a report has been made by Lucius Junio Gallio,[8] my friend and proconsul of Achaia[9] . . . will still hold the previous settlement.

(2)

Let no foreigner enter within the screen and enclosure surrounding the sanctuary. Whoever is apprehended so doing will be responsible for his own death, which shall take place immediately.[10]

(3)

The cities which are in Asia[11] and the districts and the peoples honor Gaius Julius Caesar, son of Gaius, high priest and emperor,[12] and consul for

[6]Delphi, the famous city on the slopes of Mt. Parnassus, sacred to Apollo, god of the sun, and renowned for the oracle there, to which common people and statesmen alike turned for centuries in their quest for answers to perplexing problems of war, politics, and personal welfare.

[7]Pythian Apollo was associated particularly with the oracle located at Delphi. In an effort to demonstrate the continuity of Roman culture with that of Greece, while capitalizing on the esteem in which the shrines and oracles of Greece were still held, the emperors of Rome made a conscious effort to identify themselves with the Greek deities and to visit the sacred sites. Claudius is drawing attention to his own piety by means of the inscription erected in some public spot at Delphi. The immediate occasion was the dispute referred to, but Claudius well knew that the mention of his devotion to Apollo would not be lost on the thousands who annually visited the shrine or sought counsel from the Pythian Apollo.

[8]Gallio, brother of the even better known statesman-philosopher Seneca, was consul in the year 52–53. Assuming Paul had been active for about two years before he came to the attention of the proconsul, it is virtually certain that Paul reached Corinth in A.D. 49 or 50. If this interpretation of the evidence is correct, then we have in this date one of the few fixed points for a chronology of Paul's career.

[9]Achaia was the name given by the Romans to the southern half of the Greek peninsula, including the area as far north as Mt. Olympus, the central region around Delphi, Athens, Corinth, and the Peleponnesus to the south. Paul refers to his first converts at Corinth as his "first-fruits in Achaia" (I Cor. 16:15).

[10]The temple precincts in Jerusalem were divided into a number of courts, of which the inner three were accessible to the following groups respectively: male Jews (the court of Israel); the priests (the Holy Place); and the High Priest (the Holy of Holies, or Holiest Place). Pompey horrified the Jews in 63 B.C. by entering the Holiest Place, but under the Roman policy, which permitted subject peoples full autonomy in their own religious affairs, the priests were at liberty to state publicly and enforce strictly the prohibition against Gentiles entering any part of the temple other than the outer court, which was designated appropriately the Court of the Gentiles. Several copies of this inscription were originally in position along the balustrade that marked the limit beyond which only Jews could go.

[11]Asia was the Roman designation for the province that included most of eastern Asia Minor, except for the regions bordering the Black Sea to the northeast and those along the Taurus Mountains to the southeast. The coast from Troas to Cnidos and the interior as far east as the Anatolian Plateau were included.

[12]Julius was, of course, the first to be so designated. And even though the veneration of the emperor was viewed with deep suspicion as an oriental error, so that it did not become widely accepted in Rome until well into the second century A.D., Caesar—and Augustus after him—were happy to promote the idea in the eastern provinces, where it had a long tradition reaching back to Alexander and beyond, and where it served an important function in giving the local populace an emotional tie to the distant ruler in the West.

the second time; he is a manifest god,[13] sprung from Ares and Aphrodite,[14] and universal[15] savior[16] of human life.

INSCRIPTION FROM THE THEODOTOS SYNAGOGUE[17]

Theodotos, son of Vettenos, priest and archisynagogos, son and grandson of archisynagoi, built the synagogue for the reading of the Law and for the searching of the commandments; furthermore, the Hospice and Chambers and the water installations for the lodging of needy strangers . . .

LETTERS

Beginning in the later nineteenth century, scholars began to study and decipher the writings on bits of papyrus found in tombs and trash heaps of cities and villages, especially in Egypt, where the dry climate enabled the papyrus (writing material made from reeds) to survive. The documents are of unique importance, precisely because they are not literary productions in the sense of self-conscious writings set down to be read by a wider public or by posterity. They are the records of business transactions, official reports of little people to big government, and above all, private letters between individuals. As such they reveal, as no literary document could, how people actually lived; the fabric of basic human relationships is evident in the naive prose of these writings. The small group of letters reproduced here represents a range of human situations: letters

[13]The epithet here used of Caesar is the same as that applied by Antiochus IV, the Seleucid ruler of Syria, to himself. Neither Greeks nor Romans had any difficulty with the notion that a man who rose to power among men was in some sense a participant in divine powers or specially favored of the gods, and so worthy to be ranked among the divine beings.

[14]Various Roman leaders chose different Greek gods and goddesses with whom they sought to identify themselves. Anthony claimed identity with Dionysius, Augustus with Apollo. Here Caesar asserts that he is the offspring of the god of war and the goddess of love.

[15]The Romans, like the hellenistic rulers before them, stressed the unity of mankind. The greatness of the emperors lay in the fact that all mankind benefitted from the peace and harmony which they established, or claimed to have established, so that humanity was brought together under the blessings of the Roman authority.

[16]Savior is here used as the agent of peace and prosperity, not in a distinctively religious or otherworldly sense. Terms like these were used in relation to the emperors in order to foster a kind of religious feeling, however, in order to promote a sense of contentment in the present life rather than to prepare men for another age or a heavenly realm.

[17]As the inscription indicates, this synagogue was built with combined facilities for study, worship, and lodging. The archaeologists who discovered the inscription assigned to it a date in the reign of Trajan (in the early second century A.D.), but other scholars have insisted it must have been built before A.D. 70, since Jews were prohibited by the Romans from Jerusalem after that date. But that rule must have been relaxed by the time of Trajan. The organization of Judaism under the Pharisees at Yavneh was well advanced by this time, so the erection of a special synagogue building by this time is wholly credible, whereas it is extremely unlikely prior to 70. All the evidence from that date and earlier points to meetings in private homes or public halls.

Papyrus Fragment. A writing material made from reeds that grow in the Nile Valley was used by those in the early centuries of our era who did not expect, or could not afford, more enduring copies. In the unusually dry climate of Egypt, however, thousands of writings on papyrus have survived to the present day, including this portion of a gospel, which reads like the Gospel of John in style and point of view. It is these papyrus fragments that have provided scholars with the best supply of information about ordinary life, trade, and communication in the period of the New Testament and the centuries immediately following. *(Courtesy of the British Museum)*

home from soldiers, from absentee husbands, from estranged sons; a letter from a friend who has just returned from a journey. The stylized expressions used are often reminiscent of the language and mood of the New Testament, which lie closer to that of these informal documents than to the self-conscious diction of the true literature of the period.

Hilarion has gone to work in the big city—Alexandria, which he cannot spell properly—and has heard through a friend, Aphrodisias, that his pregnant wife has interpreted his failure to communicate with her as a sign that he is abandoning her and her unborn child. Hilarion has written to convey his love and to promise support for the child, so long as it is a male! The date is the equivalent of June 17, 1 B.C.

AN ABSENTEE HUSBAND WRITES HIS EXPECTANT WIFE

Hilarion to Alis his sister many greetings. Also to Berus my lady and Apollonarin. Know that we are still even now in Alexandrea [sic]. Be not distressed if at the general coming in I remain at Alexandrea. I pray you and beseech you, take care of the little child. And as soon as we receive wages I will send thee up. If you . . . are delivered, if it was a male child, let it [live]; if it was female, cast it out. You said to Aphrodisias, "Do not forget me." How can I forget you? I urge you, therefore, do not be upset. In the year 29 of the Caesar, Pauni 23.

Endorsed: Hilarion to Alis. Deliver.

A FAITHFUL SON GREETS HIS MOTHER AND PRODS HIS IRRESPONSIBLE BROTHER

The situation represented here is that Sempronius has left home to work abroad at a great distance. Word has reached him that his next older brother has not assumed his proper role of *paterfamilias,* nor is he even looking out properly for the welfare of their revered mother. Noteworthy are the pious reference to Serapis, the divinity so widely venerated, and the divine epithets (*theos,* god; and *kurios,* lord) applied to the parents.

Sempronius to Saturnila his mother and lady many greetings. Before all things may you fare well, together with my brothers also unbewitched. And further, I make intercession for you daily to our Lord Serapis. So many letters have I sent to you, and you have not written one back to me, though so many have sailed down. You are requested, my lady, to write me without delay concerning your welfare, that I also may live more free from cares. For this is my prayer continually. I greet Maximus and his life's partner and Saturnilus and Gemellus and Helena and those who are his household. Tell her that I have received from Sempronius a letter from Cappodocia. I greet by name Julius and those who are of his household, and Scythius and Thermuthis and her children. Gemellus greets you.

May you fare well, my lady, continually.

Sempronius to Maximus his brother many greetings. Before all things may you fare well, I pray. I heard that you are slothful in caring for the lady, our mother. You are requested, sweetest brother, do not grieve her in any way. If one of our brothers should be disobedient toward her, you should hit him with your fist. For you should now be designated as father. I know that you can please her without my writing to you [to do so], but do not be unhappy with me for writing you to offer advice. For we should worship the one who bore us as though she were a god, especially when she is good. I have written these things to you, brother, knowing the sweetness of our lords and parents. You will do me a favor if you write me concerning your welfare. May you fare well, brother.

[On the reverse side:]
Deliver to Maximus X from Sempronius X his brother

A TOURIST ON THE NILE REPORTS TO HIS FRIEND

Nearchus appears to have been a man of some means, enough obviously to be able to take an extended journey on the Nile solely for the pleasure of it. He went as far as the first cataract of the Nile at Syene (now Assuan), but journeyed also across the Libyan desert to the famous oracle of Ammon, which had helped catapult Alexander into international fame by giving divine sanction to his dreams of empire. Like untold numbers of tourists before and since, Nearchus carved a message on the ancient monuments he visited, but his aim was not to leave his name or initials, but to record his pious recollection of friends at the sacred spots.

> Nearchus (to Heliodorus) . . . Greeting.
>
> Since many [have become curious about the world] even to the point of taking a ship so that they may learn about the works accomplished by man's hand, I have done the same sort of thing and undertook a voyage up as far as Soene, at which point the Nile flows out, and to Libya, where Ammon sings oracles to all men, and I learned fine things, and I carved the names of my friends on the temples for a perpetual memory, the intercession . . .
>
> [End of the letter is missing]
> Endorsed
> To Heliodorus

A WELL-INTENTIONED BUT HEAVY-HANDED LETTER OF SYMPATHY

Irene seems eager to be genuinely supportive on hearing of the death of her friends' son, and has gone through the motions—presumably of votive offerings, priestly prayers, etc. But at the end she can only acknowledge that death must be accepted and cannot ever be explained or understood. Perhaps the fact of the letter rather than the inadequacy of its sentiments may have comforted the bereaved.

> Irene to Taonnophris and Philo good comfort.
> I am as sorry and weep over the departed one as I wept for Didymas. And I have done everything that was appropriate as have all of my [family], Epaphroditus and Thermuthion and Philion and Apollonius and Plantas. But even so, against such things there is nothing anyone can do. So comfort each other. May you be well.
>
> Endorsed:
> To Taonnophris and Philo.

A SLIGHTLY HOMESICK RECRUIT WRITES FROM HIS FIRST ASSIGNMENT

Apion is terribly pleased with himself for having survived the rough voyage to Italy, for gaining his first look at the sights of Italy in the vicinity of the Bay of Naples, for his pay in gold pieces, for his new name—much more imposing than the simple Apion—and for his assignment to a military unit with an equally imposing name, Centuria Athenonica, and for his chances of advancement. He is pleased to send greetings from his many friends in his unit to his friends and relatives back home in the Egyptian village. But he still would like to have a letter from his father.

Apion to Epimachus his father and lord many greetings. Before all things I pray that you are in health, and that you prosper and fare well continually together with my sister and her daughter and my brother. I thank the lord Serapis that when I was in peril on the sea he saved me immediately. When I came to Miseni, I received as viaticum [journey-money] from the Caesar three pieces of gold. And it is well with me but I urge you, my lord father, to write me a little letter: first, about your welfare; second, about my brother and sister; third, so that I may do obeisance to your hand, because you have taught me well and I have hopes therefore of advancing quickly, if the gods are willing. Greet Capito much and my brother and sister and Serenilla and my friends. By Euctemon I am sending you a little picture of myself. Furthermore, my name is [now] Antonis Maximus. Be well, I pray. Centuris Athenonica. The following send their greetings: Serenus the son of Agathus Daemon, and . . . the son of . . . and Turbo the son of Gallonius and . . . the son of . . .

[On the back]

To Philadelphis for Epimaxus from Apion his son.

Give this to the first cohort of the Apamenians to [?]
Julianus An . . .
the Liblarios, from Apion so that he may convey it to
Epimachus his father.

LETTER TO A WIDOW FROM HER RUNAWAY SON

This intensely human document was written by a young man who had apparently borrowed money that he was unable to repay and as a result ran away from his native village to another small town some distance away. His mother had gone searching for him, probably in Alexandria, but was unable to find him. A meddling fellow villager had chanced to meet Antonius and then reported to his distraught mother what his woeful plight was. Perhaps Antonius is suggesting that his mother pay off his debts, in which case he could return home without further disgrace. But most of all, he wants to confess his wrong and gain reconciliation with his concerned but estranged mother.

Antonius Longus to Nilus his mother many greetings. And continually I pray that you may be in health. I make intercession for you day by day to the lord Serapis. I want you to understand that I had no hope that you would go to the metropolis, so that I did not come to the city. But I was ashamed to come to Caranis, because I walk about in rags. I am writing to you that I am naked. I plead with you, mother, be reconciled to me! Furthermore, I know what I have brought upon myself. I have been chastened in a way that is appropriate. I know that I have sinned. I have heard from Postumus, who met you in the country in the vicinity of Arsinoe and told you the whole story at an inopportune time. Don't you understand that I would rather be maimed than know that I still owe a man an obol? . . . Come yourself . . . I have heard that . . . I beseech you . . . I almost . . . I beseech you . . . I will . . . not . . . do otherwise.

[The papyrus is frayed and breaks off at this point.]

[On the back]

. . . his mother, from Antonius Longus her son.

LETTER HONORING SERAPIS

To Apollonius greeting [from] Zoilus the Aspendian, . . . of the . . . , who also was presented unto thee by the king's friends. It happened unto me, while I was serving the god Serapis for thy health and success with king Ptolemy, that Serapis warned me many a time in sleep that I should sail over to thee and signify to thee this answer: That there must be made for him by thee a temple of Serapis and a grove in the Greek quarter by the haven, and a priest must oversee it and sacrifice at the altar for you. And when I had besought the god Serapis that he would set me free from the work here, he cast me into a great sickness, insomuch that I stood also in jeopardy. But having prayed to him, if he would heal me, I said that I would endure my ministry and do that which was commanded by him. Now when I was quickly healed, there came a certain man from Cnidus, who took in hand to build a temple of Serapis in this place and had brought stones. But afterward the god forbade him to build and he departed. But when I was come unto Alexandria, and delayed to make intercession with thee concerning these things, save of the affair which thou hadst also promised unto me, again I relapsed four months; wherefore I could not straightway come unto thee. It is therefore well, O Apollonius, that thou follow the command by the god, that Serapis may be favourable unto thee and make thee much greater with the king and more glorious, together with the health of thy body. Be not stricken with terror of the expense, as being of great cost to thee; nay, it shall be to thee of great profit, for I will together oversee all these things.

FAREWELL

HYMNS

The Odes of Solomon

The date, the provenance, and the original language of the Odes of Solomon cannot be determined with certainty. The two facts are that they are pseudonymous and that they were written about one millennium after the time of Solomon (tenth century B.C.). It is probable that they were written in Greek somewhere in Syria about the year 100 A.D., but they may have incorporated older Semitic material, and they were very early translated into Syriac. Because the author knew the Jewish Bible in a Greek translation, the biblical idiom that is found throughout the Odes is not a result of an awkwardly literal translation that betrays a Semitic original, but is a sign of the way biblical modes of expression have shaped his own rhetoric and literary style. They may have been composed by a Jew and subsequently slightly christianized by an interpolator, or perhaps they were written by a Greek-speaking Jewish-Christian. Some scholars think the Odes are the creation of a Gnostic of the second century A.D., and were then utilized and adapted by Christians, and a recent thorough study of the Odes has led to the conclusion that they were written by a former Essene who converted to Christianity, and whose portrayal of Christ as Redeemer-Revealer is therefore strongly colored by imagery and perspectives known from the Qumran documents. But whatever the circumstances of their origin, they are akin to the lengthy and prolix discourses of the Gospel of John both in style and in the evident belief that truth is communicated to the elect through a revealer figure who has been sent by God (Ode VIII: 8–12).

ODE 8

1. Open, open your hearts to the exultation of the Lord,
   And let your love abound from the heart to the lips.

2. In order to bring forth fruits to the Lord, a holy life;
   And to talk with watchfulness in His light.

3. Rise up and stand erect,
   You who sometimes were brought low.

4. You who were in silence, speak,
   For your mouth has been opened.

5. You who were despised, from henceforth be lifted up,
   For your Righteousness has been lifted up,

6. For the right hand of the Lord is with you,
   And He will be your Helper.

7. And peace was prepared for you,
   Before what may be your war.

(Christ Speaks)

8. Hear the word of truth,
   And receive the knowledge of the Most High.

9. Your flesh may not understand that which I am about to say
   to you;
   Nor your garment that which I am about to show you.

10. Keep my mystery, you who are kept by it;
    Keep my faith, you who are kept by it.

11. And understand my knowledge, you who know me in truth;
    Love me with affection, you who love;

12. For I turn not my face from my own,
    Because I know them.

13. And before they had existed,
    I recognized them;
    And imprinted a seal on their faces.

14. I fashioned their members,
    And my own breasts I prepared for them,
    That they might drink my holy milk and live by it.

15. I am pleased by them,
    And am not ashamed by them.

16. For my workmanship are they,
 And the strength of my thoughts.

17. Therefore who can stand against my work?
 Or who is not subject to them?

18. I willed and fashioned mind and heart,
 And they are my own.
 And upon my right hand I have set my elect ones.

19. And my righteousness goes before them,
 And they shall not be deprived of my name;
 For it is with them.

(The Odist Himself Speaks)

20. Pray and increase,
 And abide in the love of the Lord;

21. And you who are loved in the Beloved,
 And you who are kept in Him who lives,
 And you who are saved in Him who was saved.

22. And you shall be found incorrupt in all ages,
 On account of the name of your Father.
 Hallelujah.

ODE 12

1. He has filled me with words of truth,
 That I may proclaim Him.

2. And like the flowing of waters, truth flows from my mouth,
 And my lips declare His fruits.

3. And He has caused His knowledge to abound in me,
 Because the mouth of the Lord is the true Word,
 And the entrance of His light.

4. And the Most High has given Him to His generations,
 Which are the interpreters of His beauty,
 And the narrators of His glory,
 And the confessors of His purpose,
 And the preachers of His mind,
 And the teachers of His works.

5. For the subtlety of the Word is inexpressible,
 And like His utterance so also is His swiftness and His acuteness,
 For limitless in His progression.

6. He never falls but remains standing,
 And one cannot comprehend His descent or His way.

7. For as His work is, so is His expectation,
 For He is the light and dawning of thought.

8. And by Him the generations spoke to one another,
 And those that were silent acquired speech.

9. And from Him came love and equality,
And they spoke one to another that which was theirs.

10. And they were stimulated by the Word,
And knew Him who made them,
Because they were in harmony.

11. For the mouth of the Most High spoke to them,
And His exposition prospered through Him.

12. For the dwelling place of the Word is man,
And His truth is love.

13. Blessed are they who by means of Him have perceived everything,
And have known the Lord in His truth.
Hallelujah.

ODE 28

1. As the wings of doves over their nestlings,
And the mouths of their nestlings towards their mouths,
So also are the wings of the Spirit over my heart.

2. My heart continually refreshes itself and leaps for joy,
Like the babe who leaps for joy in his mother's womb.

3. I trusted, consequently I was at rest;
Because trustful is He in whom I trusted.

4. He has greatly blessed me,
And my head is with Him.

5. And the dagger shall not divide me from Him,
Nor the sword;

6. Because I am ready before destruction comes,
And have been set on His immortal side.

7. And immortal life embraced me,
And kissed me.

8. And from that (life) is the Spirit which is within me.
And it cannot die because it is life.

(Christ Speaks)

9. Those who saw me were amazed,
Because I was persecuted.

10. And they thought that I had been swallowed up,
Because I seemed to them as one of the lost.

11. But my injustice
Became my salvation.

12. And I became their abomination,
Because there was no jealousy in me.

13. Because I continually did good to every man
    I was hated.

14. And they surrounded me like mad dogs,
    Those who in stupidity attack their masters.

15. Because their thought is depraved,
    And their mind is perverted.

16. But I was carrying water in my right hand,
    And their bitterness I endured by my sweetness.

17. And I did not perish, because I was not their brother,
    Nor was my birth like theirs.

18. And they sought my death but were unsuccessful,
    Because I was older than their memory;
    And in vain did they cast lots against me.

19. And those who were after me
    Sought in vain to destroy the memorial of him
      who was before them.

20. Because the thought of the Most High cannot be
      prepossessed;
    And His heart is superior to all wisdom.
      Hallelujah.

ODE 31

1. Chasms vanished before the Lord,
   And darkness dissipated before His appearance.

2. Error erred and perished on account of Him;
   And contempt received no path,
   For it was submerged by the truth of the Lord.

3. He opened His mouth and spoke grace and joy;
   And recited a new chant to His name.

4. Then He lifted His voice towards the Most High,
   And offered to Him those that had become sons through Him.

5. And His face was justified,
   Because thus His Holy Father had given to Him.

(Christ Speaks)

6. Come forth, you who have been afflicted,
   And receive joy.

7. And possess yourselves through grace,
   And take unto you immortal life.

8. And they condemned me when I stood up,
   Me who had not been condemned.

9. Then they divided my spoil,
   Though nothing was owed them.

10. But I endured and held my peace and was silent,
 That I might not be disturbed by them.

11. But I stood undisturbed like a solid rock,
 Which is continuously pounded by columns of waves and endures.

12. And I bore their bitterness because of humility;
 That I might redeem my nation and instruct it.

13. And that I might not nullify the promises to the patriarchs,
 To whom I was promised for the salvation of their offspring.
 Hallelujah.

ODE 35

1. I rested on the Spirit of the Lord,
 And She lifted me up to heaven;

2. And caused me to stand on my feet in the Lord's high place,
 Before His perfection and His glory,
 Where I continued glorifying (Him) by the composition of His Odes.

(Christ Speaks)

3. (The Spirit) brought me forth before the Lord's face.
 And because I was the Son of Man
 I was named the Light, the Son of God;

4. Because I was the most glorified among the glorious ones,
 And the greatest among the great ones.

5. For according to the greatness of the Most High, so She made me;
 And according to His newness He renewed me.

6. And He anointed me with His perfection;
 And I became one of those who are near Him.

7. And my mouth was opened like a cloud of dew,
 And my heart gushed forth (like) a gusher of righteousness.

8. And my approach was in peace,
 And I was established in the Spirit of Providence.
 Hallelujah.

Hymns from the Acts of Thomas

Purporting to be an account of the divine choice of Thomas the apostle to evangelize the east as far as India, the Acts of Thomas is part legendary narrative and part esoteric information about the destiny of man. Written in Syria in the third century A.D. and surviving in both Greek and Syriac versions, the book does include references to authentic historical figures such as Gundaphoras, a Parthian king of the first century of our era. But the book as a whole is a compilation of incidents and speeches chosen, or rather created, for symbolic purposes in order to communicate truth as the gnostics viewed it. Accordingly, the journeys and experiences of Thomas really are intended to depict the coming of the heavenly Redeemer figure from heaven, the mystic marriage of the initiate into truth, the conflict with the demonic powers, the descent into Hades—all of them part of the stock of gnostic redemptive beliefs and aspirations.

Two hymns are included in the Acts: The Wedding of the Daughter of Light and the Hymn of the Pearl (which is produced with a few minor changes in the translation by A. J. F. Klijn, *Acts of Thomas,* Leiden, 1962). The single direct point of contact between this thoroughly gnostic hymn and the New Testament is the Parable of the Pearl of Great Price in Mt. 13:45–46, although the point of the parable has been totally altered in order to make it serve the interests of gnostic thought. The mingling of metaphors—treasure, robe, jewel, home, mirror—discloses that the hymn is an account of the journey of the soul, which has lost its true identity and has become entangled in a corrupt and alien world. When the heavenly message of redemption reaches the entrapped soul, the wanderer recalls his true origins, flees from his entanglements in this world, and returns to the splendid realms from which he came.

SECTIONS 108–113

(108) And whilst he was praying, all those who were in the prison saw that he was praying and begged of him to pray for them too. And when he had prayed and sat down, Judas began to chant this hymn.

The Hymn of Judas the Apostle in the Country of the Indians.
(1) When I was a little child,
and dwelling in my Kingdom, in my father's house,
(2) and was content with the wealth and the luxuries of my nourishers,
(3) from the East our home
my parents equipped me [and] sent me forth;
(4) and of the wealth of our treasury
they took abundantly [and] tied up for me a load
(5) large and [yet] light,
which I myself could carry—
(6) gold of Beth-'Ellaye
and silver of Gazak the great,
(7) and rubies of India,
and agates from Beth-Kashan;
(8) and they furnished me with adamant,
which can crush iron.
(9) And they took off from me the glittering robe,
which in their affection they had made for me,
(10) and the purple toga,
which was measured [and] woven to my stature.

(11) And they made a compact with me,
and wrote it in my heart, that it might not be forgotten:
(12) "If thou goest down into Egypt,
and bringest the one pearl,
(13) which is in the midst of the sea
around the loud-breathing serpent,
(14) thou shalt put on thy glittering robe
and thy toga, with [which] thou art contented,
(15) and with thy brother, who is next to us in authority,
thou shalt be heir in our kingdom."

(109:16) I quitted the East [and] went down,
there being with me two guardians,
(17) for the way was dangerous and difficult,
and I was very young to travel it.
(18) I passed through the borders of Maishan,
the meeting-place of the merchants of the East,
(19) and I reached the land of Babel,
and I entered the walls of Sarbug.
(20) I went down into Egypt,
and my companions parted from me.
(21) I went straight to the serpent.
I dwelt around his abode,
(22) [waiting] till he should slumber and sleep,
and I could take the pearl from him.
(23) And when I was single and was alone
[and] became strange to my family,
(24) one of my race, a free-born man,
an Oriental, I saw there,
(25) a youth fair and lovable,
the son of oil-sellers;
(26) and he came and attached himself to me,
and I made him my intimate friend,
(27) an associate with whom I shared my merchandise.
(28) I warned him against the Egyptians,
and against consorting with the unclean;
(29) and dressed in their dress,
that they might not hold me in abhorrence,
(30) because I was come abroad in order to take the pearl,
and arouse the serpent against me.
(31) But in some way or another
they found out that I was not their countryman,
(32) and they dealt with me treacherously,
and gave me their food to eat.
(33) I forgot that I was a son of kings,
and I served their king;
(34) and I forgot the pearl,
for which my parents had sent me,
(35) and because of the burden of their oppressions
I lay in a deep sleep.
(110:36) But all these things that befell me
my parents perceived, and were grieved for me;
(37) and a proclamation was made in our kingdom,
that every one should come to our gate,

(38) kings and princes of Parthia,
and all the nobles of the East.
(39) And they wrote a plan on my behalf,
that I might not be left in Egypt;
(40) and they wrote me a letter,
and every noble signed his name to it:
(41) "From thy Father, the king of kings,
and thy mother, the mistress of the East,
(42) and from thy brother, our second [in authority],
to thee our son, who art in Egypt, greeting!
(43) Up and arise from thy sleep,
and listen to the words of our letter!
(44) Call to mind that thou art a son of kings!
See the slavery, whom thou servest!
(45) Remember the pearl,
for which thou wast sent to Egypt!
(46) Think of thy robe,
and remember thy splendid toga,
(47) which thou shalt wear and [with which] thou shalt be adorned,
when thy name hath been read out in the list of the valiant,
(48) and with thy brother, our viceroy,
thou shalt be in our kingdom!"
(111:49) My letter is a letter,
which the king sealed with his own right hand,
(50) [to keep] it from the wicked ones, the children of Babel,
and from the savage demons of Sarbug.
(51) It flew in the likeness of an eagle,
the king of all birds;
(52) it flew and alighted beside me,
and became all speech.
(53) At its voice and the sound of its rustling,
I started and arose from my sleep.
(54) I took it up and kissed it,
and I began [and] read it;
(55) and according to what was traced on my heart
were the words of my letter written.
(56) I remembered that I was a son of royal parents,
and my noble birth asserted its nature.
(57) I remembered the pearl,
for which I had been sent to Egypt,
(58) and I began to charm him,
the terrible loud-breathing serpent.
(59) I hushed him to sleep and lulled him into slumber,
for my father's name I named over him,
(60) and the name of our second [in power],
and of my mother, the queen of the East;
(61) and I snatched away the pearl,
and turned to go back to my father's house.
(62) And their filthy and unclean dress I stripped off,
and left it in their country;
(63) and took my way straight to come
to the light of our home the East.
(64) And my letter, my awakener,
I found before me on the road;

(65) and as with his voice it had awakened me,
[so] too with its light it was leading me.
(66) It, that dwelt in the palace,
gave light before me with its form,
(67) and with its voice and with its guidance
it also encouraged me to speed,
(68) and with its love it drew me on.
(69) I went forth [and] passed by Sarbug;
I left Babel on my left hand;
(70) and I came to the great Maishan,
to the haven of merchants,
(71) which sits on the shore of the sea.
(72) And my bright robe, which I had stripped off,
and the toga that was wrapped with it,
(73) from the heights of Reken
my parents had sent thither
(74) by the hand of their treasurers,
who in their truth could be trusted therewith.
(112:75) And because I remembered not its fashion,—
and I too received all in it,
(76) on a sudden, when I received it,
the garment seemed to me to become like a mirror of myself.
(77) I saw it all in all,
and I too received all in it,
(78) for we were two in distinction
and yet again one in one likeness.
(79) And the treasurers too,
who brought it to me, I saw in like manner
(80) to be two [and yet] one likeness,
for one sign of the king was written on them [both],
(81) of the hands of him who restored to me through them
my trust and my wealth,
(82) my decorated robe, which
was adorned with glorious colours,
(83) with gold and beryls
and rubies and agates,
(84) and sardonyxes, varied in colour.
And was skilfully worked in its home on high,
(85) and with diamond clasps
were all its seams fastened;
(86) and the image of the king of kings
was embroidered and depicted in full all over it,
(87) and like the stone of the sapphire too
its hues were varied.
(113:88) And I saw also that all over it
the instincts of knowledge were working
(89) and I saw too that it was preparing to speak.
(90) I heard the sound of its tones
which it uttered with its . . .
(91) "I am the active in deeds,
when they reared for him before my father;
(92) and I perceived myself,
that my stature grew according to his labours."

(93) And in its kingly movements
it poured itself entirely over me,
(94) and on the hands of its givers
it hastened that I might take it.
(95) And love urged me to run
to meet it and receive it;
(96) and I stretched forth and took it.
With the beauty of its colours I adorned myself,
(97) and I wrapped myself wholly in my toga
of brilliant hues.
(98) I clothed myself with it, and went up to the gate.
(99) I bowed my head and worshipped the majesty
of my father who sent me,
(100) for I had done his commandments,
and he too had done what he promised,
(101) and at the gate of his . . . ,
I mingled with his princes,
(102) for he rejoiced in me and received me,
and I was with him in his kingdom,
(103) and with the voice of . . .
all his servants praise him.
(104) And he promised that to the gate too
of the king of kings with him I should go,
(105) and with my offering and my pearl
with him should present myself to our king.

The hymn of Judas Thomas, the Apostle, which he spake in the prison, is ended.

MAGICAL INCANTATIONS

Found on scraps of papyrus, scratched on potsherds, and recorded on inscriptions at the shrines of healing gods, hundreds of magical formulas and longer incantation texts have been found. Of those included here in translation, the first is a full incantation aimed at forcing a demon to assist in bringing together Urbanus—apparently sick with love, and the author or sponsor of the incantation—with Candida, his beloved. The second text is a more general appeal to the demons, phrased in the pompous, polysyllabic, word-coining style apparently admired by those addicted to magic.

The third actually describes a theurgic process by which the desired effect is to be brought about through the ritual slaying of a white cock. The situation implied in the fourth text is that a magician has been asked by someone who has seen a vision of a supernatural being what is the present and the potential significance of what he has been allowed to behold; the possibilities are nearly limitless, he is told. The magician revealing the methods of the prince of demons, Beelzeboul, is apparently a Jew, who in our fifth excerpt has disclosed the methods of his demonic highness in tricking and dominating foolish men.

The final brief document is an inscription dedicated to Asclepius, the god of healing, and was found on the island in the Tiber at Rome where a shrine to him was located in ancient times and where in more recent times there is a hospital. The inscription attests the restoration of sight to the blind by the formerly blind himself.

I

I adjure thee, demonic spirit, who dost rest here, with the sacred names Aoth Abaoth, by the God of Abraan and the Jao[18] of Jaku, the Jao Aoth Abath, the God of Israma: hearken to the glorious and fearful and great name, and hasten to Urbanus, whom Urbana bore, and bring him to Domitiana, whom Candida bore, so that he, loving, frantic, sleepless with love of her and desire, may beg her to return to his house and become his wife. I adjure thee by the great God, the eternal and almighty, who is exalted above the exalted Gods. I adjure thee by Him who created the heaven and the sea. I adjure thee by him who separates the devout ones. I adjure thee by him who divided his staff in the sea, that thou bring Urbanus, whom Urbana bore, and unite him with Domitiana, whom Candida bore, so that he, loving, tormented, sleepless with desire of her and with love, may take her home to his house as his wife. I adjure thee by him who caused the mule not to bear. I adjure thee by him who divided the light from the darkness. I adjure thee by him who crusheth the rocks. I adjure thee by him who parted the mountains. I adjure thee by him who holdeth the earth upon her foundations. I adjure thee by the sacred Name which is not uttered; in the [— —] I will mention it and the demons will be startled, terrified and full of horror, that thou bring Urbanus, whom Urbana bore, and unite him as husband with Domitiana, whom Candida bore, and that he loving may beseech her; at once! quick! I adjure thee by him who set a lamp and stars in the heavens by the command of his voice so that they might lighten all men. I adjure thee by him who shook the whole world, and causeth the mountains to fall and rise, who causeth the whole earth to quake, and all her inhabitants to return. I adjure thee by him who made signs in the heaven and upon the earth and upon the sea, that thou bring Urbanus, whom Urbana bore, and unite him as husband with Domitiana, whom Candida bore, so that he, loving her, and sleepless with desire of her, beg her and beseech her to return to his house as his wife. I adjure thee by the great God, the eternal and almighty, whom the mountains fear and the valleys in all the world, through whom the lion parts with the spoil, and the mountains tremble and the earth and the sea, [through whom] every one becomes wise who is possessed with the fear of the Lord, the eternal, the immortal, the all-seeing, who hateth evil, who knoweth what good and what evil happeneth in the sea and the rivers and the mountains and the earth, Aoth Abaoth; by the God of Abraan and the Jao of Jaku, the Jao Aoth Abaoth, the God of Israma, bring and unite Urbanus, whom Urbana bore, with Domitiana, whom Candida bore—loving, frantic, tormented with love and affection and desire for Domitiana, whom Candida bore; unite them in marriage and as spouses in love for the whole time of their life. So make it that he, loving,

[18]The names of the deity ending in *-oth,* but especially the name Jao (or Iao), recall Hebrew spelling and specifically the Hebrew name for God, Yah or Yahweh. The context of the incantation is clearly that of Roman paganism, but from hellenistic times on, there was widespread syncretism, according to which worshippers asserted the identity of the gods behind the diversity of the names.

shall obey her like a slave, and desire no other wife or maiden, but have Domitiana alone, whom Candida bore, as his spouse for the whole time of their life, at once, at once! quick, quick!

II

I invoke you, ye holy ones, mighty, majestic, glorious Splendours, holy, and earth-born, mighty arch-demons; compeers of the great god; denizens of Chaos, of Erebus and of the unfathomable abyss; earth-dwellers, haunters of sky-depths, nook-infesting, murk-enwrapped; scanning the mysteries, guardians of secrets, captains of the hosts of hell; kings of infinite space, terrestrial overlords, globe-shaking, firm-founding, ministering to earthquakes; terror-strangling, panic-striking, spindle-turning; snow-scatterers, rain-wafters, spirits of air; fire-tongues of summer-sun, tempest-tossing lords of fate; dark shapes of Erebus, senders of necessity; flame-fanning fire-darters; snow-compelling, dew-compelling; gale-raising, abyss-plumbing, calm-bestriding air-spirits; dauntless in courage, heart-crushing despots; chasm-leaping, overburdening, iron-nerved demons; wild-raging, unenslaved; watchers of Tartaros;[19] delusive fate-phantoms; all-seeing, all-hearing, all-conquering, sky-wandering vagrants; life-inspiring, life-destroying, primeval pole-movers; heart-jocund death-dealers; revealers of angles, justicers of mortals, sunless revealers, masters of daimons, air-roving, omnipotent, holy, invincible [magic words], perform my behests.

III

Keep yourself pure for seven days, and then go on the third day of the moon to a place which the receding Nile has just laid bare. Make a fire on two upright bricks with olive-wood, that is to say thin wood, when the sun is half-risen, after having before sunrise circumambulated the altar. But when the sun's disc is clear above the horizon, decapitate an immaculate, pure-white cock, holding it in the crook of your left elbow; circumambulate the altar before sunrise. Hold the cock fast by your knees and decapitate it with no one else holding it. Throw the head into the river, catch the blood in your right hand and drink it up. Put the rest of the body on the burning altar and jump into the river. Dive under in the clothes you are wearing, then stepping backwards climb on to the bank. Put on new clothes and go away without turning round. After that take the gall of a raven and rub some of it with the wing of an ibis on your eyes and you will be consecrated.

IV

This is the holy operation for winning a familiar spirit. The process shows that he is the god; a spirit of the air was he whom you saw. He will perform at once any commission you may give him. He will send dreams, he will bring you women and men without need of a material link; he will remove, he will subdue, he will hurl winds up from the bosom of the earth; he will bring gold, silver, bronze, and give it to you, if you need it; he will also free from bonds the prisoner in chains, he opens doors, he renders you invisible, so that no human soul can see you; he will bring fire, carry water, bring wine, bread, and any other food you want: oil, vinegar, everything except fish, as many vegetables as you want; but as for pork, you must never

[19]*Tartaros* is the underworld, the abode of the dead, dark and chaotic.

command him to bring that. And if you wish to give a banquet, state your intention and order him to make ready with all speed any suitable place you have chosen for it. He will forthwith build round it a room with a gilded ceiling, and you will see its walls shining with marble, and you will partly believe it to be a reality and partly only an illusion. And he will provide precious wine too, such as is necessary to the spendour of the banquet, and he will hastily summon demons and provide you with servants in livery. All this he will do in the twinkling of an eye. . . . He can bind ships and loose them again; he can ban wicked demons in any quantity; he can soothe wild animals and instantly break the teeth of wild reptiles; he can send dogs to sleep and make them noiseless; he can transform into any shape or form as a winged creature, a water-creature, a four-footed beast or a reptile. He will carry you through the air and throw you down again into the waves of the sea and the ocean streams; he will make rivers and seas fast in a moment, so that you can walk on them upright, if you wish . . . and if you wish to draw down the stars, and make warm cold, and cold warm, he will do it for you; he will make lights shine and go out; he will shake walls and reduce them by fire; he will be serviceable to you in all that you may desire, you happy mystic of holy magic.

V

And I summoned again to stand before me *Beelzeboul,* the prince of demons, and I sat him down on a raised seat of honour, and said to him: "Why are thou alone, prince of the demons?" And he said to me: "Because I alone am left of the angels of heaven that came down. For I was first angel in the first heaven, being entitled *Beelzeboul.* And now I control all those who are bound in *Tartarus* . . ."

I Solomon said unto him: "*Beelzeboul,*[20] what is thy employment?" And he answered me: "I destroy kings. I ally myself with foreign tyrants. And my own demons I set on to men, in order that the latter may believe in them and be lost. And the chosen servants of God, priests and faithful men, I excite unto desires for wicked sins, and evil heresies, and lawless deeds; and they obey me, and I bear them on to destruction. And I inspire men with envy, and murder, and for wars and sodomy, and other evil things. And I will destroy the world. . . ." I said to him: "Tell me by what angel thou art frustrated." And he answered: "By the holy and precious name of the Almighty God, called by the Hebrews by a row of numbers,[21] of which the sum is 644, and among the Greeks it is *Emannuel.* And if one of the Romans adjure me by the great name of the power Eleêth, I disappear at once."

I Solomon was astounded when I heard this; and I ordered him to saw up Theban marbles. And when he began to saw the marbles, the other demons cried out with a loud voice, howling because of their king *Beelzeboul.*

[20]"Beelzeboul" is one of a series of variant spellings for the chief of demons. It has been conjectured that originally this name was *Baal* (or Beel)-*shamayim,* meaning "lord of the heavens," but that it was corrupted to *Baal-zebul,* meaning "lord of the dung," or *Baal-zebub,* meaning "lord of the flies," after the deity worshipped in the Philistine city of Ekron who had the power to drive away insects.

[21]Since in both Hebrew and Greek letters were used for numerals, the practice developed of attaching significance to the sum of the numerical values of the letters in a word or a name. Then the sum could be used by those in the know for the name or word thus represented. A similar practice lies behind the mysterious 666 used in Rev. 13 as a cryptic reference to the blasphemous "beast"—probably one of the Roman emperors.

4

The Philosophical Context

Although the New Testament writers seem to hold negative views of philosophy as a type of merely human wisdom,[1] they were inevitably influenced by popular philosophy of the period, and incorporate aspects of it in their writings.

STOICISM

Stoicism arose as a philosophical system in the early third century B.C., taking its name from the public porticos (in Greek, *stoa*) in which the teaching was carried on. Nature is considered to be a material substance controlled by an all-powerful, provident deity who shapes all events—what we would call both human and natural occurrences. Human reason enables all persons to recognize this power and summons them to submit to its control. Wisdom is the knowledge of what is just and unjust, and conforms to the Law of Nature. Human awareness of what is according to the Law of Nature is the quality known as *conscience*. To live in accord with conscience is to gain self-control, and thereby to be free of the passions. One can live calmly in the face of adversity knowing that even what seems evil or cruel can be used of the gods to achieve admirable goals, including self-discipline in the person who endures suffering. And it can be seen as part of the divine plan that is being worked out in the universe. The later Stoics thought of the god as living within the individual,

[1]Paul declares in I Cor. 1:21 and 2:1–4 that no one comes to know God through the wisdom of this world, uttered as it is "in lofty words." In Col. 2:8 there is a warning against "philosophy and empty deceit."

experienced as the power of a divine spirit within. Yet ethical responsibility was considered to be not merely individual, but aimed at the welfare of humanity as a whole.

PLATONISM

Both hellenistic and early Christian thinking were profoundly influenced by some of the major facets of Plato's philosophy: the assumption that there is an eternal, divine mind whose power and purpose shape the structure and destiny of the universe; that all visible phenomena are but imperfect copies of the heavenly forms or paradigms of reality, which endure independently of time and decay; in all creation, human beings alone have the capacity to discern the ultimate reality of the universe and through reason to come to understand it. Earlier we noted how this view of reality influenced Jewish wisdom tradition (Wisdom of Solomon). It is even more fully evident in the writings of Philo of Alexandria and Plutarch, who were major thinkers and writers in the Jewish and pagan traditions, respectively, during the first century B.C.

CYNICISM

Dating back to at least as early as Diogenes of Sinope (412–323 B.C.), the designation *Cynic* (from the Greek word for *dog*) was given to a philosophical school that called for complete freedom from what its adherents regarded as the false hopes and values of society: wealth, family stability, fine food and clothing, and popular esteem. Seneca's scornful portrait of the typical "philosopher" is clearly a dig at the Cynics. Diogenes, of whom we have anecdotes in the writings of Diogenes Laertius,[2] exemplifies the scorn of power and reputation that was typical of the Cynics. They were persuaded that only by divesting themselves of these values could one achieve true freedom. The Epistle of Heraclitus, which purports to come from the time of that philosopher (sixth century B.C.), but which is likely to be dated from around 100 B.C., carries forward this pattern of denouncing established authority in favor of the true autonomy of the individual.

STOICISM

Of the extensive Stoic material that has survived, representative of the earlier stages of that philosophical school are excerpts from two third-century B.C. Stoics, Cleanthes and Chrysippus. Cleanthes's *Hymn to Zeus* is

[2]See pp. 187–89.

justly famous, and Chrysippus's statement sums up beautifully the Stoic view of natural law.

CLEANTHES, *HYMN TO ZEUS*

Most glorious of immortals, O Zeus of many names, almighty and everlasting, sovereign of nature, directing all in accordance with law, thee it is fitting that all mortals should address . . . Thee all the universe, as it rolls circling round the earth, obeys wheresoever thou dost guide, and gladly owns thy sway. Such an agent thou holdest in thy invisible hands—the two-edged, fiery, everliving thunderbolt, under whose stroke all nature shudders. No work upon earth is wrought apart from thee, lord, not through the divine ethereal sphere, nor upon the sea, except whatever deeds wicked men do in their own folly. Indeed, thou knowest how to make even the rough smooth, and to bring order out of disorder; even unfriendly things are friendly in thy sight. For so thou hast fitted all things together, the good with the evil, that there might be one eternal law over all . . . Deliver human beings from destructive ignorance. Banish it from their soul, and grant them to obtain wisdom, on which you rely in your governing all things with justice.

CHRYSIPPUS, *ON NATURAL LAW*

The natural law is king over everything, divine and human alike. It must be the authority that determines what is good and what is evil, the leader of human beings destined to live in communities; it lays down standards for right and wrong, and it does so by commanding what is to be done and forbidding what is not to be done.

Seneca, Moral Epistles

Born in Spain, the son of a distinguished rhetorician and writer (also named Seneca), the so-called younger-Seneca spent most of his life in Rome, where he was a philosopher and advisor to the emperor Nero. Accused of conspiracy against the emperor, he was ordered to commit suicide, and did. Of his many writings, which include *Tragedies* and *Moral Essays,* his best known works are his *Moral Epistles.*

In the first excerpt, Seneca is discussing the nature of the Good. He declares that there are three different kinds of things that can be called "good." In the other excerpts he considers the nature of virtue, how philosophers should behave (including some sarcastic remarks about those professional philosophers, the Cynics), the source of true goodness, and the presence of God within.

ON THE GOOD (EP. LXVI)

[As for things adjudged to be good] certain of them, according to our philosophical tenets, are primary, such as joy, peace, and the welfare of one's country. Others are of the second order, moulded in an unhappy material, such as the endurance of suffering, and self-control during severe illness. We shall pray outright for the goods of the first class; for the second class we shall pray only if the need shall arise. There is still a third variety, as, for example, a modest gait, a calm and honest countenance, and a bearing that suits the man of wisdom. Now how can these things be equal when we compare them, if you grant that we ought to pray for the one and avoid the other? If we would make distinctions among them, we had better return to the First Good, and consider what its nature is: the soul that gazes upon truth, that is skilled in what should be sought and what should be avoided, establishing standards of value not according to opinion, but according to nature,—the soul that penetrates the whole world and directs its contemplating gaze upon all its phenomena, paying strict attention to thoughts and actions, equally great and forceful, superior alike to hardships and blandishments, yielding itself to neither extreme of fortune, rising above all blessings and tribulations, absolutely beautiful, perfectly equipped with grace as well as with strength, healthy and sinewy, unruffled, undismayed, one which no violence can shatter, one which acts of chance can neither exalt nor depress,—a soul like this is virtue itself. There you have its outward appearance, if it should ever come under a single view and show itself once in all its completeness. But there are many aspects of it. They unfold themselves according as life varies and as actions differ; but virtue itself does not become less or greater. For the Supreme Good cannot diminish, nor may virtue retrograde; rather is it transformed, now into one quality and now into another, shaping itself according to the part which it is to play. Whatever it has touched it brings into likeness with itself, and dyes with its own colour. It adorns our actions, our friendships, and sometimes entire households which it has entered and set in order. Whatever it has handled it forthwith makes lovable, notable, admirable.

THE NATURE OF VIRTUE (EP. LXXIV)

The strength and beginnings of all goods exist in virtue herself. What does it matter if running water is cut off and flows away, as long as the fountain from which it has flowed is unharmed? You will not maintain that a man's life is more just if his children are unharmed than if they have passed away, nor yet better appointed, nor more intelligent, nor more honourable; therefore, no better, either. The addition of friends does not make one wiser; nor does their taking away make one more foolish; therefore, not happier or more wretched, either. As long as your virtue is unharmed, you will not feel the loss of anything that has been withdrawn from you. You may say: "Come now; is not a man happier when girt about with a large company of friends and children?" Why should this be so? For the Supreme Good is neither impaired or increased thereby; it abides within its own limits, no matter how Fortune has conducted herself. Whether a long old age falls to one's lot, or whether the end comes on this side of old age—the measure of the Supreme Good is unvaried, in spite of the difference in years.

Whether you draw a larger or a smaller circle, its size affects its area, not its shape. One circle may remain as it is for a long time, while you may contract the other forthwith, or even merge it completely with the sand in which it was drawn; yet each circle has had the same shape. That which is straight is not judged by its size, or by its number, or by its duration; it can no more be made longer than it can be made shorter. Scale down the honourable life as much as you like from the full hundred years, and reduce it to a single day; it is equally honourable. Sometimes virtue is widespread, governing kingdoms, cities, and provinces, creating laws, developing friendships, and regulating the duties that hold good between relatives and children; at other times it is limited by the narrow bounds of poverty, exile, or bereavement. But it is no smaller when it is reduced from prouder heights to a private station, from a royal palace to a humble dwelling, or when from a general and broad jurisdiction it is gathered into the narrow limits of a private house or a tiny corner. Virtue is just as great, even when it has retreated within itself and is shut in on all sides. For its spirit is no less great and upright, its sagacity no less complete, its justice no less inflexible. It is, therefore, equally happy. For happiness has its abode in one place only, namely, in the mind itself, and is noble, steadfast, and calm; and this state cannot be attained without a knowledge of things divine and human.

The wise man is not distressed by the loss of children or of friends. For he endures their death in the same spirit in which he awaits his own. And he fears the one as little as he grieves for the other. For the underlying principle of virtue is conformity; all the works of virtue are in harmony and agreement with virtue itself. But this harmony is lost if the soul, which ought to be uplifted, is cast down by grief or a sense of loss. It is ever a dishonour for a man to be troubled and fretted, to be numbed when there is any call for activity. For that which is honourable is free from care and untrammelled, is unafraid, and stands girt for action.

HOW PHILOSOPHERS SHOULD BEHAVE (EP. V)

I commend you and rejoice in the fact that you are persistent in your studies, and that, putting all else aside, you make it each day your endeavour to become a better man. I do not merely exhort you to keep at it; I actually beg you to do so. I warn you, however, not to act after the fashion of those who desire to be conspicuous rather than to improve, by doing things which will rouse comment as regards your dress or general way of living. Repellent attire, unkempt hair, slovenly beard, open scorn of silver dishes, a couch on the bare earth, and any other perverted forms of self-display, are to be avoided. The mere name of philosophy, however quietly pursued, is an object of sufficient scorn; and what would happen if we should begin to separate ourselves from the customs of our fellow-men? Inwardly, we ought to be different in all respects, but our exterior should conform to society. Do not wear too fine, nor yet too frowzy, a toga. One needs no silver plate, encrusted and embossed in solid gold; but we should not believe the lack of silver and gold to be proof of the simple life. Let us try to maintain a higher standard of life than that of the multitude, but not a contrary standard; otherwise, we shall frighten away and repel the very persons whom we are trying to improve. We also bring it about that they are unwilling to imitate us in anything, because they are afraid lest they might be compelled to imitate us in everything.

THE SOURCE OF TRUE GOODNESS (EP. XXIII)

I pray you, do the one thing that can render you really happy: cast aside and trample under foot all those things that glitter outwardly and are held out to you by another or as obtainable from another; look toward the true good, and rejoice only in that which comes from your own store. And what do I mean by "from your own store"? I mean from your very self, that which is the best part of you. The frail body, also, even though we can accomplish nothing without it, is to be regarded as necessary rather than as important; it involves us in vain pleasures, short-lived, and soon to be regretted, which, unless they are reined in by extreme self-control, will be transformed into the opposite. This is what I mean: pleasure, unless it has been kept within bounds, tends to rush headlong into the abyss of sorrow.

But it is hard to keep within bounds in that which you believe to be good. The real good may be coveted with safety. Do you ask me what this real good is, and whence it derives? I will tell you: it comes from a good conscience, from honourable purposes, from right actions, from contempt of the gifts of chance, from an even and calm way of living which treads but one path. For men who leap from one purpose to another, or do not even leap but are carried over by a sort of hazard,—how can such wavering and unstable persons possess any good that is fixed and lasting? There are only a few who control themselves and their affairs by a guiding purpose; the rest do not proceed; they are merely swept along, like objects afloat in a river.

ON THE GOD WITHIN US (EP. XLI)

We do not need to uplift our hands towards heaven, or to beg the keeper of a temple to let us approach his idol's ear, as if in this way our prayers were more likely to be heard. God is near you, he is with you, he is within you. This is what I mean, Lucilius: a holy spirit indwells within us, one who marks our good and bad deeds, and is our guardian. As we treat this spirit, so are we treated by it. Indeed, no man can be good without the help of God. Can one rise superior to fortune unless God helps him to rise? He it is that gives noble and upright counsel. In each good man

A god doth dwell, but what god know we not.

If ever you have come upon a grove that is full of ancient trees which have grown to an unusual height, shutting out a view of the sky by a veil of pleached and intertwining branches, then the loftiness of the forest, the seclusion of the spot, and your marvel at the thick unbroken shade in the midst of the open spaces, will prove to you the presence of deity.

PLATONISM IN JEWISH AND PAGAN THOUGHT

In the first selection from Philo of Alexandria's *On the Creation,* the writer interprets the biblical statement that humans were created in the image of God as affirming the Platonic notion that earthly phenomena are copies of the heavenly archetypes. The mind of humans aspires to ascend to the celestial realm where it may gain the direct vision of God. The same basic point is made in a curious allegorical interpretation of Gen. 15:10, where we are told that Abraham, while making an offering to God, did not divide the birds in two that he had brought as a sacrifice. Philo wants us to know that the birds are merely figures for forms of reason.

Plutarch, in the course of explaining a mysterious *E* that was found at the shrine of Apollo at Delphi, discusses directly the nature of Being itself.

PHILO: ON THE CREATION

XXIII. After all the rest, as I have said, Moses tells us that man was created after the image of God and after His likeness (Gen. 1:26). Right well does he say this, for nothing earth-born is more like God than man. Let no one represent the likeness as one to a bodily form; for neither is God in human form, nor is the human body God-like. No, it is in respect of the Mind, the sovereign element of the soul, that the word "image" is used; for after the pattern of a single Mind, even the Mind of the Universe as an archetype, the mind in each of those who successively came into being was moulded. It is in a fashion a god to him who carries and enshrines it as an object of reverence; for the human mind evidently occupies a position in men precisely answering to that which the great Ruler occupies in all the world. It is invisible while itself seeing all things, and while comprehending the substances of others, it is as to its own substance unperceived; and while it opens by arts and sciences roads branching in many directions, all of them great highways, it comes through land and sea investigating what either element contains. Again, when on soaring wing it has contemplated the atmosphere and all its phases, it is borne yet higher to the ether and the circuit of heaven, and is whirled round with the dances of planets and fixed stars, in accordance with the laws of perfect music, following that love of wisdom which guides its steps. And so, carrying its gaze beyond the confines of all substance discernible by sense, it comes to a point at which it reaches out after the intelligible world, and on descrying in that world sights of surpassing loveliness, even the patterns and the originals of the things of sense which it saw here, it is seized by a sober intoxication, like those filled with Corybantic frenzy, and is inspired, possessed by a longing far other than theirs and a nobler desire. Wafted by this to the topmost arch of the things perceptible to mind, it seems to be on its way to the Great King Himself; but, amid its longing to see Him, pure and untempered rays of concentrated light stream forth like a torrent, so that by its gleams the eye of the understanding is dazzled.

PHILO: WHO IS THE HEIR?

230 XLVIII. Having said what was fitting on these matters, Moses continues, "the birds He did not divide" (Gen. 15:10). He gives the name of birds to the two words or forms of reason, both of which are winged and of a soaring nature. One is the archetypal reason above us, the other the copy of it
231 which we possess. Moses calls the first the "image of God," the second the cast of that image. For God, he says, made man not "the image of God" but "after the image" (Gen. 1:27). And thus the mind in each of us, which in the true and full sense is the "man," is an expression at third hand from the Maker, while between them is the Reason which serves as model for our
232 reason, but itself is the effigies or presentment of God. Our mind is indivisible in its nature. For the irrational part of the soul received a sixfold division from its Maker who thus formed seven parts, sight, hearing, taste, smell, touch, voice and reproductive faculty. But the rational part, which was named mind, He left undivided. In this he followed the analogy of the

233 heaven taken as a whole. For we are told that there the outermost sphere of the fixed stars is kept unsevered, while the inner sphere by a sixfold division produces the seven circles of what we call the wandering stars. In fact I regard the soul as being in man what the heaven is in the universe. So then the two reasoning and intellectual natures, one in man and the other in the all, prove to be integral and undivided and that is why we read "He did not divide the birds."

PLUTARCH: THE *E* AT DELPHI

19. "What, then, really is Being? It is that which is eternal, without beginning and without end, to which no length of time brings change. For time is something that is in motion, appearing in connexion with moving matter, ever flowing, retaining nothing, a receptacle, as it were, of birth and decay, whose familiar 'afterwards' and 'before,' 'shall be' and 'has been,' when they are uttered, are of themselves a confession of Not Being. For to speak of that which has not yet occurred in terms of Being, or to say of what has already ceased to be, that it is, is silly and absurd.

Nature, when it is measured, is subject to the same processes as is the agent that measures it, then there is nothing in Nature that has permanence or even existence, but all things are in the process of creation or destruction according to their relative distribution with respect to time. Wherefore it is irreverent in the case of that which is to say even that it was or shall be; for these are certain deviations, transitions, and alterations, belonging to that which by its nature has no permanence in Being.

20. But God *is* (if there be need to say so), and He exists for no fixed time, but for the everlasting ages which are immovable, timeless, and undeviating, in which there is no earlier nor later, no future nor past, no older nor younger; but He, being One, has with only one 'Now' completely filled 'For ever'; and only when Being is after His pattern is it in reality Being, not having been nor about to be, nor has it had a beginning nor is it destined to come to an end. Under these conditions, therefore, we ought, as we pay Him reverence, to greet Him and to address Him with the words, 'Thou art'; or even, I vow, as did some of the men of old, 'Thou art One.' "

CYNICISM

EPISTLE OF HERACLITUS IV

Heraclitus to Hermodorus, Greeting,

Do not now grieve any longer about your own affairs, Hermodorus. Euthycles, the son of Nicophon, who despoiled the goddess two years ago, has charged me with impiety, thus reproaching in his ignorance a man outstanding for wisdom. The accusation was that I wrote my own name upon the altar which I set up, thus making myself, who am but a man, into a god. I shall then be accounted among the impious by an impious man. What would you expect? Shall I seem to be pious to them when I hold opinions about the gods opposed to what they think? Indeed, if the blind were to judge what is sight, they would say that blindness is seeing!

You stupid men, teach us first what god is, so that you may be trusted when you speak of comitting impiety. Also, where is god? Is he shut up in temples? You are a fine sort of pious men, who set up god in darkness! A man takes it as an insult if he is said to be stony; but is a god truly spoken of whose honorific title is "he is born from crags?" You ignorant men, don't you know that god is not wrought by hands, and has not from the beginning had a pedestal, and does not have a single enclosure? Rather the whole world is his temple, decorated with animals, plants, and stars.

I inscribed upon the altar, "To Heracles the Ephesian," thus making the god your fellow citizen, and not, "To Heraclitus." If you do not understand letters, your ignorance is not my impiety; learn wisdom and understand. Don't you want to? I won't force you. Grow old in ignorance, delighting in your own vices.

Was not Heracles a man? Indeed, he was even murdered of his guests, as Homer fabricated it. What, then, deified him? It was his own virtue and the most noble of his deeds, when he had successfully concluded so many labors. Therefore, sirs, am I not myself virtuous?

I have made a mistake in asking you, for even if you answer the negative, nevertheless I am virtuous. I, too, have successfully completed many very difficult labors. I have overcome pleasures; I have overcome money; I have overcome ambition; I overthrew cowardice; I overthrew flattery; fear does not contradict me; drunkenness does not contradict me; grief fears me; anger fears me. The struggle is against these opponents, and I have been crowned victor, not by Eurystheus, but by controlling myself.

Will you not stop insulting wisdom and attributing to us faults and indictments proper to yourselves? If you could be reborn and live once again five hundred years from now, you would find Heraclitus still alive, but of yourselves, you would not find even the trace of a name. On account of Culture I shall never be silenced and shall live as long as cities and lands. Even if the city of the Ephesians should be sacked and all the altars destroyed, the souls of men will be my memorials. I, too, shall take to wife a Hebe, but not the Hebe of Heracles. He will always be with his own, but another will be mine. Virtue bears many daughters, and she gave one to Homer, another to Hesiod, and Culture betroths Renown to each individual who is in some way virtuous.

Euthycles, am I not pious, who alone know god? Are not you both bold and impious; bold because you think you know him, and impious because you think him to be who he is not? If an altar of a god is not established, he is not a god, according to your reasoning; while if an altar is established for one who is not a god, then he becomes a god, so that stones are witnesses of gods! In fact, his works bear witness to what he is like. Do not night and day witness to him? The seasons are his witnesses; the whole fruitful earth is his witness. The orb of the moon, his handiwork, is his heavenly testimony.

Bibliography

TRANSLATIONS OF ANCIENT SOURCES

Works by the following writers quoted in the book are available in Latin or Greek with English translation in the Loeb Classical Library, which is published in the United States by Harvard University Press:

Apuleius	Lucian
Cicero	Philo
Diogenes Laertius	Plutarch
Epictetus	Seneca
Eusebius	Suetonius
Josephus	Virgil
Livy	Pliny

The extra-canonical writings of Judaism are available in *The Old Testament Pseudepigrapha,* edited by James H. Charlesworth (Garden City, N.Y.: Doubleday, The Anchor Bible, 1983–84). The so-called Apocrypha are available in the Revised Standard Version of the Bible. *The Dead Sea Scrolls in English,* edited and translated by Geza Vermes (Baltimore: Penguin Books, 1962). A valuable introduction to this literature is George Nickelsburg, *Jewish Literature between the Bible and the Mishnah* (Philadelphia: Fortress, 1981).

Studies of the period from the third century B.C. to the second century A.D. include:

CHADWICK, HENRY. *The Early Church.* Baltimore: Penguin Books, 1967, 1980.

HENGEL, MARTIN. *Judaism and Hellenism.* 2 vols. Philadelphia: Fortress, 1974.

NEUSNER, JACOB. *From Politics to Piety: The Emergence of Pharisaic Judaism.* Englewood Cliffs, N.J.: Prentice-Hall, 1973.

———. *The Rabbinic Traditions about the Pharisees Before 70.* Leiden: E. J. Brill, 1971.

Ogilvie, R. M. *Roman Literature and Society.* Totowa, N.J.: Barnes and Noble, 1980.

Reinhold, Meyer. *Diaspora: The Jews Among the Greeks and Romans.* Sarasota, Fla.: Samuel Stevens, 1983.

Russell, D. S. *The Jews from Alexander to Herod the Great.* New York: Oxford University Press, 1967.

Index

I

J

K

L

M